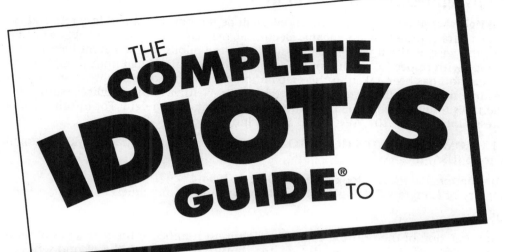

THE COMPLETE IDIOT'S GUIDE® TO

Financial Aid for College

by David Rye

D1398087

alpha books

A member of Penguin Group (USA) Inc.

International Standard Book Number: 0-02-863994-4
Library of Congress Catalog Card Number: Available upon request.

05   04   8   7   6

Interpretation of the printing code: The rightmost number of the first series of numbers is the year of the book's printing; the rightmost number of the second series of numbers is the number of the book's printing. For example, a printing code of 01-1 shows that the first printing occurred in 2001.

Printed in the United States of America

Publisher
Marie Butler-Knight

Product Manager
Phil Kitchel

Managing Editor
Cari Luna

Senior Acquisitions Editor
Renee Wilmeth

Development Editor
Doris Cross

Production Editor
Billy Fields

Copy Editor
Diana Francoeur

Illustrator
Jody Schaeffer

Cover Designers
Mike Freeland
Kevin Spear

Book Designers
Scott Cook and Amy Adams of DesignLab

Indexer
Lisa Wilson

Layout/Proofreading
Terri Edwards
Donna Martin
Mark Walchle

Contents at a Glance

Contents

Part 2 Planning Is Everything   37

4 So, Kid, You Want to Go to College?   39

C Alphabetical State Financial Aid Listings   321

Forewords

David Rye invites you to participate in the college financial aid application process. Quite frankly, you're an idiot if you don't. Millions of Americans do it annually. And so can you with a little help. In this insightful and practical book, David Rye illuminates what it takes to apply for and get the financial aid your kid needs for college. The book is filled with how-to examples and solid advice to avoid the pitfalls that are inherent in applying for financial aid. It begins by introducing you to what financial aid is all about and shows you how you can get in on the action, even if you don't think you qualify.

You'll learn how to estimate the amount of money you'll need for your kid's college education so that you'll know how much aid to apply for. And it doesn't end there. The author shows you where you can go and how to apply for literally thousands of college scholarships. The information you'll need to make it all happen is conveniently listed in the back of the book in a comprehensive directory and state-by-state listings of financial aid offices and agencies. This is the only book you'll need to learn how to apply for financial aid.

Dr. T. K. Nelson

Dr. Tim Nelson is a successful two-time entrepreneur, speaker, and student aid consultant. He is currently president of Western Publications.

There's good news and there's bad. First the bad. There are a lot of college students in serious debt. Forty-five percent of kids have education loans averaging $18,363. Generally, it takes about 7 years to pay off college debt. And the sticker price for a bachelor's degree is rising faster than a jet plane heading for Las Vegas.

Now here's the good news. There's more money available for financial aid than ever before. In fact, $50 billion in grants and loans are distributed each year, and 7 out of 10 full-time students receive some form of assistance.

What does this mean for you?

Despite the soaring cost of a college education, there's no reason why any student need abandon his dream of higher education due to money concerns. And in fact, students should pick the schools they want (and of course, that want them) because in most cases, students can find the money they require.

And it's most important to realize that all those dollars aren't just for families that can easily demonstrate financial need. Consider this: Between 1989-1995, not only did need-based funding rise 114 percent, but the amount of merit scholarship funds distributed increased 97 percent. At Washington University in St. Louis, Missouri, for example, 10 percent of the freshman class received merit scholarships that covered anything from half of the tuition costs to full tuition plus a stipend towards room and board!

So while it will cost lots of money to go to college (no surprise), with some time and effort, you can find the necessary financial help. Plus, and here's the important kicker: Even if you come out of college thousands of dollars in debt, it pays off in the long run. A worker with a bachelor's degree earns 77 percent more than a high school graduate.

So how do you get the $$$ you need? First, it takes time and effort. For many, the research and paperwork can be daunting and discouraging. You'll have to investigate a wide range of opportunities, collect and organize your family's financial data, maybe write an essay or two, perhaps be interviewed. But always remember that the payoff is worth it. You will literally be well rewarded for your troubles. And *The Complete Idiot's Guide to Financial Aid for College* will be a significant help. It offers clear instructions, state-by-state guidelines, insider tips, and steady reassurance. It even teaches you how to negotiate for a better financial aid package than the one you were offered.

Don't let the scarcity of funds in your own bank account deny you the opportunity for a better life. Your college career depends on finding the money you need—and with time and effort, you will.

Good luck!

Marian Edelman Borden

Author of *Unbelievably Good Deals and Great Adventures that You Absolutely Can't Get Unless You're a Student* (Contemporary Books, 2001).

Introduction

Each year, colleges and universities routinely deliver the painful news of yet another tuition increase. Now at over $35,000, the average cost of a public institution is soaring. You'll pay at least $80,000 or more if your kid wants to go to a private institution. How are you going to pay for that education? Are you willing to bite the bullet and take drastic financial steps like selling your house to come up with the money you'll need to ensure your child's future? Fortunately, there are a number of alternative ways to fund your kid's education so that you won't have to jeopardize your own financial well-being.

This book explains it all in easy-to-understand terms. We show you not only how to plan for college expenses, but how to apply for grants, scholarships, and low-interest loans to pay for them. In this unique and comprehensive guide, you'll learn how to do everything that's required to get the money you need. We've even included the necessary forms. In addition, we'll show you how to ...

> ➤ Pick colleges that offer the best financial aid packages.

> ➤ Plan ahead to improve your chances of receiving financial aid.

> ➤ Negotiate to get the best financial aid offer that you can.

> ➤ Take advantage of the new tax laws to build a college savings plan.

> ➤ Find the best low-interest financial aid loan programs.

> ➤ Get your kids involved in the process so they'll appreciate college that much more.

The Complete Idiot's Guide to Financial Aid for College takes you through the process step-by-step with lots of examples and explanations along the way; we want to get you the financial aid you deserve. You'll be amazed at how easy it is if you follow our advice. We encourage you to get your son or daughter involved in the process from start to finish. In the end, your kids will have a better appreciation of what their college education is going to cost and they'll study a lot harder to earn their degrees.

How to Use This Book

The chapters are laid out to guide you sequentially through the college financial aid application process. Treat each chapter as you would a steppingstone. Read Chapter 1 and complete what it tells you to do, and then go on to the next steps in the subsequent chapters. The book is divided into five parts.

Part 1: The Lowdown on Financial Aid

You'll learn what college financial aid is all about and about the different types of financial aid programs you can apply for. You'll also find the answers to many of the questions you have about funding your kid's college education.

Part 2: Planning Is Everything

Where does your kid want to go to college? We'll show you how to get the most bang for your buck in this section. In the process, you'll discover how to determine the amount of money to apply for when you estimate the cost of sending your kid to the college of his or her (your) choice. We'll also show you how to get your kid involved in the application process right from the beginning so that he or she will have an appreciation of what it costs to go to college these days.

Part 3: Seek and You Shall Find—Money

In this section, we show you how to first determine what's out there in the way of financial aid before you go looking for sources. We start off with federal aid programs and move on to the state, corporate, and community aid sources. You'll also learn how to apply for low-cost educational loans and how to save money on taxes.

Part 4: From Applications to Offers

Filling out the college financial aid application forms is about as much fun as filling out your tax return forms. In this section, we make it as painless as possible by giving you an overview of what's in a financial aid package and showing you how to properly fill out the forms. You'll also learn about financial aid offers, how to negotiate and appeal them, and what options you have if your application is rejected.

Part 5: Okay, You're Accepted and You Have Aid: Now What?

These chapters guide you through the ins and outs of finding additional financial aid—and having fun while doing it! For students, there's a wealth of advice on how to cut college expenses where it doesn't hurt so that they can have more to spend on the important stuff.

Watch for Road Signs

In addition to all the information and explanations we offer throughout this book, we include road signs to make it even easier and more interesting to learn about the financial aid process. There are four types of road signs to watch for. Each provides useful information in the form of short asides designed to help you focus on important ideas that deserve a little more attention. Here's what they look like:

Insight

This box gives you another perspective on the principles and practices covered in a chapter, and defines less familiar financial aid terms. By providing you with an example or some background, the Insight box helps you focus on the bigger picture.

Warning

Mistakes are always possible when applying for financial aid. The Warning box alerts you to what might go wrong and how to minimize errors so that your application won't be turned down.

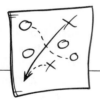

Action Plan

Here we direct you to specific steps that you may want to include in your financial aid Action Plan.

Help

Use the ideas in this Help box to simplify the task of applying for financial aid and increase your chances of getting it.

How to Use Our Directory of General Financial Aid Resources

Successfully qualifying for financial aid for your kid's college education is easier than you think. By the time you finish reading this book, you'll know everything you need to know to make it happen. And because we've included a comprehensive Directory and an alphabetical listing by state of state financial aid resources in the back of the book, you won't have to waste your time trying to find additional financial aid reference books or Web sites to complete the process. The Directory is full of information about how to contact federal and private financial aid sources; where to find aid for veterans, women, and minorities; which forms to fill out; and much more. In the appendix which follows you can find all the important state offices and agencies listed by state. We wish you the best of luck in your quest for college financial aid!

Acknowledgments

To all the friends I made while writing this book, thanks for helping me along the way: Jim and Roey Fitzpatrick, Reta and Dan Rye, Maida Naden, Dale Mosier, Tim Nelsen, Doug Hoagland, Kristi and Kori Grote, Cheri Dengel, and Jack Washburn. A special thanks goes to senior acquisitions editor Renee Wilmeth, who gave me the inspiration to write this book.

Trademarks

All terms mentioned in this book that are known to be or are suspected of being trademarks or service marks have been appropriately capitalized. Alpha Books and Macmillan USA, Inc., cannot attest to the accuracy of this information. Use of a term in this book should not be regarded as affecting the validity of any trademark or service mark.

Part 1

The Lowdown on Financial Aid

Paying for college can be a bummer, but don't let "sticker shock" stop your kids from attending the schools that are right for them. These chapters give you an overview of what financial aid is all about and get you started on seeking the scholarships, loans, grants, and tuition money you need.

Chapter 1

What's Financial Aid All About?

In This Chapter

➤ Discovering what the financial aid process is all about

➤ Learning what types of financial aid are available to you

➤ Identifying scholarship assistance companies which make fraudulent claims

Financing education is not a pleasant topic. Most parents probably wish that it weren't a consideration at all. Unfortunately, each year many students face limited choices because of the lack of financial planning for college. In order to best prepare for the future, families need to understand what it costs to go to college and what financial aid is available to them.

Financial aid makes up the difference between what a family can afford and what it will cost to send their kid (or kids!) to the college of their choice. The belief is that students who can't afford the full cost of education should still have the chance to go. In the past, financial aid was synonymous with grants and scholarships, also known as "gift aid." Today, education loans are the main source of financial aid. The recent shift in financial aid, from grants to loans, raises much concern.

College graduates may be required to pay off the cost of their education for many years to come. Unfortunately, there doesn't seem to be much hope for change in the near future. It isn't just students who have been forced to borrow. Parents are also borrowing money to meet their share of the costs.

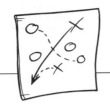

Action Plan

"The Smart Student Guide to Financial Aid" is a Web site that offers a host of information about financial aid, including a free newsletter and several tips on getting financial aid. The address is www.ivillagemoneylife.com/money/articles/0,4029,15461~344,00.html, also listed under Lenders in Appendix B.

Insight

What's the difference between **grants, scholarships,** and **loans?** Loans have to be repaid whereas grants and scholarships do not. Grants are usually awarded on the basis of need. Scholarships are usually awarded to students who demonstrate or show potential for distinction, either academically or in a specific skill, such as music or athletics.

Where's the Money Coming From?

Families trying to finance rising college costs have many questions. What about financial aid? Is there money for everyone? If not, who will receive whatever assistance is available? If a family isn't eligible for much financial aid, what kinds of planning will help meet the rising costs of higher education? It's important that families develop a financial plan for college costs.

More and more students are unable to attend the college of their choice because their families haven't planned for financing their college costs. Perhaps you had the foresight to set up a special college education savings account when your kids were young. Maybe you didn't! Who else can help you pay college expenses? Fortunately, there are other sources of education funds out there.

Uncle Sam's Contribution

Uncle Sam is the largest source of need-based aid. Most of the aid is made available through the U.S. Department of Education (ED). Since the federal government is the largest source of student aid, it pays to know all you can about its major programs. The ED provides aid primarily through *grant programs* in which students are awarded "free" money to apply toward tuition or federally subsidized low-interest *loans.*

The Federal Aid Umbrella

In recent years, the federal government has increased the amount of loan money, but decreased the amount of money for grants. The need to increase spending on educational programs across the board is one of the few programs politicians of both parties can agree on. Since the sources of federal funds are constantly changing, get the latest copy of *The Student's Guide: Federal Financial Aid Programs* by calling

1-800-4-FED-AID (433-3243). It's free, and it lists all current federal financial aid programs. Also be aware that eligibility for various types of federal aid can change from year to year. Just because you didn't qualify for a program last year doesn't mean you won't make it this year.

State Coffers

State funds for financial aid vary widely between the states, and there are often restrictions. To qualify, you typically have to be a resident of the state. States go through annual cycles of generosity and stinginess depending upon how well their financial year is going. So, it's impossible to predict how much aid you might be able to get from year to year.

Hidden College Funds

School aid, which is often called *institutional aid,* can come directly from a state college in the form of need-based and non–need-based dollars. Any amount of financial assistance provided to you by a college will depend on the individual school's policies. This money includes everything from *merit scholarships* for athletic, academic, or special achievement; to scholarships earmarked for specific fields of study, such as nursing.

In the last few years, hundreds of millions of dollars in endowments have been flowing into colleges. Some of this endowment money has been earmarked for scholarships.

Insight

Merit scholarships are awarded to students based upon their individual merit rather than their financial need. Merit could be based on academic achievement, athletic capabilities, or a range of other distinctions that are considered important to the institution.

Private Stashes

Private sources of financial aid come from community associations, businesses, interest groups, and other organizations. Funds from these sources generally come in the form of scholarships or loans. Be prepared to do some legwork to find private source money. However, it can be well worth your while. Many employers help put students through college by participating in *cooperative education programs,* where students alternate school semesters with work semesters. Not only does this provide your kids with a chance to build their professional skills, it also helps finance their education. Most of the employers that participate in cooperative education programs offer students flexible work hours to accommodate their class schedules.

Types of Financial Aid

Financial aid consists of three kinds of assistance: grants and scholarships, work-study loan programs, and student loans. Grants and scholarships are only a small part of the available funds. *Work-study programs* give students the chance to earn money working part-time while they're in school. There are a number of government-sponsored low-interest loans to consider, and these are covered in Chapter 15, "The Inside Scoop on Student Loans." Most financial aid comes in the form of student loans.

Insight

In **cooperative education programs** students alternate semesters of work and study. **Work-study programs** provide part-time jobs for undergraduate and graduate students with financial need, allowing them to earn money to help pay education expenses. They are also known as FWS (federal work study) programs because they are sponsored by the federal government, which makes them different from co-op programs. Co-op work-study programs are usually sponsored by private organizations.

Grants Are Great

Grants do not have to be repaid and are need-based. *Pell Grants* are need-based grants of up to $2,340 funded by the federal government. Students must be undergraduates to be eligible for a Pell Grant. *Supplemental Education Opportunity Grants* are campus-based federal grants that are based on financial need and that award up to $4,000 per year.

Make sure you read Chapter 9, "Grant Me a Grant," which provides details on how to apply for grants. Grants are a special form of scholarship. Chapter 11, "Playing the Scholarship Game," deals specifically with how and where to apply for scholarships.

Scholarships Are Everywhere

Some students receive *merit scholarships* for outstanding achievement, athletic skill, special talents, or their academic record. Scholarships are awarded without regard to a family's ability to pay. The idea is that outstanding accomplishments, within and outside the classroom, deserve recognition. However, less than 5 percent of all financial aid is in the form of merit scholarships.

Athletic Scholarships

Colleges offer *athletic scholarships* to attract certain students to play for specific teams. Many parents and students are unrealistic about the availability of these well-publicized awards. Athletic scholarships are quite rare, and only unusually gifted athletes receive them. Unfortunately, coaches in high school and athletic leagues often raise unrealistic expectations about the availability of athletic scholarships.

Merit Scholarships

Scholarships are generally given to students with a mix of talents. A student with unique skills in a specific area, such as music, might find a college interested in recruiting him or her through a merit-based scholarship that recognizes both the academic credentials as well as the personal qualifications of the student. Although there are fewer academic scholarships than athletic ones, the number of academic scholarships has been steadily increasing over the last five years. The bottom line is that any scholarship is tough to win. In reality, all colleges look at the "total you" when they consider you for a scholarship. Can you make it academically? Do you have demonstrated leadership qualifications? Do you have special skills (athletic or musical, for example) that you can apply while you attend college?

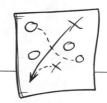

Action Plan

Check out Scholarship Search at www.collegeview.com to locate possible scholarship opportunities. Also see Scholarships, Grants, and Fellowships in Appendix B.

Low-Interest Loans

Federal student loans are one way to pay for college. Although the loans must be repaid with interest, they have deferment options and favorable terms for repayment, which typically does not start until after graduation. These loans generally have low interest rates and are not based on your credit history.

Federal Direct Loan Program

Many schools are now participating in the *Federal Direct Loan Program*. In this program, schools rather than banks act as the lending institutions and the federal government supplies the funds. Some students prefer the Federal Direct Loan Program to the traditional *Federal Family Education Loan Program (FFELP)* because it seems to simplify the process and to speed up the disbursement of funds.

Help

If you're interested in applying for a student loan, make sure you read Chapter 15, which provides you with everything you need to know to apply.

Family Education Loans

The majority of federal student loans are funded through the FFELP. This program differs from the Direct Loan Program in that the school is not the lender; rather, private lenders, such as banks, credit unions, and other financial institutions, supply and manage the loan funds. The federal government guarantees the loans against default to help keep the interest rates down.

Stafford Loans

Subsidized and unsubsidized *Stafford Loans* are available through both the FFELP and the Federal Direct Loan Program. Eligibility for a *subsidized* Stafford loan is based on financial need. The federal government pays the interest accrued on such loans until a student graduates. An *unsubsidized* Stafford Loan is not based on financial need, and the student is responsible for paying interest from the date of origination. For both types of loans, the annual amounts vary. For dependent students, the amounts that can be borrowed each year range from $2,625 to $5,500, depending on how many years the student has been in school. For independent students, the annual borrowing amounts range from $6,625 to $10,500.

Help

Stafford Loan rates, amounts, and terms are constantly changing. You can learn more about Stafford Loans through their Web site at www.student.services. wiu.edu/mifina/stafford/. For the latest information on these and other loans, check the loan Web sites given in the Loan Programs section of Appendix B.

Parent Loans

Parent Loans for Undergraduate Students (PLUS) are available through the FFELP and Federal Direct Loan Program. Parents can borrow up to the total amount of their student's entire education costs, minus any financial aid that their student has received. These loans require a credit check.

Perkins Loans

Federal Perkins Loans are campus-based loans that offer a low interest rate and are available to undergraduate and graduate students who have great financial need. The school acts as the lender but uses partial funds from the federal government to cover the loan. Undergraduate students can borrow up to $4,000 annually; graduate students can borrow up to $6,000 annually.

Work-Study Programs

Work-study programs are campus-based programs in which federal dollars are distributed through colleges to eligible students who are assigned part-time jobs. To qualify for the program, students must be able to demonstrate a need for financial aid and be enrolled at least half-time in an undergraduate or graduate program. Most of the employment is on the college campus, although some campuses arrange for off-campus jobs through community service programs. The pay is at least minimum wage, and often higher.

This need-based federal program lets students earn money that gets paid directly to them while in school. And these jobs might be related to the student's field of study so that he or she will be getting some practical experience. Some schools do not allow freshmen to participate in work-study programs. Talk to the school's financial aid officer about opportunities that might be available.

Service-Learning Programs

Service learning combines service to the community with student learning in a way that improves both the student and the community, according to the National and Community Service Trust Act of 1993.

Service learning is a method whereby students learn and develop through active participation in thoughtfully organized service that is conducted in, and meets the needs of, communities. It's coordinated with an elementary school, secondary school, institution of higher education, or a community service program. Service learning is integrated into and enhances either the academic curriculum of the students who are enrolled or the education components of the community service program in which they are participants. Such programs, which provide structured time for students to reflect on their service experiences, can foster learning, even though the learning may not be directly related to their academic work.

Insight

Service-learning programs were designed to help foster civic responsibility.

The Connection Between Community and College

Service learning is part of the academic curriculum in a college. In community organizations, youth develop practical skills, self-esteem, and a sense of civic responsibility. Examples of service-learning projects include preserving native plants, designing neighborhood playgrounds, teaching younger children to read, testing the local water quality, creating wheelchair ramps, preparing food for the homeless, developing urban community gardens, starting school recycling programs, and much more.

Why Service Programs Are Important

A national study of Learn and Serve America programs suggests that effective service-learning programs improve academic grades, increase attendance in school, and develop personal and social responsibility. Whether the goal is academic improvement, personal development, or both, students learn critical thinking, communication, teamwork, civic responsibility, mathematical reasoning, problem solving, public speaking, vocational skills, computer skills, scientific methodology, and research and analytical skills.

Tips on Applying for Financial Aid

But is there any way to "beat the system" when applying for financial aid? Can families rearrange their finances so that they can receive more financial assistance? There are two things to remember before these questions can be answered.

First, you should always be honest and accurate when applying for financial aid. There are severe penalties if dishonesty is discovered.

Second, the federal government often changes the rules and regulations that determine how financial aid is awarded. Today's savvy financial aid strategy may be obsolete next year.

Don't be dishonest or manipulate your income and assets in an attempt to secure more money. Instead, structure your entire college financial-planning process to maximize your resources, keep debt levels manageable, and meet college expenses in a rational and comprehensive way.

Before you apply for financial aid, however, there are certain peculiarities of the current formula for financial aid and need analysis that you should understand. The tips in the following sections will help you get your fair share of the action.

The Federal Formula

The current federal formula expects students to contribute 35 percent of their assets each year to meet their college costs. That same formula requires that parents contribute only 5.6 percent of their assets to meet their kids' college expenses. For example, if your family has assets of $10,000, it's better to have them in the parents' names, rather than in the kids'. As parents, you would have to contribute 5.6 percent, or $560, by the current need-analysis formula. Your student would be expected to contribute $3,500, or 35 percent, toward meeting school bills.

Consider Using Your Home

Home equity loans allow parents to borrow against the value of their house to pay for their kids' college education. Parents can take out a second mortgage and establish a line of credit based upon the equity they've built up in their house. Unlike the interest on other consumer loans, the interest on home equity loans is tax deductible.

Although financing college costs with home equity loans would not work for everyone, it's an effective college-financing plan for homeowners.

Some parents use the funds from a home equity loan to prepay four years of college costs to save on tuition increases.

Watch Your Assets

Investigate ways of reducing your income and assets, including investing in retirement accounts and life insurance policies.

Delay taking any profits from investments or real estate holdings; that way, they won't be included as part of the family's income for the year preceding college enrollment.

Timing is important. Because financial aid awards are based on the previous tax year—in other words, the year *before* the college year—make sure that you shift any income and assets in advance of the college year.

Your Expected Contribution

A family's contribution is reduced by the number of family members in college at the same time. If two kids are simultaneously enrolled, the expected family contribution is reduced by almost 50 percent for each one. The same is true if two parents are simultaneously enrolled in higher education courses.

Watch for Fraud

When school is about to start, advertised offers for "guaranteed" scholarships, grants, and loans may look very attractive to college-bound students who didn't apply or qualify for financial aid. However, the Better Business Bureau (BBB) of Wisconsin warns students to be cautious of unethical scholarship companies.

Some scholarship companies promise a "guaranteed match" of students to sources of funding, regardless of the students' academic qualifications, scholastic credentials, or family economic status. Their advertisements and sales pitches assert that there are millions of dollars in unclaimed scholarship money waiting to be tapped. However, in the BBB's experience, many of these promises prove empty, and few if any students receive funds. In exchange for an upfront fee, which can range from $50 to several hundred dollars, these scholarship companies only supply lists of possible scholarship sources.

Here are some points to keep in mind if you're considering getting help from a scholarship company:

➤ Even though the company making the offer may claim that scholarships are "guaranteed," only the sources actually granting the funds can guarantee approval.

➤ Unethical scholarship companies do not assist students in obtaining loans and do not screen applicants. After buying the lists from the firm, the student is responsible for researching and contacting each organization listed as a possible funding source.

➤ Many ads by these companies offer a "money back guarantee" to students who do not receive any scholarship funds. Students who are unsuccessful in obtaining funds may find that refunds are difficult, if not impossible, to obtain. In many cases, companies require that students prove through documentation that they were turned down by every source on the list.

If students do decide to seek the help of a scholarship service company, the Better Business Bureau recommends that they first check the service's references. Reference checks can be made through high school guidance offices, reference sections of libraries, or the financial aid office of the college the student is planning to attend.

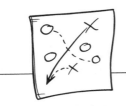

Action Plan

You can obtain a reliability report on a scholarship company by calling the Better Business Bureau of Wisconsin at 1–800–273–1002.

The Least You Need to Know

➤ Financial aid is available to millions of American families. Don't make the mistake of assuming you don't qualify. You won't know until you apply!

➤ There are literally thousands of financial aid sources out there for the people who are willing to search for them. You may even find a pot of gold at the end of the rainbow!

➤ If you research financial aid possibilities and do some advance planning, you won't have to overburden yourself with debt to send your kids to college.

➤ Beware of scholarship service companies that guarantee scholarship funds.

Chapter 2

Staking Out Your Financial Aid Claim

In This Chapter

➤ Discovering what the eligibility requirements are for financial aid

➤ Learning how the application process works, and why it's important to apply even if you think you don't qualify

➤ Exploring financial aid myths and misconceptions

➤ Learning how to calculate what college will cost and how much you can expect to pay

➤ Dispelling financing myths

A recent survey published in *Business Week* found that a huge majority of parents who are paying tuition bills say the current financial aid system doesn't meet the needs of the beleaguered average American family. To be honest with you, I believe that it never will because, quite simply, the cost of going to college now and in the future is outstripping the funding that's available for college aid. In this chapter, I show you techniques that you can employ to enhance your chances of getting a larger piece of the action.

Eliminate Frustration: Do Your Research

Now that Cheri Rye's second child is in college, Cheri is somewhat of a professional at applying for financial aid. And, as is the case for many parents who face the fact that college expenses are more than their budgets allow, Cheri's learning curve was a steep one. Even though she had ready access to a wealth of information about financial aid from books, magazine articles, Web sites, and high school financial aid experts, anxiety was her biggest obstacle.

When she looked at the cost of tuition in relation to her income, paying it seemed a terrifying prospect, particularly because the idea that her children wouldn't go to college was not an option. "The first time I filled out the aid forms for my daughter Lisa, I was physically sick," she recalls. "I was told that if you make a mistake you get rejected by the system and go to the end of the line."

Well, Cheri knows better now, and her distress is history. Her daughter Lisa is halfway through her undergraduate degree at a good college. So when she began seeking financial aid for her daughter Jennifer, Cheri was somewhat less apprehensive. By the time Jennifer was securely enrolled in college, Cheri was on a first name basis with the college's financial aid administrator.

Warning

If you don't get to know your financial aid administrator (FAA) or officer, you're in trouble. The help of the FAA will be essential if questions arise when you're filing for aid. FAAs can also point you to numerous financial sources that you hadn't thought of.

Ronald Shunk probably has heard all there is to hear about the frustration and confusion surrounding financial aid from a parent's perspective. For 10 years, he answered parents' questions on *USA Today*'s Financial Aid Hotline, and he is currently Director of Financial Aid at Gettysburg College in Gettysburg, Pennsylvania. "What impresses me is that many callers into my Hotline don't have even a fundamental understanding of financial aid and don't know where to begin."

With all the information about financial aid available, why do parents panic the first, and even the second, time around?

Cheri's experience and that of other parents who have been through the process indicate some common concerns. Ronald explains: "It's because most of them don't take the time to understand the application process before they apply. When they make a mistake and their application gets rejected, they get frustrated and blame everybody but themselves."

Who Gets the Money?

Generally, all college financial assistance is based on "need." Financial aid services used by colleges and universities have a standard formula to determine whether you and your children qualify for various forms of assistance. All institutions granting assistance are required by federal law to use the formula.

This formula uses a family's income, assets, and expenses to calculate the *expected family contribution* (EFC). In theory, the expected family contribution remains constant from school to school. The individual institutions then subtract this number from the cost of attending their institution in order to come up with an estimate of "need." The amount of "need" will vary depending on that institution's cost of attendance.

In determining a family's need, the standard formula takes into account more than just a family's annual income. Equity in the home, the value of a family-owned business, savings, stock holdings, and other assets that may be potential sources of funding for education are factored in as well. The formula also considers whether other siblings are in college, requiring the family's support.

Do You Need the Money?

Many colleges, including some of the most selective, are opposed to merit-based assistance. These colleges give only need-based assistance and feel that only students who demonstrate need deserve assistance. Their concern is that merit awards reduce the money available to help those who really need it. To determine your kid's eligibility for need-based aid, the "expected family contribution" is subtracted from the total cost of attending the college. The difference is the family's need for assistance. Therefore, the need increases as the total cost goes up. The total cost varies from one college to another. For example, private colleges are generally more expensive than public institutions.

What's Considered Total Cost?

Total cost includes tuition and fees as well as other associated expenses, such as the cost of books and other supplies. If a student plans to live on campus, room and board will be considered and allowance made for traveling home at least once during the school year. If the student will be commuting, transportation is included. In other words, the amount is the total cost of attending college for one year.

Insight

The **Expected Family Contribution (E**... amount of money ... and his or her fam... pected to contribu... student's cost of c...

Help

For more information about educational and living expenses at college, check out the College Cost Web site at www.finaid.org/calculators/costprojector.phtml listed under Budgeting in Appendix B.

More Expensive May Be Cheaper

More-expensive colleges tend to have more money available, so the "sticker price" at any college may be very misleading. Students should explore every college that interests them on the assumption that they will receive financial aid if they need it. But they should keep in mind that while the college's financial aid office will attempt to meet the total "need for assistance," there's no guarantee that the college will be able to do so.

Colleges that can provide assistance to meet the full need of each student are the exception. Some colleges meet the need of as many students as possible, whereas others meet a portion of the need of all students. In either case, there's no guarantee that a student's needs will be met.

Misconceptions About Need

One common misconception is that having savings or assets will automatically exclude a family from financial aid. Many parents assume that aid won't be offered until all savings and assets have been exhausted. This is simply not true. Some parents assume that owning a home or having significant savings makes them ineligible. Having home equity and money in the bank does not mean that students will not qualify for assistance. In fact, home equity isn't even considered by some colleges in determining eligibility.

What You're Expected to Pay

What you'll be expected to pay, or your EFC, is a combination of what you and your student will be expected to contribute toward a college education. The parents' contribution is based on the number of family members in college, and it allows for living expenses. This allowance is conservative and reflects a minimum budget for any family. As a result, it is rare to find a family that can meet its expected contribution from current income. Most families meet this expense through a combination of savings, current income, and loans.

Income is the major factor in establishing a family's contribution. Assets and savings are also considered, but no more than 6 percent of parents' assets are included in any given year. Parents should be honest about their ages, since the 6 percent maximum assessment would be lower for older parents who are closer to retirement. There are three general family income categories that are considered in determining your EFC, or what you are expected to pay.

Low-Income Families

Families with incomes under $25,000 are eligible for assistance. Families sho municate this to their children so that they do not assume they cannot affor As an example for their children, parents might consider putting spare chan coffee can labeled "college fund." The amount saved may not make a dent ir total cost of college, but it sends a powerful message about the importance o tion.

Middle-Income Families

Middle-income families should understand where they stand in relation to others applying for financial aid. Income alone can be deceiving. Family size, number of children in college, unusual expenses, and savings and other assets will also be considered. Currently the "statistical" middle class consists of the 3 out of 5 families with incomes between $25,000 and $70,000.

Middle-income families usually qualify for financial assistance, but they will also be expected to make a significant EFC. This may require a number of sacrifices and a possible change in lifestyle. Going out to eat may become a rare luxury, and these families should probably get accustomed to driving the same car for a while.

Help

Use a Financial Aid Calculator to help you determine your eligibility. There are several calculators available on the Web. Check Appendix B for helpful sites found under "Financial Aid Resources" or "Financial Planning."

Wealthy Families

Families with incomes above $70,000 make up one-fifth of the population in the United States. According to the government, high-income families should be in the best position to contribute toward their children's education, but even they may struggle to meet college costs. If you're in a high-income category or believe you will be when your kids reach college age, you should begin long-term college financial planning as early as possible.

Is Your Kid Eligible?

Although the process of determining a student's eligibility for federal student aid is basically the same for all applicants, there is some flexibility. For instance, if your FAA believes that, based on the documentation you provided, it's appropriate to change the student's status from dependent to independent, he or she can do so.

ne cases, your FAA may consider circumstances that might affect the amount of
EFC, and adjust your "cost of attendance" or the information used to calculate
EFC accordingly.

se circumstances could include a family's unusual medical or dental expenses, or
ion expenses for children attending a private elementary or secondary school.
, an adjustment may be made if you, your spouse, or either of your parents (if ap-
ble) has been recently unemployed. If conditions such as these apply to you or
family, contact your FAA.

with your FAA if you feel you are subject to any other special circumstances
ight affect the amount of your expected contribution. But remember, there
be very good reasons for the FAA to make any adjustments, and you'll have
provide adequate proof to support those adjustments. Also, remember that the
FAA's decision is final and cannot be appealed to the U.S. Department of Education.

To quickly determine whether you qualify for federal financial aid, follow these easy
steps:

1. Take 5 percent of the value of your total family assets, including home equity,
   savings, and investments, and add this figure to your adjusted gross income
   from last year's tax return.

2. Divide that result by the anticipated annual college expense.

3. If the result is 6 percent or less, you could qualify for financial aid.

4. If the final number is higher, you may have a difficult time convincing financial aid officers of your need.

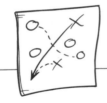

Action Plan

You can calculate your expected family contribution by using several of the Web sites listed in Appendix B under "Federal Financial Aid."

Note: No matter what you prejudge your chances to be, you should still go through the application process. Many different factors enter into the final outcome. Public and private institutions alike offer varying amounts of aid, and you may be pleasantly surprised. If you do not receive aid from your chosen institution, there are other alternatives.

Stepping into the Application Process

No doubt about it, the financial aid process can leave you bewildered. I've put together a brief summary that will be helpful as you explore the world of federal aid. Later chapters will get into more of the details of how to apply for college aid, but for right now, here are the basic steps in applying for aid:

Warning

Don't hang back waiting to be admitted to a college before filing your financial aid request forms. Too many students make this mistake. For any college you're even thinking about attending, submit your application as soon as possible, even if it's before you're allowed to apply for financial aid. If you think that it should be financial aid money first and application second, you may find yourself in last place. Colleges will first review financial aid requests received from students whose applications have already been accepted.

Step 1: Complete the Application

To get the process started, you and your parents must fill out and submit a *Free Application for Federal Student Aid* (FAFSA) sometime between January 1 and March 1 in order to qualify for funds starting in September of the coming school year. That means that you will need to include information from your parents' tax return (last year's return) to complete the form. If they wait until the April 15 cutoff date to complete and file their return, it will be too late for you to apply for financial aid. The FAFSA form is available through your high school, from the financial aid office of the college, or on the Internet. There's a copy of the FAFSA in Appendix B.

Step 2: Evaluate the Student Aid Report

You'll receive your *Student Aid Report (SAR)* four to six weeks after submitting the FAFSA. The SAR indicates whether you are eligible for a Pell Grant, and it outlines your Expected Family Contribution (EFC). The EFC is determined by subtracting parent and student contributions from the *cost of attendance (COA)* at the college of your choice. Remember, the EFC varies depending on several factors, including your family's income, assets, size, and whether the student is a dependent or independent. It also varies according to the COA, since the COA is different for each college.

Step 3: Receive and Consider Offers

Next, you will get an award letter from the college you've applied to or are currently attending. This letter will outline how much financial aid you are eligible for. If you receive a rejection letter, don't give up. Chapters 20, "What Does an Offer Look Like?"

and 21, "Negotiating a Better Offer," show you how to compare and negotiate the best offer possible. I also show you how to turn a rejection letter into an offer.

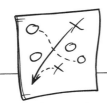

Action Plan

Prioritize your efforts by beginning with the federal government. But don't forget to explore Appendix C for state financial assistance programs, and use the Web sites you'll find throughout Appendix B to locate other sources.

Warning

Don't limit your options. Don't automatically rule out high-cost colleges. The financial aid system works proportionally, making up the difference between what you can afford to pay and what college costs. Check out the information that's available under "College Financial Aid" in Appendix B.

Dispelling Financial Aid Myths

You've heard it all before. Everything you've heard about what it's going to take to pay for your kid's college education is driving you crazy. Before you go crazy, make sure you can separate the facts from the most common myths.

Millions of Scholarship Dollars Go Unclaimed

False! The statement that private scholarship dollars go unclaimed is unfounded. This is what professional scholarship search services would like you to believe because they want you to pay for their services. You can do your own search for scholarships.

Your Family's Income Is Too High to Qualify

False! Income is only one of the criteria on which financial aid is based. If the school's costs exceed your family's means, you may qualify for some form of financial aid. Remember, there are some scholarships that are based on merit and not family income.

Don't Consider High-Tuition Colleges

False! As a general rule, the higher the total school costs, the easier it is to demonstrate eligibility for financial aid. Also, the stated costs at a school can be deceiving. Aid is often available to offset some of their higher costs. You should apply to the school and wait to see the financial aid award letter before you make a decision. You may get a favorable response.

Financial Aid Funds Are Dwindling

False! A recent statistic published in *The Arizona Republic* indicates that in 1965 $600 million was available for financial aid, but in 1997 that figure had soared to $55 billion. It is true, however, that loans and work-study are now a larger percentage of the total financial aid award than they used to be.

Moving Forward

With some of the myths out of the way, you're now ready to tackle the process of financing your kid's education. Paying for school isn't much fun to think about, but it is something you need to do. There are lots of sources available to help you afford school, but to tap into them, you have to know they exist!

Do You Need Help?

An increasing number of school counselors, instructors, and administrators familiar with the complex world of financial aid for education offer their expertise to students, parents, and guardians, for a fee. These private educational consultants can help a client choose the best possible colleges, given the student's academic abilities and interests, and assist in applying for, and obtaining, financial aid.

Although it certainly is not necessary to have this kind of professional advice, and consultants cannot guarantee the availability of funds, in some cases it can make researching and considering all the options much easier. The time to consider hiring an educational consultant is early in the student's junior year of high school. Ask the school guidance counselor for recommendations on private consultants in your area. Set up meetings with the prospective consultants. Examine and check out their credentials with local academic references.

Warning

The fees charged by a consultant may vary widely, depending on the type of assistance provided. Remember, most of the information and assistance from a consultant should be available free of charge from a college financial aid office.

Other Sources of Money

Other sources of financial aid include corporations, businesses, professional associations, philanthropic organizations, credit unions, labor unions, religious organizations, fraternities and sororities, and civic organizations. As the college years approach, students and parents need to be alert to announcements for financial support offered by these organizations.

No one knows a student's educational progress or potential better than the student's teachers and counselor. High school counselors can help you research sources of aid and complete college applications and financial aid forms. Keep in contact with them. Guidance counselors can help explore various available choices.

Maintain communication with these professionals in order to keep current. In addition, counselors can help identify the most appropriate possibilities for individual students. With years of experience in counseling many different students, guidance professionals have a unique perspective.

Admissions Counselors

College admission counselors can also provide help. Just keep in mind that there are thousands of two- and four-year colleges and universities and trade, technical, and career schools with different requirements, expectations, and policies. So advice from a counselor at one college may not apply to others.

Special-Programs Operatives

There are a variety of special programs that serve disadvantaged students, including Upward Bound and Talent Search, among many others. Often hosted by colleges, these programs are a wonderful source of support for students and families. They often help students preserve educational options. If there is no college nearby or if your local college does not sponsor such a program, check with the nearest Educational Opportunity Center for further information. Libraries have books on financial aid available from private, state, and federal sources. Employers may offer employee tuition benefits and assistance for family members. Several million dollars in employee education benefits go unused each year.

Warning

The College Board Web site has loads of useful resources for the college-bound student and many links to the College Board's online services. Their Web site is listed under "Scholarships, Grants, and Fellowships" in Appendix B.

Financial Aid Officers

Since funds are limited, college financial aid administrators or officers are usually quite eager to help families in early financial planning. These professionals have information on a variety of aid packages you may be eligible for. Consider attending a local financial aid night at the high school. Keep your eye out for other programs on financial aid and planning. Each state has an agency that administers state scholarships and other forms of financial aid. In recent years, these agencies have become involved in a variety of outreach programs to families.

Don't forget that financial aid procedures and policies do change. State financial aid offices can provide you with information about the types of financial aid they offer. You can find financial aid offices and other state agencies listed by state in Appendix C. It's very important for families to have the most current information available. In this area, what is true today may not be true tomorrow. Stay informed!

In conclusion, it's important for all families to have a good sense of what their expected contribution might be. Taking the time to secure a realistic estimate of college costs will help you plan more effectively.

The Least You Need To Know

➤ Just about everybody is eligible for some form of financial aid. At this point, you should have a general idea of the amount of aid you can qualify for and where to begin looking for it.

➤ You should be familiar with the four basic steps of applying and qualifying for college financial aid.

➤ The myths about financial aid are just that. Now that you know the facts, you can take a realistic approach to searching for the aid you need.

Chapter 3

Answers to All Your Financial Aid Questions

In This Chapter

➤ Exposing many of the myths that have plagued all aspects of the financial aid process

➤ Knowing why the confidential information you disclose on a form won't be shared with others

➤ Learning the basics of getting started

➤ Finding out where to get any additional information you need

---

"A friend of a friend of a friend of mine told me ... about financial aid." That's how the myths that surround financial aid get started. This chapter helps to expose the myths by answering the most common questions that parents and students ask about financial aid. It also addresses the most common questions about how to get started in the financial aid process. Where appropriate, I point you to other places in this book where you can find more information about a topic.

Why Does College Cost So Much?

Parents who went to college 30 years ago and are now putting their own children through college are shocked when they compare today's fees to what they paid. And when other parents who didn't have a college experience learn the price of a college education for their kids, they too are shocked and automatically assume that they can't possibly get enough aid to get their kids through school.

Although the cost of college today is indeed stunning, the reality is that *all* families are eligible for *some* level of federal assistance, and many state-funded institutions offer state financial aid.

Colleges are responding to the competition to attract good students, so there is more merit-based aid available now.

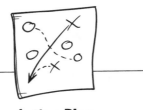

Action Plan

Just about anybody can get some form of financial aid. You just have to be willing to properly complete the necessary forms, provide the required documentation to support your application, and follow up on the process.

"Institutions have dramatically increased their financial aid budgets, and there is a much higher proportion of financial aid than 10 years ago," asserts Robert Baum, author of the bestseller *Logic*.

How Much Money Goes Into Financial Aid Annually?

Unfortunately, too many students feel they are denied their chance to go to college simply because they can't afford the rising costs of higher education. Many students and parents do not know that more than $35 billion in financial aid is available each year. You have to start by filling out a few simple forms, which are covered in Part 3 of this book, "Seek and You Shall Find—Money."

If I Apply, Will Strangers Pry Into My Personal Business?

The financial aid process feels intrusive. People are used to paying income taxes because they do it every year and know what's expected. But applying for financial aid is, for most people, a new experience. With pages and pages of instructions and applications to fill out, financial aid forms are intimidating.

In addition, people are disinclined to share so much of their personal financial profiles with people they don't know. To the first-timer, the forms seem worse than they are. However, when you start filling them out, you'll find they're not as complicated as you'd anticipated, nor is the information requested more than what's commonly requested by the IRS. In Chapter 19, "Decoding the Forms," we show you how to fill out the main federal aid form, the FAFSA.

Isn't Asking for Financial Aid the Same as Asking for Welfare?

Many people are embarrassed to ask for assistance because it means they aren't making six-figure incomes. Often, parents hesitate to ask difficult questions about financial aid and don't want to bring up the subject of their personal income to financial aid staff. They don't feel comfortable soliciting guidance about their money from strangers.

Don't hesitate to seek out high school counselors and financial aid officers who can give you the information you need. Financial aid officers are very service- and people-oriented. They're aware of the need to educate qualified students and their parents about how to get financial aid. That's their job! Competition for top students is tight, so it's also in the best interest of colleges to attract top-ranked students with financial aid packages.

Does Each College Have a Different Financial Aid System?

All colleges operate on different systems. Talk to the representatives at the financial aid office at each of the colleges where your child will apply. They're the best sources of information in terms of what is available and what their policies are. Find out how each institution allocates aid and what criteria they use to award it. Then get the appropriate forms from each institution, fill them out, and send them in. Many applications are available through your student's high school guidance counselor's office. Make sure you review all of the material in Chapter 4, "So, Kid, You Want to Go to College?" It will give you a better idea of what questions to ask the guidance counselor and the financial aid people working for the colleges your child is thinking about attending.

How Can I Get the Most Out of the System?

Parents can easily become overwhelmed because of the perceived volume of facts and figures involved in seeking financial aid. Many rely on hearsay and secondhand knowledge to educate themselves about the process of paying for college. However, there are abundant helpful resources out there, especially for parents and families with computers. Parents can research not only government and university resources for aid, but also private sources of scholarships and grants.

How Do I Know If I'm Eligible for Financial Aid?

You won't know if you're eligible unless you apply. Most students qualify for some kind of financial assistance. Here are the basic qualifications a student needs in order to qualify for financial aid:

➤ Demonstrate financial need, or merit for some scholarships.

➤ Have a high school diploma or a General Education Development (GED) certificate.

➤ Be enrolled in an eligible degree or certificate program and be making satisfactory progress.

➤ Be a U.S. citizen or eligible noncitizen.

➤ Have a valid Social Security Number.

➤ Register with the Selective Service, if applicable.

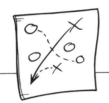

Action Plan

Students: In addition to exploring the information available on the Internet, contact your high school counselor or the financial aid department at the college of your choice. These sources can provide you with invaluable information.

Is My Kid Eligible for Special Aid?

Find out if your child is eligible for merit-based aid. Merit-based financial awards are based on students' scores and grades as well as on how they spend their free time.

Exemplary academic and extracurricular performance increases a student's chances of qualifying for merit-based financial aid. To become eligible for these scholarships, your child must strive to excel in a variety of school activities, and his or her honors and awards should be recorded in school files.

Merit–Based Scholarship Myths

There's a rumor that only students with high academic achievement win merit-based scholarships. The real story is that scholarships are awarded to students with all sorts of talents and interests. In fact, many of the best scholarships are awarded to students who devote their time to such diverse fields as music, art, community service, writing, and even foreign languages, to name a few. Many of these scholarships are based, not on students' grades, but rather on their accomplishments in specific areas.

Many scholarships that *do* take students' grade point averages into consideration do it to create a cutoff point in order to limit the number of applicants. If you make the grade-point cut, the judges turn their attention to what you've been able to accomplish in your life.

Every scholarship contest is judged differently, and anywhere from a single judge to hundreds of judges can be responsible for evaluating entries.

Athletic Scholarships

Just as the letter grades on your transcript aren't necessarily a prerequisite, and certainly aren't the only one, for winning scholarships, varsity letters earned on the playing field don't make the great impact people think they do.

Although a few merit-based contests are targeted at athletes who excel on and off the field, in the vast majority of scholarship contests, athletic prowess is just another element of a student's record, equivalent to having a skill in any other field.

Extracurricular Activities

Are we saying that the student who has the most extracurricular activities generally wins? As is the case in many other aspects of life, winning scholarships is about quality, not quantity.

Some people think that to win a scholarship you must have devoted your entire high school career to participating in extracurricular activities. On the contrary, most scholarship winners distinguish themselves by the devotion they've demonstrated to a particular activity or activities, rather than by how much time they've spent on many activities.

How to Be a Contender

Scholarship contests demand a modified approach from the college admissions process because contests are characterized by more direct, head-to-head competition. While college admissions officers generally compare students to a standard, scholarship contests compare students to one another. Because of this heightened competitive environment, students who devise creative techniques to stand out from the crowd have a distinct advantage.

Each scholarship contest has it own biases. This is not to say that scholarship judging is unfair. Rather, it's just that each contest is looking for students with particular qualities. The subjective process of valuing certain qualities over other ones tilts the playing field far from level. In this way, the perfect application for one particular scholarship contest may place you out of the money for another. Because of these biases, it's essential to define each contest's ideal applicant and to develop a strategy that emphasizes personal attributes consistent with that ideal. To paraphrase George Orwell, "Everyone is equal, but some are more equal than others."

Third-Party Organizations

Contests administered by third-party organizations often recruit judges from the ranks of current or former teachers, school administrators, and organization staff members. Most third-party organizations have run numerous scholarship contests, and the judging administered by them tends to be highly objective and in compliance with published judging criteria.

High-profile national contests administered by these types of organizations may also employ "blue-ribbon panels" for final judging. The panels generally include celebrities, government officials, and other notable individuals. For example, judges for the 1997 Prudential Spirit of Community Awards program included Senator Robert Kerrey of Nebraska, actor Richard Dreyfuss, and Robert Goodwin, President and CEO of the Points of Light Foundation.

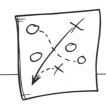

Action Plan

Merit is often only in the eyes of the beholder or, in the case of scholarships, in the eyes of the judges. If you understand what the judges are looking for and tailor your approach to each scholarship you apply for, you'll dramatically increase your chances of winning.

On the local level, such blue-ribbon panels typically include television and radio personalities, successful entrepreneurs, and professional athletes.

In contests that employ blue-ribbon panels for judging, a limited number of finalists are usually preselected via more mundane judging channels, and then presented to the blue-ribbon panel for final evaluation.

Corporations

For contests administered by a participating corporation rather than by the third-party organization, public relations personnel may be the ones to select the winners. When judging is conducted by a public relations department, other factors, such as geographical balance, can sneak into the (unpublished) judging criteria.

Service Organizations

Scholarship programs sponsored by service organizations, fraternal lodges, and veterans' associations are likely to be judged by members of the particular organization. In this way, the key tenets and values of the sponsoring organization frequently play a role in the judging.

Perhaps the most subjective judging occurs when scholarships are sponsored by small family or historic institutions, each of which has a unique set of biases and viewpoints.

How Many Aid Sources Should I Explore?

Explore as many sources of financial aid as you can. The amount of aid you receive will be determined partly by the cost of the school you attend, so don't rule out any school as being too expensive.

Once the financial aid office has determined your need and you've been notified of the amount and type of aid you'll receive (grants, scholarships, or loans), begin negotiating financial aid options with the schools that have accepted your child. Should you need more aid, seek out and apply for loans such as those offered by banks and credit unions. See Chapter 15, "The Inside Scoop on Student Loans," for more on loans.

When Should I Submit Applications?

Submit applications for aid well before their deadlines. Paying for education is often a family effort. When students begin working on their applications, parents should organize their income, asset, and tax records. Family need is determined by a federal formula that considers this information as well as tuition and other costs. See Chapter 18, "What's Inside a Financial Aid Package?" for more on how the formula works.

All applicants for federal aid must complete a need-analysis form, and some colleges also require that students submit some type of financial aid form. These forms cannot be submitted before January 1 or after May 1, and it's best to submit them as soon after January 1 as possible.

The sooner you apply, the better chance you have of being considered for aid with early award dates. Always contact the financial aid administrator at each school to verify specific deadline dates.

Warning

Don't think that getting financial aid will be an easy undertaking. Students who understand the details of financial aid and the application process reap the most benefits.

Where Can I Get More Information and Guidance?

The following individuals and organizations are good sources of information and advice about financial aid:

1. High school counselors can help you research sources of aid, complete college applications, and obtain financial aid forms.

2. College financial aid officers have information on a variety of aid packages you may be eligible for.

3. State financial aid offices can provide you with information about the types of financial aid they offer. They are listed in Appendix C.

4. Libraries have guides that list the financial aid available from private, state, and federal sources.

5. Employers may offer employee tuition benefits and assistance for family members.

Warning

Even though grants, scholarships, loans, work-study programs, and financial aid packages may be more plentiful than ever before, the key is not to wait until the last minute, or even the last year, when your child graduates from high school, to become aware of the high costs of sending him or her to college.

Other sources of financial aid include private and public business, professional associations, philanthropic organizations, credit unions, labor unions, religious organizations, fraternities and sororities, and civic organizations. As the college years approach, students and parents need to be alert to announcements for financial support offered by these organizations.

You'll find the addresses, phone numbers, and Web sites of many financial aid sources listed in Appendix B.

When Should I Begin Planning for My Kid's Education?

Do it now! You can never begin too early to plan to meet future college expenses. Most financial analysts recommend that as soon as your child is born, you should initiate some form of college financial program. Early planning gives families options and can make the difference in the college selection process.

How Can I Find Out If I Qualify for Assistance?

No one can tell a family with certainty whether they will qualify for federal financial aid. The federal government frequently changes the rules and regulations that determine eligibility. Some schools have a service that provides families with an estimate of what their aid will be if the student is accepted. Ask all the schools you're considering if they have this service. If you know at the time of application what you can realistically expect to receive from all sources, you can determine whether you can afford to send your kid to that particular school and what your financial contribution is expected to be.

Is There an Income Cutoff for Federal Aid?

There is no income cutoff to receive federal financial aid. All families, regardless of income, should file the application for federal aid. Always remember, eligibility for funding from all sources is determined in part by costs. Attending an expensive school may actually mean that a family will qualify for more aid than if the student attended a lower-cost institution. That's why it's so important for students to make college selections based primarily on the academic strengths and other appealing factors of the institutions—not on what they cost.

Another good reason why all families should file for federal financial aid is that most colleges and universities will not consider a student for institutional aid unless a federal application form is on file.

Do I Need to Reduce My Asset Base to Qualify?

The federal aid formula that is used to determine a family's ability to contribute to a college education expects parents to hand over as much as 47 percent in profits realized from investments, such as stocks and bonds. If you're thinking about unloading stocks or bonds, it's unwise to do so right before your son or daughter begins college. Time your investments so that profits don't show up on your income tax return for the year preceding the one in which you apply for aid.

Isn't the Federal Government Reducing Financial Assistance Programs?

No. The federal government still provides about 75 percent of all aid awarded. Although it's true that aid from the federal government has not kept pace with annual tuition increases, it's incorrect to state that the federal government no longer supports higher education.

Financial assistance is still available; however, funding sources have shifted from grants to loans, and at some schools, employment allocations have decreased. Although deficit budgets will probably prevent the federal government from substantially increasing financial aid to college students, there are many other sources of funding, including state and institutional programs (see Chapters 10, "State Aid Programs," and 11, "Playing the Scholarship Game"). It's the responsibility of the family to locate those sources.

What Are the Alternatives to Federal Aid?

Starting a savings plan and investment program a long way in advance to finance your kid's college education may mean that aid won't be needed. If it is, as is often the case, there are many ways to finance college costs.

Most schools and many states award scholarships based on academic achievement. Many private organizations offer financial assistance to students who meet specific criteria. Banks generally have college financing programs. The PLUS program (see Chapter 15) is awarded on the basis of creditworthiness, not financial need.

What's the Best Savings Plan?

No one single savings or investment program is best for all families. Each family must design a savings plan that will best meet its particular financial needs. The age of the kid and the parents, and the financial resources of the family, will help determine the appropriate college savings program. The federal formula currently used to determine a family's ability to pay for college assesses greater weight to current income than to assets, so families are not unjustly penalized for having started to save early for their kid's college education.

Prepayment plans allow families to purchase a fixed, discounted tuition at many colleges. The money is then invested by the institution or the state to cover the future cost of tuition.

Prepayment plans relieve families of the anxiety of escalating tuition bills. However, since these plans are a new type of financing option, don't invest any money in one before you find out whether the plan covers all college costs or just tuition expenses.

Also, determine the maximum amount you can invest, and what happens to your investment if your kid decides not to attend that college, or any college, or drops out after the first year.

What Are Tuition Stabilization Plans?

Tuition stabilization plans are similar to prepayment plans, but the amount paid into the plan is generally less than four years of tuition. Most tuition stabilization plans require the family to pay a portion of the educational costs in advance. The advantage of this type of plan is that tuition is capped for all subsequent years that the student is enrolled at the college.

Help

Find out as much as you can about financing a college education. If you bought this book, you've already learned something about financial aid, and where to go to learn more.

Who Can Help Me Get Through This Process?

The first person to look to for help is you. The process of finding the money for your kid to attend college will seem very complicated unless you take the time to investigate, educate yourself, and explore all of your financial options.

Compare college costs. Seek the advice of your accountant, banker, or investment broker. Get to know a financial aid counselor at the local college or university. The more knowledge you have, the less complicated the process will be.

The Least You Need To Know

➤ There are a lot of myths out there about college financial aid. Know how to separate fact from fiction.

➤ Doing as much research as you can will help you get through the process and reap greater aid benefits.

➤ Understanding the basic steps you need to take to get started is key. If there's something you don't understand about the system, ask questions until you get the answers you need.

Part 2

Planning Is Everything

Tuition increases over the last several years are enough to scare any parent with kids to put through college. Only a few families can afford to foot the bills by themselves; yet if the kids don't get through college, they'll have a tough time surviving in today's job environment. Before you give up the hope of sending a kid of yours off to college, take the first painful step: Find out what it's going to cost so you can sit back and determine where you're at financially. How much can you afford to spend, how much do you need in the form of financial aid to make ends meet, and what kind of financial plan will you have? That's what these chapters are all about.

Chapter 4

So, Kid, You Want to Go to College?

In This Chapter

➤ Discovering why it's important to get your kids to start thinking about college at an early age

➤ Making sure your kids take the proper level of courses in high school so they're better prepared to get into college

➤ Learning what kids need to do in their freshman year of high school to get ready

➤ Finding out how to preplan for important tests like the SAT in order to improve your kid's results

---

If you have older kids, you've probably asked them the question, "So, you want to go to college?" Chances are they didn't have the foggiest idea of whether they wanted to go at all, much less what they wanted to do when they got there. And, the situation seemed to get worse as they got older. At least when they were little, they would tell you they wanted to be a cowboy or a nurse or a racecar driver. As parents, many of us keep trying to get a feel for our son's or daughter's potential interest in going on to college. We know that they have a better chance of making it in the real world if they have a college degree.

Even though parents know college is going to be an expensive proposition, many of them encourage their kids to think about the benefits of a college education. If you have a child who's considering college, you should begin to coach him or her on how to prepare for it early on, at the beginning of freshman year in high school at the latest.

Minimum Course Work Required

Students and parents often wonder how the level of course work affects college admission. In other words, would colleges rather see a B in an honors course or an A in a regular course? The answer isn't straightforward, but usually colleges prefer a B in an honors course. Students should choose courses based on their abilities. If a student is good in math or science, then he or she should take challenging courses in these areas.

However, the same individual might be better off taking "easier" courses in subjects where he or she isn't as strong. In any case, students should avoid taking unreasonably difficult courses in which they have no chance of getting good grades. A grade of D or F in a challenging course will hurt a student's chance of admission to a college. It could also cause enough frustration to discourage a student from pursuing higher education altogether.

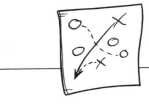

Action Plan

College admission officers use high school profiles that list the courses offered and other school data to evaluate an applicant's record.

Parents and students often worry about their high school's limited course offerings, but most colleges evaluate each applicant in light of the courses available at the student's school. For example, colleges will take into account that a small rural high school might not be able to offer advanced courses in many subjects. However, students who do have the opportunity to take more advanced courses will have an advantage, and they will be better prepared for college work. The minimum course work required for admission to most colleges is outlined in the following sections.

Language Arts

Colleges require four years of English. Fortunately, at most high schools, this is also a requirement for graduation. If a student can do work at a more challenging level, such as an honors course or one specifically labeled college prep, he or she should be encouraged to do so.

Math

Students are often prevented from pursuing certain options because they didn't take the appropriate math courses. The minimum requirement for most colleges usually includes three years of math, including Algebra I and II and Geometry. Students who are able should take Advanced Algebra, Trigonometry, Pre-calculus, or Calculus.

Science

Most colleges look for at least three years of study in science. Two years of science, usually Biology, Physics, or Chemistry, are typically required. Taking courses that are beyond the minimum requirements, such as Physiology, Biochemistry, or Anatomy, will give a student more options.

Social Sciences

Colleges expect a minimum of two years of study in Social Sciences or History. As is the case with English, students will satisfy the minimum requirement in this area by meeting high school graduation requirements. However, students with ability and interest should certainly be encouraged to take more courses.

Foreign Languages

Most colleges expect a minimum of two years of study in a single foreign language, and prefer more. Students who cannot meet this requirement for reasons such as a serious learning disability may be offered alternative programs and opportunities. Students should concentrate on a single language and not jump from one language to another. As is the case with math, insufficient foreign language preparation can limit a student's choices. Advanced work will enable a student to consider colleges that require more than the two-year minimum in language study.

Other Courses

Finally, colleges expect students to have some exposure to the fine arts and the performing arts, as well as an introduction to the world of computers. Once again, these courses may also be required for high school graduation.

All students enter high school with the potential to continue their education after graduation. Not everyone will attend college, but all students should be encouraged to keep their postsecondary school options open. They should plan a program of study during high school that preserves choices after graduation. Those students who think ahead will have many opportunities available to them.

Advice for High School Freshmen

Some simple steps taken early in high school can have great value in broadening your kids' college and financial aid prospects.

Make sure they understand the level of courses they'll need to take in high school to qualify for college. Help them select high school courses with advice from their guidance counselor. Encourage them to focus on building strong academic, vocabulary, mathematics, and critical thinking skills. These skills can have a positive effect on their college entrance exam scores.

Suggest to your kids that they discuss their academic plans with their guidance counselor. Talk to your kids to get their ideas about what they want to do and where they want to go to college. Help them research the types of colleges that might be of interest to them and send for catalogues and brochures.

Constantly encourage your kids to study hard, get excellent grades, and become involved in extracurricular activities that will help them learn skills that they can't learn in classrooms.

Insight

The **College Scholarship Services Profile (CSS)** is an institutional need-analysis service developed by the College Scholarship Services. It assesses all of your family's assets, including equity in your home. The profile also assesses student income and expected summer earnings contributions.

Some schools require you to fill out their own aid application in addition to a *College Scholarship Services Profile* (*CSS*) and a FAFSA. Be sure to find out whether the school you're interested in requires this. Some do because they figure a family's expected contribution and ultimate need using two different systems; they'll use the Federal Methodology system for the FAFSA and the Institutional Methodology system for the CSS. Some colleges will even request financial data on parents' retirement accounts, cash values of insurance policies, and the like to satisfy their award policies.

The one good thing about the CSS profile is that there's a relatively short waiting period for finding out how much money you and your family will have to contribute. That's because you send the CSS forms in at the same time you file your application for admission. The quick response time will help if you're shopping for an affordable college.

Advice for High School Sophomores

Okay, you've just started your sophomore year of high school, and you want to go to college. But college is three years off, so you don't need to think about it now. Wrong. *Now* is the time to start practicing for the Scholastic Aptitude Test (SAT) by taking preliminary tests. The score you get on the SAT can literally make or break your chances of getting into the college of your choice. So get with it, kid, and always remember what Yogi Berra said: "Practice makes perfect." You can learn all about the SAT, ACT, and other tests in Chapter 6, "Take the Tests."

Sophomore Fall Checklist

Sophomores should take the PSAT and the PLAN tests. They are preliminary preparation tests for the SAT and the ACT. High scores on these preliminary tests can qualify you for academic recognition and possible scholarships. Both tests are scheduled from October through December. You'll need to register and prepare several weeks in advance, so ask the counseling center at your high school about test dates as soon as you begin your sophomore year.

The PSAT and SAT have similar questions, so consider the PSAT as practice for the SAT. Your PSAT scores from your junior year qualify you for the National Merit Scholarship Competition. Take the test seriously, and take it as often as you can so you can become familiar with the format and the questions. Your final test score will benefit from taking these practice tests.

The Scholastic Aptitude Test is used to measure a student's ability in math, verbal comprehension, and problem solving. SATs are administered during the junior and senior years in high school.

The ACT Assessment Test is designed to assess high school students' general educational development and their ability to complete college-level work. The tests cover four skill areas: English, mathematics, reading, and science reasoning.

Sophomore Winter Checklist

Meet with your guidance counselor to review the results of the PSAT and PLAN tests. Review the material that's included with your results.

➤ Read challenging books over winter break to strengthen your vocabulary.

➤ Visit your college guidance office to research colleges, view literature, read guidebooks, and discover Internet resources.

➤ Read good books over spring break to strengthen your vocabulary.

Sophomore Spring Checklist

Visit your guidance counselor to discuss registering for the June SAT Subject Test. There's some disagreement about whether students should take the test as early as sophomore year, before they've had a chance to learn more about a subject. Taking more tests also means more expense, but we strongly recommend taking the SAT Subject Test in June of your sophomore year. This specialized test evaluates you on academic course work that you've already completed.

Discuss with your guidance counselor options for enrolling in summer school or in a summer course or program at a local college or community college.

Action Plan

Read a variety of fiction, nonfiction, and drama over summer break to strengthen your vocabulary and for pure enjoyment.

Warning

At many colleges, scholarship and grant applications need to be received early in the student's senior year in order to be considered for the freshman year of college, so don't delay. Learn everything you can about scholarships by visiting the Web sites that are listed under Scholarships in Appendix B and by state in Appendix C. You'll discover a variety of sources for financial aid that you didn't know existed.

Sophomore Summer Checklist

Some colleges require three SAT Subject Tests, which are given in early June. Two of the tests should be in a math and a writing subject. You'll be taking these tests again in your junior year, and you'll have the option of sending your best scores to colleges. PSATS will be taken in October. Consider taking a summer PSAT/SAT prep course.

Advice for High School Juniors

Going to college is almost a requirement for increased earning potential and career satisfaction. The opportunity to study at the college of your choice is both an honor and a privilege. To find the most appropriate schools in which to invest your time and to find the best sources of financial aid to fund your education, follow a few simple steps to make negotiating the course to college more manageable and more promising.

Junior Fall Checklist

Complete the necessary requirements to take or retake the SAT or the ACT tests. Take practice tests again before going to the exams so you can be familiar with the format of the questions.

➤ Start evaluating your college choices. You're looking for qualities ranging from academics to dorm life, and you'll want to know which schools offer what you want. Be prepared to identify what is important to you, such as a specific degree program, a big city or small town campus, a college that's close to home or far away, an atmosphere that's culturally diverse, or a school with special recognition. This search can be free and is always fun.

➤ Apply for every scholarship you think you have a chance to win. College can be very expensive and most likely will require financial assistance from numerous sources. The more informed you are on sources of college funding, the easier it will be to attend the college of your choice. Know where to start so you can find and qualify for grants, loans, and scholarships.

➤ Discuss and review your courses for this year and your plans for next year with your guidance counselor. Make certain you'll be meeting your college requirements with the courses you're taking and have completed.

➤ Register for the October PSAT. This PSAT will qualify you for the National Merit Scholarship Competition. With high PSAT and SAT scores, good grades, and a recommendation from your school, you may become a National Merit Scholarship Finalist. Finalists qualify not only for academic distinction, but also for scholarships.

Warning

Watch out for the avalanche of "junk" mail that will start appearing in your mailbox during your junior year. Everybody who has anything to do with the financial aid process will contact you for a variety of related reasons, offering consulting services, scholarship search services, and many other "deals." Some of what you receive will probably contain false advertising claims, but there may also be some mail worth following up on, so don't throw it all in the trash.

Junior Winter Checklist

Begin financial aid research by exploring grants, scholarships, and work-study programs with college financial aid offices and with your high school counselor.

➤ Do research on your own via the Internet.

➤ Review your PSAT test results with your guidance counselor and consult with him or her about taking the ACT or the SAT. You'll have to determine which tests are required for the colleges you're considering.

➤ Make sure you have a Social Security Number. If necessary, visit the Social Security office in your area to obtain one.

➤ Prepare a preliminary list of colleges you would like to investigate and possibly attend. Visit with your guidance counselor to discuss your list of colleges.

➤ Write to the colleges on your list, and ask for catalogues, community activity information, and special financial aid options.

➤ Register for the March SAT.

➤ Purchase a SAT prep guidebook to read over winter break, and consider taking an SAT prep course.

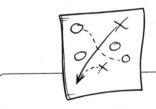

Action Plan

Contact each school to explore the financial aid possibilities. Write to the school's financial aid office as soon as you apply for admission. Applying for financial aid should not affect your chances of getting accepted.

Junior Spring Checklist

Make sure your spring checklist includes the following items, and don't let spring fever keep you from getting them done!

➤ Check the SAT I and ACT test dates.

➤ Narrow the list of colleges that you're considering down to perhaps a top-five.

➤ Contact the colleges on your short list, and request admission literature.

➤ Consider your summer plans, including summer job options, summer school, and a summer course or program at a local college or community college.

Junior Summer Checklist

Enroll in summer school at a local college, apply for an internship, or work as a volunteer in the field of your career choice.

➤ Review literature received from the colleges on your short list.

➤ Pursue other information resources about these colleges. Visit the college's Web site.

➤ Consider planning visits to colleges during the summer.

➤ Inquire about attending an interview session with one of the college admissions counselors. They book up quickly so set up appointments as early as possible. Include family members on your college tours. Incorporate these visits with your family's summer vacation plans.

➤ Begin preparing for the application process by assembling your portfolio, collecting writing samples, and drafting application essays.

➤ If applicable, contact the coaches at the college to inquire about athletic scholarships.

Advice for High School Seniors

Now that you're a high school senior and on the fast track to college, it's time to find out just how fast you really can run. You have to take the SAT and perhaps the ACT before the year is over, so now's the time to fine-tune your testing skills. Go to the library or local bookstore and get a good book that shows you how to ace these tests. If you like computers, you can also get application software that will show you how to improve your overall score. You're an idiot if you don't practice taking these tests before you take the real thing!

Senior Fall Checklist

Register for the October or November SAT and ACT tests. You can do this through your high school's student guidance office or online. (See the "Scholastic Aptitude Tests" section in Appendix B for Web site addresses.)

➤ Send for college applications and information from the schools on your short list. Check on application deadlines and any special requirements.

➤ Ask teachers, coaches, and employers to write you a letter of recommendation. Give these people at least two weeks to write you the best letters they can, and be sure to thank them.

➤ Visit with your guidance counselor to review your list of colleges, making sure your choices are appropriate for your academic and personal record.

➤ Update your personal records.

➤ Visit the scholarship Web sites listed in Appendix B to discover and research private scholarships. Apply for every scholarship you think you have a chance of winning.

➤ Visit your library, bookstore, and the Internet to research any additional sources of scholarships and financial aid.

➤ Plan visits and set up interviews at those colleges you did not visit during the summer.

➤ Develop a schedule of admissions and financial aid deadlines for yourself.

➤ Update your personal profile to include any changes or last-minute additions.

➤ Visit your guidance counselor to make sure your transcript and test scores have been sent to the colleges you selected.

➤ If you're sure about which college you want to attend, submit applications for early decision/early action programs.

➤ Prepare applications for your backup college choices.

➤ Check with your high school guidance office, bank, or public library to find out about any scheduled financial aid presentations.

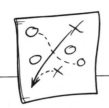

Action Plan

Obtain a Free Application for Federal Student Aid (FAFSA) form at high schools, colleges, and libraries, or by calling 1-800-4-FEDAID (333-7243). FAFSA is also available online, along with additional college information. Visit them at www.fafsa.ed.gov/ (also see the "FAFSA" section in Appendix B).

Warning

Be prepared. Students and parents should file their income tax returns early in the year in which they're applying for financial aid. You'll need information from income tax forms to complete your financial aid applications.

Senior Winter Checklist

Discuss and review your final list of colleges with your school counselor.

➤ File all remaining college applications. Have your test scores sent to those colleges.

➤ Obtain all financial aid forms that may be required by the colleges you've applied to.

➤ Update your personal profile to include any changes or last-minute additions.

➤ Complete the FAFSA form, make a copy of it, and submit it as early in January as you can.

➤ Parents and students should compile income tax information and then complete and file income tax returns early to complete the FAFSA application.

➤ Check to determine whether any other financial aid forms are required by your state or the colleges you are applying to.

Senior Spring Checklist

Review your list to make certain that you've submitted all required financial aid forms. Many private scholarships have March 1 application deadlines.

➤ Update your personal profile, and apply for any new scholarships.

➤ If required, send copies of your income tax returns to financial aid offices.

➤ Receive your Student Aid Report (SAR). (It should arrive about four weeks after you submit the FAFSA.) Contact your school's financial aid office to ask whether they need a copy of the SAR.

➤ Sign and return financial aid forms.

➤ Receive admissions notifications and compare your financial aid packages.

➤ Choose a college. Send final transcript and student loan applications to your chosen college.

➤ Contact your financial aid office to check status.

➤ Contact admissions and financial aid offices of schools whose enrollment offers you've decided to decline, informing them of your final decision. Never burn your bridges with any college you apply to!

Warning

Monitor your applications to be certain that all materials are sent and received on time and that they are complete. Be aware of all deadlines. Miss a deadline and your application will automatically be rejected.

Now that you've chosen a specific college, you may discover other sources of aid for that school.

Senior Summer Checklist

Complete any remaining financial aid forms. Check your Scholarships.com mailbox. New awards are added regularly. It's never too early to start looking for next year.

Ten Financial Aid Tips

The financial aid tips that we include in this section are certainly not meant to be all-inclusive. They will, however, help you stay on top of the financial aid process so you can get the best possible support out of the program.

1. Prioritize your efforts, beginning with the federal government. Explore the private sector for additional financial assistance programs. Use Web sites like Scholarship.com to locate the private sector funds to apply for.

2. Contact each school to explore the financial aid possibilities by writing their financial aid office as soon as you apply for admission. Applying for financial aid will not affect your chances of getting accepted.

3. Be prepared. Students and parents should file their income tax returns early. You'll need information from income tax forms to complete your financial aid applications.

4. Try to get to know the financial aid administrators (FAAs) at the various colleges that you've applied to. Take notes whenever you talk to them so that you'll remember their names and what you've talked about in the past. The help of the FAAs will be valuable if questions arise later on in the year.

5. Submit a FAFSA even if you don't think you'll qualify for aid. Being rejected for federal aid is sometimes a prerequisite for private awards. Some schools require you to fill out their own aid application as well as a CSS profile. Be sure to find out what each school needs.

6. Apply for aid as early as possible. Deadlines vary, but your application for Federal Student Aid can be sent any time after January 1. An early application will help you get the best financial aid package possible.

7. Take advantage of tuition prepayment discounts. Many colleges offer up to a 10 percent discount for early payment.

8. Money from grandparents could be paid in your name directly to the school. This avoids gift tax liability.

9. Investigate company-sponsored tuition plans. Many employers will invest in the education of their employees or children of employees.

10. Apply for financial aid each and every year you are in school. Even if you receive aid during one year, you must reapply to get it for the next year. Use the renewal FAFSA form to reapply for aid and save time. See your FAA for assistance.

To get the most out of financial aid, parents and students need to have a plan that starts in the student's freshman year. Go to your public library, and check out the latest scholarship books. There are lots of them out there, and the research librarian can help you find them. They will give you listings of available scholarships and contact addresses for applying. Check out the Internet for scholarship opportunities. If you don't have access to the Internet at home, use the public library or your high school's computer lab.

The Least You Need to Know

➤ Parents and kids should start thinking about college as early as possible.

➤ Students should choose courses that match their capabilities and will result in good grades.

➤ Important tests, such as the PSAT, PLAN, SAT, and ACT should be taken several times to improve results.

➤ High school students who make plans using the checklists in this chapter will greatly increase their chances of acceptance at colleges of their choice, and of obtaining financial aid.

Chapter 5

Where Do You Want to Go, Kid?

> ## In This Chapter
>
> ➤ Gathering the information you need for determining which college is right for you
>
> ➤ Finding out how to ask the right questions to be sure you're informed about every aspect of financial aid
>
> ➤ Comparing college alternatives using failsafe selection criteria

This chapter is about ways to get the most out of every dollar you spend on college. Look for colleges that have innovative programs to help you meet their ever-increasing tuition cost. Many even have unique programs that will help you find room and board at very competitive rates. Remember: Tuition is just one part of the total cost line.

Choose Wisely, Kid

The process of choosing a college or university can be both exciting and frustrating at the same time. If you're a parent, the last thing you want is to face a confrontation with a son or daughter who wants to attend a college that you don't think is right for him or her or, worse yet, one that you flat-out can't afford.

Although it's not the intention of this book to get into the philosophical reasons for selecting one college over another, it is within its charter to discuss the value issues that parent and student should consider jointly. Then, you can select the college

options that make sense in terms of meeting both your budgetary and educational objectives. This chapter covers all of those issues.

Start by Gathering Information

Write for school catalogues, their financial aid brochures, and any other information they may have, such as the placement of their graduates. It may be more appropriate to request information over the phone because you'll have a chance to query the person you're talking to about what information is available. After you've obtained the information, you and your family can compare the various schools and decide which ones deserve further investigation.

> **Warning**
>
> This chapter makes some general assumptions about the subject matter that is discussed. For example, what may be an advantage to one student is a disadvantage or has no effect on another student.

Your in-depth investigation might include a visit to the campus and interviews with the admissions officer, the financial aid administrator, and the placement director. Make sure you ask the admissions officer questions regarding the academic quality of the programs that are of most interest, and find out what the student/faculty ratio is.

Questions to Ask the Admissions Officer

When you meet with the admissions officer, your objective should be to find out everything you can about what the college requires before they will admit a student into their institution. For example, you might ask:

How much emphasis is placed on a student's high school GPA or SAT score?

Which high school extracurricular activities are more important?

Ask the admissions officer to profile for you their "ideal" student applicant so that you can get a good picture of exactly what they're looking for.

Questions to Ask the Financial Aid Administrator

Questions that you pose to the FAA should cover the types of financial assistance programs that are available, application deadlines, and any special aid programs they offer. Also ask:

➤ How are awards made, and how does the appeals process work?

➤ What percentage of students receive financial aid, and what is the average amount of annual assistance per student?

These two critical financial aid numbers, when compared with the annual cost for the college, will give you a good idea of how much financial aid you can expect.

Action Plan

A quick formula for calculating the amount of financial assistance you can expect is to compare the percentage of students on financial aid and the average amount of aid per student with the annual cost of the college. For example, if one of your top colleges is, on average, awarding $4,300 to 57 percent of its students and another one of your top choices is awarding less than half that, you can narrow your selection process based on the probability of the award you may receive.

Other questions you may want to ask an FAA are …

➤ What's the total cost of attending your school for one year?

➤ What's been the average increase in tuition over the past three years?

➤ How do you calculate a student's financial need?

➤ Do you have a "need-blind" admissions policy, meaning that equal opportunity is given to students for admission regardless of their financial needs?

➤ Do you meet the full need of every admitted student?

➤ What percentage of the freshman class is paying full tuition?

➤ What scholarship opportunities are available?

➤ Is my financial aid package renewable each year?

➤ What applications are required, and what are the deadlines?

➤ When will I receive my financial aid award letter?

Questions to Ask the Placement Director

When you meet with the placement director, ask:

➤ What placement services are available?

➤ What is the profile of recent graduates? (For example, what percentage had Bachelor's versus Master's degrees?)

➤ What percentage were able to find jobs through the placement office?

➤ What was the average starting salary in the various career fields?

If you can't get answers to these basic questions, then you're probably dealing with a school that has a mediocre placement office. Or, worse yet, they may not even have one. If it's not possible to visit all of the schools, get the information over the phone.

Look for Creative Payment Plans

The fact of the matter is that more and more colleges are looking for ways to take the sting out of paying the costs. For many of them, this means offering plans that make it possible to get around paying for college in one formidable annual chunk.

Many colleges now offer a range of innovative payment programs. Some of the programs are as simple as allowing you to pay for tuition and room and board in interest-free, equal installments over 12 months instead of having to fork over whopping payments at the start of every quarter or semester.

Some colleges offer tuition stabilization programs. If you're willing to pay them the full four-year tuition up front, future tuition hikes do not apply to you.

Action Plan

Never forget the fact that your kid is still the customer when he or she starts searching for the right college to attend. The college business is a competitive business, although you'll seldom hear college administrators admit this fine point. All colleges need students in order to survive. Consider yourself a consumer: Tell them what you're willing to pay for their service, and listen to what they have to say.

Become a Wise Consumer

For both parents and kids, getting a college education is a major investment of time and money, so make sure that the school your student attends is right for him or her. When choosing a school, a student should consider things like:

➤ The quality of instructors and school facilities.

➤ Information about students at the school, such as ...

➤ The percentage of students who complete the program.

➤ The percentage of students who find jobs within a short time after graduation.

➤ The percentage of students who default on their student loans.

The school is required to inform you of its aid procedures and deadlines, and how and when you'll receive your aid award. Be sure that you've read and understood the school's satisfactory-progress policy, and keep copies of your enrollment agreement, the school's catalogue, and all loan documents that you've received.

Count Your Credit

If you have an excellent credit history, some colleges offer very low interest loans for financing your kid's four-year education over as many as ten years. The point is that there are as many flexible college finance programs out there as there are colleges.

As you and your son or daughter begin your search for viable college alternatives, make sure you ask the question: "Do you offer flexible finance programs?" If they tell you "No," scratch them off your list and proceed to your next college option.

It May Be Cheaper at the Top

As a result of doing such extensive research into the financial aid possibilities available for his second child, my friend George was literally stunned to find out how much aid he was eligible for. And even more surprising was that top institutions were among his most viable choices.

George had uncovered a little-known fact: The more expensive the institution, the more likely it is to offer need-based financial aid. He said, "When we looked through the guidebooks, we found colleges that met about 90 percent of our need." George discovered that he had more choices for his children than families whose incomes were $20,000 to $30,000 higher than his.

For example, let's say your EFC (expected family contribution) toward college tuition is $10,000, and you're eligible to receive $1,000 in aid. For a college costing $20,000 in tuition, you could be eligible for

Help

College Opportunities On-Line is brought to you by the National Center for Education Statistics in the U.S. Department of Education. It was authorized by Congress in 1998 to help college students, future students, and their parents understand the differences between colleges and how much it costs to attend college. The site is www.nces.ed.gov/, found in the "Career Guidance" section in Appendix B."

$11,000 in aid. The amount you're expected to contribute is the same, regardless of the total cost at either school. What changes is the amount that different colleges will provide you in financial aid.

If you can get your kid into an Ivy League college, and if you have financial need, the college might actually cost you less than a state-supported university. Ivy League institutions don't typically give merit-based aid, so if you can get accepted and have need, they may provide you with enough money to make up the difference. It's all based on your financial resources.

Too many students eliminate colleges from their "preferred list" before determining their financial aid eligibility. Before they address cost issues, students should make choices based on the attributes of the colleges and where those choices fit into their career plans. That's the whole philosophy of financial aid. Thus, highly talented students from low-income families may qualify for significant amounts of aid and have the opportunity to attend institutions they otherwise might not have even considered. If you can be admitted, you can figure out a way to go.

At the other end of the misinformation scale, families often assume there is some income cutoff level that turns off the financial aid tap. That's not true, because even though financial aid is driven by a family's ability to pay, that ability is affected by special circumstances, size, and how many of their children are attending college.

Selection Criteria

Less-selective colleges focus on whether applicants meet minimum requirements and whether there is room for more students. Grades are not overlooked, but acceptable grades might be the only requirement beyond an interest in college study. The SAT I or ACT may be required, but test scores might be used for course placement rather than admissions decisions. Other factors might be considered, but they probably won't play a major part.

At more-selective colleges, course work, grades, test scores, recommendations, and essays will be considered. There may be additional considerations, but the major factor will be whether a student is ready for college-level study. Students could be denied admission because of some weakness in their academic preparation, less-impressive grades or test scores, or a lack of interest in higher education.

At the most-selective colleges, as many as 10 or 15 students might apply for each spot. Each applicant usually has the necessary academic qualifications, but they can't all be accepted. Their admissions officers look carefully at every aspect of a student's high school experience. Applicants must have academic strength and impressive SAT or ACT scores. Since so many applicants are strong academically, other factors become quite important in the admissions decision.

Although the most-selective colleges receive a great deal of publicity, there are actually very few of them.

Extracurricular Activities Do Count

The importance of what a student does outside of school has been exaggerated. Selective colleges may look at extracurricular activities, but they're only interested in applicants who've shown long-term commitments to one or two activities. These colleges aren't trying to enroll a class of well-rounded students; they want to admit a well-rounded *group* of students. An applicant with achievements in a specific area may have an advantage, but it's hard to tell which areas might be of interest to a college in any given year.

Fill a College's Need

At the most-selective colleges, you must fill a need in the freshman class. Otherwise, you might not be admitted, despite outstanding academic records. That need might be something as arbitrary as the student's home state, intended major, desire for housing on campus, or ability to play a specific musical instrument in the college orchestra.

If there's housing for only part of the freshman class, then admissions decisions must reflect this limitation. If there's room for only 25 new engineering majors, but 75 new accounting majors can be accommodated, this must also be considered as admissions decisions are made. On the other hand, if a college wants geographic distribution and an ethnic balance of students, admissions decisions will reflect those needs.

Basically, the admission process is unpredictable and holds many potential surprises.

Warning

Don't believe what you hear about the importance that colleges place on your extracurricular activities. Less-selective colleges rarely look beyond test scores and grades, and those that are more selective tend to change their interest in specific activities from year to year.

Find the Right Match

Remember that "more selective" does not necessarily mean "better." Our society often associates exclusivity with higher value. However, college is one area where that notion is wrong. If you focus on the most-selective colleges, you risk overlooking your personal needs. Try to find colleges that provide a good match with your interests, objectives, characteristics, and needs. Such colleges may be found anywhere. If you consider only the most competitive college within your area, you may overlook more appropriate possibilities.

The best-prepared student will have the most options. That doesn't necessarily mean attending the most-competitive college. The overriding concern should be finding the right match. If you're well prepared, you will have many options to choose from.

Some Do's and Don'ts

Parents: Be candid with your kids about the financial aid process. Many parents are reluctant to discuss finances with their children because they don't want to unduly concern them. The degree to which you involve your children should be based on your assessment of how much they should know. But your children will be better prepared to help make wise family decisions if they have information about the factors you are dealing with. They'll have to become involved sooner or later in their college years as they take over paying back college and graduate school loans.

The Do's

Keep these do's in mind as you and your son or daughter go through the process of choosing a college:

➤ Do make sure the information you're using to apply for aid reflects your parental status. This tip applies to a divorced as well as either a custodial or a noncustodial parent. Some institutions don't specifically ask about this on their forms. It could make a difference in the financial aid you might receive.

➤ Do have an organized plan in place to keep track of applications. Note deadlines and what you have to do to follow up. Some high school counselors can give you forms that will help you compare financial aid packages.

The Don'ts

The list of don'ts is longer:

➤ Don't wait to apply for financial aid until your child is admitted. This common misperception among parents sets them to scrambling when an offer of admission is made. At this late date, a lot of the available money has already been allocated. Many families don't realize how time-sensitive admissions are. Your financial package could get cut by as much as 50 percent if you don't meet deadlines.

➤ Don't assume you have to wait until you get current tax information to begin applying for financial aid. Estimates of your income that are based on the previous year are acceptable. Many people miss out on the full funding they could have gotten because they were waiting for tax returns.

➤ Don't assume you'll be penalized because you've saved for college tuition. Legally, you can be asked to contribute only 5.6 percent of your savings toward tuition. You will get slightly less aid, but you'll also end up borrowing less money and paying less interest.

➤ Don't start the process of seeking aid when your financial house is a mess. Clean up your credit history before starting to apply for loans. Have all your financial records handy and in order.

Online Applications

Save time and paper by submitting your school application online. At the College Quest www.petersons.com/schools/ccq-6.html, you can apply to more than 1,200 colleges using a single application. You enter all of your application information once, and then it's available for use on each new application that you open. Once you've completed your applications, you can print and mail them, or you can submit them electronically and securely to colleges that accept electronic applications.

College Admissions Criteria

For many years, admissions policies were "need-blind," reflecting the belief that students who needed financial aid should be treated the same as those whose families could afford the total cost.

However, much has changed in recent years. A number of colleges still maintain "need-blind" admissions policies, but other colleges include the family's financial situation in the admissions process. This doesn't mean that only students with enough money are admitted, but rather that these colleges know they can't satisfy the financial aid needs of all applicants.

Most colleges accept the strongest applicants without regard to need. Then, as financial aid resources begin to run out, students who don't have as much academic strength are evaluated for their family's ability to pay. This may sound unfair, but so is accepting a student who cannot afford the school without financial help.

Other colleges have a policy of meeting a portion of every accepted student's need. A certain amount

Help

CollegeNET was launched in 1995 and lets college applicants complete, file, and pay for their admissions applications entirely through the Internet. Over 350 colleges and universities have contracted with CollegeNET to serve as their official Web-based admissions application site. For Web sites to check out, see the College Admission Requirements section in Appendix B or CollegeNet's Web site at www. collegenet.com/.

of need is left unmet for all. Unfortunately, students and parents have no control over the policies or the resources at any college. If a student needs financial aid to attend college, he or she should consider each school's policy when deciding where to apply. Each college has a different approach to admitting qualified applicants and has different factors that it considers.

At most colleges, admissions criteria might include:

Courses taken in high school.

Counselor or teacher recommendations.

Ethnicity.

Overall grade point average.

Answers to application questions and the quality of submitted essays.

Location of the student's home.

Personal interview.

Alumni relationship.

Rank in class.

Activities outside the classroom.

Major that the student is applying for.

Admissions test results.

Special talents and skills.

Family's ability to pay for college expenses.

These are not arranged to reflect any specific priorities. In fact, there is no general agreement about how criteria should be ranked. Most likely, the chief admissions factor is a student's high school record—both the student's grades and the courses taken.

Colleges evaluate applications in very different ways, depending on how selective, or competitive, the college is. At one extreme are "open admission" colleges. These schools require only a high school diploma and accept students on a first-come, first-served basis. At the other extreme are very selective colleges that consider all of the factors listed. These colleges admit only a small percentage of applicants each year. Most colleges fall somewhere in between.

International Considerations

The idea of an international experience excites many American students until they find out how difficult it is to get any financial aid from foreign institutions. Obtaining aid at a foreign institution is challenging for United States citizens because you're obviously competing with students who are citizens of that institution's country. About 100,000 Americans study away from United States shores each year, and many have been able to find the financial aid they needed to make it abroad. If you wish to study abroad, be prepared to work hard at locating aid sources.

See Chapter 14, "Adult, Graduate, and International Programs," for more on studying abroad, and on study for foreign students in the United States. Also check out the Web sites listed in the "International" section of Appendix B. The best one I've found is FinAid at www.petersons.com/finaid.com.

Selecting the Winner

Choosing the right school is difficult; even narrowing your choices down to a few likely candidates can be an exercise in frustration. With thousands of schools in the United States, how will you ever find the right one for you?

CollegeQuest at www.petersons.com/ is an online service that can help get you through the selection process. This service offers profiles of every undergraduate institution accredited in the United States, along with specially designed tools to help you manage the college admissions process. CollegeQuest also allows you to search for schools by location, major, difficulty level, and other factors, and then compare them side-by-side and apply online. The Web site provides informative articles about college selection and admissions.

If you're thinking about graduate or professional school, see Chapter 14, and look to the Graduate School Channel at www.petersons.com/graduate/ for detailed information on 35,000 programs, including business, law, medical, and dental school. *Peterson's* is an annual publication that offers a wealth of information about planning for college, and about distance learning programs, and also has a discussion area for graduate students. Check out their site: www.petersons.com/. You'll find more Web sites in Appendix B under "College Admission Requirements."

Action Plan

Network with your friends. Reach out for information that your friends and their friends have discovered in their respective searches for the perfect college to attend. If you have the opportunity, take a "walkabout" on the campuses of your preferred colleges and survey the current students who are also on "walkabouts." Ask them what they think about the college to get invaluable insight and information.

The Least You Need To Know

➤ To make sure you pick the college that's right for you, look at the full spectrum of offerings for each college that you're considering.

➤ Don't let high tuition at your favorite institutions scare you. Find out what they're willing to offer you in their financial aid package.

➤ Know what your favorite college is looking for in their admissions requirements so that you can customize your application accordingly.

➤ Going online to CollegeNet and CollegeQuest is the best way to get information and to file applications in the least amount of time.

Chapter 6

Take the Tests

In This Chapter

➤ Learning what admissions tests are all about and why you must take them

➤ Discovering how you can improve your score with a little practice

➤ Understanding how test scores are used to get you into college and to win you merit scholarships

---

There are many thousands of high schools in this country, each with its own grading policy. Years ago, colleges determined that they needed a common measure, such as a standard test, to evaluate applicants. Many college students and parents are confused about the role that college admissions tests play in both the admissions and the merit scholarship awards process. To better understand these tests, students and parents should consider all the factors that influence scores, and that is the topic of this chapter.

By the time many students start to think about college admissions tests, it's too late. These tests measure skills developed over a long period of time—skills that cannot be acquired through short-term preparation. "Last minute" courses may help students demonstrate their abilities, but they won't help students develop the skills that the college admissions tests measure.

What can students do early on that may have an impact on test results? Check out the section "Scholastic Aptitude," in Appendix B, "Directory of General Financial Aid Resources."

The Almighty Scholastic Aptitude Test (SAT)

The *Scholastic Aptitude Test (SAT)* is taken by over two million high school students each year. Scholastic Aptitude Test (SAT) scores, course grades, and other information about your academic background helps college admission officers evaluate how well prepared you are to do college-level work. Because courses and grading standards vary widely from school to school, scores on standardized tests such as the SAT help colleges to compare the academic achievements of students from different schools.

The SAT is divided into two parts, one for verbal skills and one for math. The maximum possible score on the SAT is 800 points per part, for a total of 1600 points. The minimum possible score is 200 points per part.

Colleges often require applicants to take the SAT as a prerequisite for admission. This test is designed to measure verbal and math-reasoning skills that students have developed over time. The SAT I helps predict a student's success in college. Some colleges require students to take the American College Test (ACT), although many will accept either the SAT I or the ACT. While these two tests are somewhat different, the objectives are similar. Each provides an indication of a student's potential for academic success. The ACT test measures a student's ability in math, verbal comprehension, and problem solving. Usually students take this test during their junior or senior year of high school.

What Exactly Is the SAT I?

The *SAT I* is a three-hour, multiple-choice test used by many colleges as a factor in undergraduate admissions and placement decisions. It has seven sections, placed in random order.

The test contains three scored math sections, with a total of 60 questions. Two of the math sections are 30 minutes each, and the third section runs 15 minutes.

The math questions appear in three different formats:

➤ Five-choice problem-solving questions

➤ Multiple-choice quantitative comparison questions

➤ Grid-in questions

Quantitative comparison questions ask you to compare two columns and determine which one is greater. *Grid-ins* are the only nonmultiple-choice questions on the test; you're asked to find a numerical answer and mark it on a grid.

The SAT I also contains three scored verbal sections for a total of 78 questions. Two of the verbal sections are 30 minutes each, and the third is 15 minutes.

The two 30-minute sections consist of sentence completions, analogies, and critical reading; the 15-minute section consists only of critical reading questions.

The seventh section on the SAT is an experimental section composed of either math or verbal questions. It's used to test questions for future tests and is not scored. There is no reliable way of knowing which of the seven sections is experimental, since the seven sections are randomly ordered.

You'll find more about the verbal and math sections later in this chapter.

Insight

The **Scholastic Aptitude Reasoning Test (SAT I)** is a three-hour test, primarily multiple-choice, that measures verbal and mathematical reasoning abilities that develop over time. Colleges often require SAT I scores as part of the admissions application. **Scholastic Aptitude Subject Tests (SAT II)** are one-hour, primarily multiple-choice tests in specific subjects. Unlike the SAT I, which measures more general abilities, Subject Tests measure knowledge of particular subjects and the ability to apply that knowledge. Many colleges require or recommend one or more of these tests for admission or placement. SAT scores are one of the main selection criteria used by college admissions officials to assess a student's academic qualifications and abilities.

How Important Is the SAT?

Unfortunately, your SAT score is often one of the most important pieces in your admissions portfolio. If your score falls below a school's acceptable range, the admissions officers may look very critically at the other parts of your application; if your scores exceed the school's acceptable range, you'll have a leg up in the applicant pool for that college.

Larger schools tend to rely heavily, or even base their admissions decisions entirely, on SAT scores and high school grade-point averages. Smaller and more-selective schools tend to place more weight on other factors, such as your interview (if one is required), your essays, and your extracurricular activities. Some schools have begun to de-emphasize the SAT, and a few have even made it optional as an entry requirement.

What Is the PSAT?

The *PSAT* is a test that's very similar to the SAT. In fact, the PSAT is composed of previously administered SAT questions. It is given to high school students in their sophomore and junior years. The test is used to help select National Merit Scholars, but unless you're one of the very few who are in contention for these scholarships, it's really only a practice test. Colleges will not see your PSAT scores; only your high school will. If you're interested in doing well on the SAT, make sure you practice by taking the PSAT first.

Help

There are many Web sites that address every aspect of SAT and ACT testing. They are listed in the "Scholastic Aptitude Tests" section in Appendix B.

Who Created the SAT?

The SAT I and SAT II are written and administered by the College Entrance Examination Board (better known as the "College Board"). The people who work at the College Board are average folks who just happen to make a living writing and administering tests. The SAT math sections will test only basic arithmetic, algebra, and geometry. But the questions are often confusingly worded, and the Educational Testing Service (ETS) has planted plenty of trick choices to seduce you into picking incorrect answers. You may get the feeling at times that the ETS has rigged the game against you—and you're right.

Preparing for the Test

The best academic predictor for most college admissions offices is the student's high school record. In other words, high school courses and grades are usually the most accurate and comprehensive factors considered in the admissions process. The admissions tests do give the college another valuable piece of evidence about a student: potential. Since the SAT and ACT tests measure potential rather than achievement, it's possible for students to prepare for them.

Long-Term Preparation

True success on these tests is based on long-term preparation. Experiences in the classroom will affect how well a student does on admissions tests. But students spend only six hours or so each day for 180 days a year in school, so what they do outside the classroom is important, too.

Students who have strong reading habits do well on the verbal part of the SAT. There is no substitute for reading about a variety of subjects on a regular basis. Both the SAT and ACT contain questions and reading passages that reflect subjects that students encounter in many areas, including the social sciences, humanities, literature, and physical sciences. Students who read a lot generally do better.

Admissions tests emphasize critical reading skills and vocabulary strength. Students develop most of their vocabulary through reading experiences, but they may also benefit by learning to attack new words. Knowing prefixes, suffixes, and root words will be helpful in some situations. Studying a foreign language can help a student figure out new words.

Students who hope to do well on the math portions of these tests should take challenging math and science courses to help them further develop the math reasoning and problem-solving skills that will be measured.

Warning

Unfortunately, by the time most students begin to worry about admissions tests, it's too late to do much about preparing for them. Preparation should begin well before the required test date, like in the first year of high school.

Short-Term Preparation

During the later high school years, students should begin short-term preparation for taking college entrance tests. They should take practice tests such as the PSAT, which gives students a chance to become familiar with the SAT format and types of questions. After they take the test, students receive a score report, which shows how they did on each type of question. They should use the report to pinpoint where they need to do more work. Taking the PSAT will help students feel more relaxed about taking the SAT. There's a similar warm-up for the ACT.

Test Preparation Courses

Students may also consider taking a test preparation course. However, they need to realize that these "coaching" courses aren't meant to help them develop the skills the tests measure; they try to help students demonstrate skills they already have.

Coaching courses usually try to help students keep the test in perspective so they'll be more relaxed. The courses also teach test-taking strategies. Some students need help in these areas, and their scores should improve after taking a coaching course.

There are free guides and practice tests available in most high school guidance offices. Also, counselors and teachers are usually happy to help students prepare.

Some students' test scores won't improve when they take a special preparation course simply because they have modest abilities in the areas being tested. Their scores may even go down, adding to their frustration and probably diminishing their self-confidence.

What's Inside the SAT?

As explained earlier, the SAT I is a three-hour test that consists of six scored sections and one unscored equating section for test research. The majority of the test is multiple choice; however, there is a variety of question types.

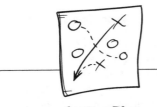

Within the two main parts of the exam, the questions are arranged in order of difficulty from least to most difficult. It is to your advantage to answer the easier questions first and then tackle the more difficult ones in your remaining time.

Action Plan

Check out the sample PSAT questions at www.review.com/. Web site addresses are listed in Appendix B under Scholastic Aptitude Tests.

The Verbal Part

The verbal part of the exam is primarily a test of your vocabulary skills. The *critical reading section* is composed of word essays taken from a variety of topics, including social sciences, natural sciences, and the humanities. The passages can be either fiction or nonfiction. The critical reading section is intended to measure reading comprehension skills. There are three types of questions in the critical reading section:

1. **Explicit questions**   These ask you to refer to specific facts or words in the passage.
2. **Inferential questions**   These ask you to draw conclusions from the passage.
3. **Line reference questions**   These ask you to refer to a specific line in the passage.

To enhance your reading comprehension skills, you should be reading articles in quality periodicals and newspapers. When you finish an article, always ask yourself, "What was the main point of what I just read?" There will be at least two paired passages in the critical reading section of the exam. The questions based on the pair of passages will ask you to compare or contrast them.

The *analogy section* of the exam tests your vocabulary skills and your ability to recognize relationships between words. When answering analogy questions, remember that you're looking for similar relationships between pairs of words, not for words that have similar meanings. Don't think about the original paired words independently of one another; always think about the relationship between them.

Remember that words can have more than one meaning and that some words can be used as more than one part of speech. The correct answer pair must be the same part of speech as the original pair. If the original pair consists of a verb and a noun, then the answer will also be a verb and a noun.

The *sentence completion section* of the exam tests your vocabulary skills and your ability to understand sentence structure. Note the use of conjunctions such as *not, but, though,* and *although,* which change the direction of the sentence. The two parts of the sentence will contrast with each other, and the answer you choose should fit the logic of that contrast. If a sentence has two blanks, make sure both answers fit the logic of the sentence.

Some of the sentence completion questions will have two blanks, rather than just one. To solve these questions, do them one blank at a time. Pick one blank or the other, whichever seems easier to you, and figure out which word should go in the blank. Often, but not always, the second blank is easier to figure out. Then cross off all of the choices that don't work for that blank. If more than one choice remains, pick a word for the other blank and see which of the remaining choices works best.

Take a look at this example, and select the appropriate words to fill in the two blanks:

The scientific community was _____ when a living specimen of the coelacanth, which they feared had become _____, was discovered by deep-sea fishermen.

(A)	perplexed	common
(B)	overjoyed	dangerous
(C)	unconcerned	exterminated
(D)	astounded	extinct
(E)	dismayed	alive

Let's review some of the logical steps you would go through when you search for the correct answer (that is, the two words to insert) to this question: Who is the audience that's addressed by the opening words of the sentence? The answer is "the scientific community," which we know intuitively is not perplexed (Answer A), unconcerned (Answer C), or dismayed (Answer E) as a group in general. We have quickly ruled out three of the five choices for the fill-ins.

Wouldn't it be logical to conclude that the scientific community would be overjoyed (Answer B) or astounded (Answer D) at the discovery? That's a tough call, until we take the time to look at the second insert word to find the correct answer (Answer D). They feared that the animal was extinct rather than that it was dangerous; to be dangerous it would still have to be running around the earth in great numbers.

The point of this exercise is to show you how to carefully dissect the important segments of a sentence so that you can quickly arrive at the right answer and move on to the next part of the test.

The Math Part

The math part of the exam will test your knowledge of arithmetic, geometry, algebra, and logical reasoning. Most of the questions on the math portion of the exam will be questions you recognize from your school textbooks. However, there may be questions that are unfamiliar to you and that require you to think about a problem in an unfamiliar way. Here are some examples of math questions that might appear on your SAT test:

A. If a student scores 70, 90, 95, and 105 on four tests, what is the average test score?

B. If a student has an average score of 80 on four tests, what is the total of the scores received on those tests?

C. If a student has an average of 60 on tests whose totals add up to 360, how many tests has the student taken?

D. If the average of 4 and x is equal to the average of 2, 8, and x, what is the value of x?

E. The average (arithmetic mean) of four numbers is 80. If two of the numbers are 50 and 60, what is the sum of the other two numbers?

F. What percent of 5 is 6?

G. 60 percent of 90 is the same as 50 percent of what number?

H. A group of 30 adults and 20 children went to the beach. If 50 percent of the adults and 80 percent of the children went swimming, what percentage of the group went swimming?
(A) 31% (B) 46% (C) 50% (D) 62% (E) 65%

The answers to the questions are ...

A. 90

B. 320

C. 6

D. x = 8

E. 210

F. 120%

G. 108

H. 31%

The *student-produced response section* of the exam (also known as grid-in) is unique. There are no answer choices to select from. The most important thing to understand about this section is how to enter your answers on the answer sheet grid. You use a pencil to shade the area on the grid that you feel is the answer to the question.

The standard *multiple-choice section* of the exam will cover a variety of mathematical concepts. Read each problem carefully. Translate any word problems into mathematical notation, and begin to solve the problem. Review the answer choices, and find the solution that fits best. If you're unsure of an answer, use the process of elimination. If you're completely unsure of the correct answer and cannot make an educated guess, skip the question and move on. There is no penalty for omitted questions. However, there is a penalty of one-fourth point for an incorrect answer.

The *quantitative comparison questions* deal with the concepts of equalities, inequalities, and estimation. This should be the quickest type of math question to answer. Remember, you don't need to calculate values; just compare them. Review the answer choices, and find the solution that fits best. There are only four answer choices (A–D) on this section. A selection of (E) will not be scored. If you're unsure of an answer, use the process of elimination. If you're completely unsure of the correct answer and cannot make an educated guess, skip the question and move on. The penalty for an incorrect answer on this section is the most severe of all the math sections. There is a one-third point deduction.

Warning

Before you take the SAT, be sure you know what the penalties for incorrect answers are in each section. It will help you decide whether to make a guess or just not answer a difficult question.

How Much Time Should You Spend on Each Question?

It depends. The amount of time needed varies from student to student, from section to section, and even from question to question. As a result, it is very important to monitor the time you spend on each type of SAT question while taking practice exams. This will allow you to make informed decisions about the order in which you should answer questions, and you will be able to determine when you're wasting too much time on a single question.

In the case of the verbal portion, most questions increase in difficulty as you progress through each section of the test.

The easier analogy and sentence completion questions may require only a few seconds' work, whereas the later (or harder) ones may take a minute or more to answer. The critical reading questions are not arranged in order of difficulty, but the reading passages often are. In other words, if two reading passages are contained within a single verbal section, the latter passage, as well as the questions associated with it, will probably be the more challenging of the two. Also, critical reading questions generally take more time to answer than other questions on the verbal section. An entire passage generally takes 10 to 15 minutes. So, what does this all mean for you?

Essentially, if you find yourself struggling to finish the verbal section within the given time limits, you should probably answer the questions in the following fashion:

1. Answer the easier sentence completions first.
2. Move on to the easier analogies.
3. Return to the sentence completions that require more effort.
4. Go back to the analogies that require more effort.
5. Finally, tackle the critical reading passages.

The math questions are also arranged in order of difficulty. For the most part, however, you will not have subgroupings of question types comparable to those in the verbal portion of the SAT.

In two of the sections you'll be given regular multiple-choice problems; on the third section you'll first need to answer the quantitative comparison questions and then the grid-ins. In both cases, however, the subsections are a mixture of problems designed to test your knowledge of arithmetic, algebra, and geometry. So you may want to focus your attention on questions that deal with your areas of strength before working on questions involving mathematical topics that are relatively difficult for you—even if the questions that are easier for you appear later in the exam.

How Does SAT Scoring Work?

Scoring on the SAT is very different from what you're accustomed to in school. In school you usually receive a certain number of points when you answer a question correctly, and you lose an equal number of points when you answer a question incorrectly or when you skip it. On the verbal part of the SAT, you receive one point for each correct answer and you lose a quarter point for each incorrect one. Questions that you skip don't count against you, but they won't count for you, either.

A scoring sheet for an SAT test will have the following basic formula for each verbal section:

The scoring system is designed so that one correct answer compensates for four incorrect choices. The reason for this is fairly simple: If you randomly guessed from among five multiple-choice solutions provided for a problem, you would have a one-in-five chance of choosing the correct answer. Given these odds, a student who made random guesses throughout this portion of the exam should end up with a *raw score* of zero on the test. If you can eliminate even one answer, however, you've put yourself in a position that betters those odds.

Insight

The **raw score** is, as the name implies, the score you get on the SAT after your wrong answers are deducted from your right answers. Fortunately, your right answers receive more points than your wrong answers, as we explained in the introduction to this section.

Theoretically then, you should be able to improve your score through random guessing when you're choosing from among four or fewer answers. (However, our experience shows that students who are able to eliminate only one or two answers don't really have enough information to answer the question; they usually guess wrong and are thus better off skipping to the next question.)

If, however, you can eliminate all but two (or maybe three) answers, take the chance and guess. Think of it this way: If you guess one answer correctly for every two you get wrong, you're still ahead in the game (unlike when you make a random guess without eliminating, in which case you should simply break even). This is because the one correct answer netted you one point, whereas the two incorrect answers cost you only a half point combined. The resulting half point will round up to a whole point, canceling out your incorrect guesses. In other words, you should consider guessing if you can narrow your choices to three answers, and always guess if you can eliminate all but two answers.

Although the same scoring scale applies to the regular math sections of the SAT, the quantitative comparison and grid-in portions of the math exam are slightly different.

Quantitative comparisons have only four answer choices, and you will lose a third of a point for each incorrect solution. Why? The logic is the same as for the five-answer questions: If you randomly guessed from among four multiple-choice answers, you would have a one-in-four chance of choosing the correct solution. Given these odds, a student who made random guesses throughout this portion of the exam should end up with a raw score of zero.

As with the five-choice questions, eliminating one answer should theoretically put you at an advantage. Eliminating two choices gives you a 50/50 shot in this portion of the exam. The grid-in section carries no guessing penalty. Of course, since your answers are self-generated, it's very unlikely that you'll get the correct answer by just taking a shot in the dark. On the other hand, if you've worked on a grid-in problem but feel unsure about your solution, you should still enter it on the answer grid since there is no penalty.

To Guess or Not to Guess

If you're faced with a verbal question you cannot answer, you'll have to decide whether to guess or skip the question entirely. All incorrectly answered questions on the verbal section of the SAT I result in the deduction of one quarter point from your final score. There is no deduction for omitted questions.

If you're faced with a math question you can't answer, it's a little more complicated. Deciding whether to answer or skip a question will depend on which type of question you're working on and your sense of what is being asked. For incorrectly answered questions, the point deductions are as follows:

Student-Produced Response = no deductions

Standard Multiple Choice = $1/4$-point deduction

Quantitative Comparisons = $1/3$-point deduction

Skipping should always be done in conjunction with elimination. When you cannot eliminate enough choices to comfortably guess, skip that question.

When you skip a question, it's a good idea to circle the question number in the test book so that you can find it later. If you do return to the question during your review, and answer it, darken in the circle so that you know it's been taken care of. If you are skipping the question, be especially careful about filling in the next answer on the answer sheet, making sure that you've left a blank and haven't messed up the order of answers. This is not an error you'll have time to fix later on!

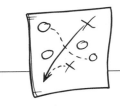

Action Plan

Because of the SAT's scoring system, if you have no idea what the answer to a question is, you're better off skipping it.

Many students are unwilling to skip questions for fear of costing themselves points. When you take an English or math test at school, your teacher deducts points for each question you leave blank, in addition to deducting for the ones you have wrong. Remember that on the SAT you receive one point for each correct answer and lose only a fraction of a point for incorrect answers. There are no penalties for skipping, so it makes sense to skip the questions you're likely to get wrong.

The questions you'll be most likely to skip are those in the last third of the analogies and the sentence completions, as well as in the last fifth of the regular math and quantitative comparisons. These questions require more-proficient vocabulary and math skills, take the most time to answer, and thus give you the least chance of success.

It's true that if you don't answer enough questions you can't expect a high score; on the other hand, answering too many questions incorrectly will also adversely affect your score. If you wisely choose the questions to skip, you can skip over half of the 78 verbal questions and still score in the low 500s. If you had answered all those questions and gotten them wrong, your score would have dropped into the 400s. You can even skip 20 of the 78 verbal questions and still score in the low 600s. Again, if you had attempted all those questions and gotten them all wrong, your score would have dropped into the 500s.

For example, suppose you're realistically hoping to score a 500 on the math portion of the SAT. You need a raw score of approximately 31 to do that. If you carefully select just 31 problems from the entire test and get them all right, your score should be between 500 and 520. Now suppose you answer all the questions, getting 31 right and 29 wrong. Your raw score drops to 24:31 − ($^1/_4$ × 29) = 233/4, which rounds up to 24. This translates to a *scaled score* of 470–480. Of course, if you're realistically aiming for an 800 (or something close to it), you should answer all the questions. If you're shooting to score somewhere closer to average (500) on a section, you should focus your attention on those questions you have a good chance of answering correctly. This is particularly true on the math portion of the test.

Practice Tests

Taking practice exams prior to the actual SAT I is an important part of your exam preparation. An essential aspect of preparing for the SAT I is knowing how to pace yourself. Taking the practice tests should give you a good sense of whether you're answering questions within the allotted time.

Another important aspect of taking practice tests is understanding how to mark your answer sheet correctly.

After you've finished the tests, scoring them, using the SAT scoring system, will allow you to measure how guessing or skipping a question affects your overall score.

We strongly recommend that you use actual SAT examinations when you practice for the test. Even with the changes to the exam, you should use compilations of old-format tests produced by the College Board rather than the mock exams produced by other organizations. Why? The mock examinations are not similar enough to actual SATs.

Help

The College Board provides a sample of the examination in its publication *Taking the SAT*, which should be available in your high school guidance office. Additional tests are contained in *Real SATs* and *Introducing the New SAT*. Both documents are published and available by contacting the College Board (www.collegeboard.org/html/copyright000.html.

Fine-tuning your verbal and math skills is a good way to prepare for the SAT, not to mention your college career! However, when it comes to your SAT score, some skills will do you more good than others. There are concepts you can learn, techniques you can follow, and tricks you can use that will help you get the best score possible. Here are 10 tips to help you out:

1. **Make a study plan and follow it.** The right SAT study plan will help you get the most out of this book in whatever time you have.

2. **Learn the directions in advance.** If you already know what to do for each question type, you won't have to waste precious test time. You'll be able to jump right in and start answering questions as soon as the proctor says "Go!"

3. **Make educated guesses.** If you can eliminate one or more answer choices, you have everything to gain by guessing.

4. **Know what to expect.** Learn the SAT question types in advance. They won't change, and you won't have any surprises on test day.

5. **In analogy questions, figure out the relationship by summarizing it in a sentence.** Analogies are about word relationships, so making up a sentence can help you make the connection.

6. **In sentence completions, look for clue words.** These words will reveal the meaning of the sentence and point you in the right direction.

7. **Save critical reading questions for last.** These reading questions take more time than others, but you don't get any more credit for them. So tackle the rest of the section first.

8. **If a multiple-choice math question stumps you, work backward from the answers.** The right answer has to be one of the five choices. And since the choices are arranged in size order, start with (C). That way you'll have to do the fewest calculations.

9. **In quantitative comparisons, consider all the possibilities.** Think what would happen if you plugged in 1, 0, a fraction, or a negative number for *x* in the expressions you're comparing.

10. **In grid-ins, blacken the bubbles.** If you don't, the computer won't give you any points.

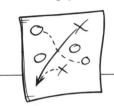

Action Plan

To register for the PSAT or SAT I, ask the college admissions counselor at your high school for an SAT I registration form. The test is offered nationally seven times each year. You can also call the College Board at 609-771-7600, or, if you're ready to take the test, you can register online at www.chinmaya-chicago.org/ sat_registration99.htm.

How Test Scores Are Used

Myths and misconceptions abound about the college admissions process:

What are colleges really looking for?

How do they make admissions decisions?

How much control do students have in this process?

Are there steps students can take that might affect their chances of being admitted?

Check out the "College Admissions Requirements" section of Appendix B for the answers to these and other pertinent questions about what colleges look for and how they make admissions decisions.

Students who have poor grades often have fewer choices. With this in mind, some students do not enroll in challenging classes. On the other hand, these students may not meet minimum course requirements for many colleges. With better planning, all students can have access to the appropriate courses. Also see Chapter 5, "Where Do You Want to Go, Kid?" for more on required course work.

The Least You Need to Know

➤ Students should start preparing to take college aptitude tests in their freshman year of high school.

➤ There are numerous practice tests and preparation courses kids can take to build their skills for taking the real tests.

➤ Know how test scores are used by colleges for admitting purposes, and impress upon your kids how important these tests are to their future.

Chapter 7

What's College Going to Cost?

In This Chapter

➤ Getting a college to help you determine what it will cost

➤ Discovering the hidden cost of going to college

➤ Determining the best college value for your kid

➤ Considering ways that kids can help finance their college education

---

By the time your kids are seniors in high school, they should have completed a school search and conducted comparative analyses of colleges they want to attend. The next step is to apply to the schools that meet their academic needs and your financial abilities. A careful analysis of school costs at this time is essential. You should know what it will cost for your kid to attend each of the schools he or she is considering and what resources will be needed to meet those costs. This chapter covers the steps for arriving at an accurate estimate of what it costs to go to college.

Get All of the Facts

Once your kids decide on a career path, the next step is to locate appropriate colleges that offer the specific programs they're seeking. Take the following factors into consideration. Establish the importance of each one, to you and to your college-bound kid. Then use your own ranking system to determine which school is right for both you and your son or daughter.

Gather Information

Make comparisons of what the different colleges and universities cost and have to offer by writing for their catalogues, financial aid brochures, and information on the placement of their graduates.

After obtaining this information, you and your family can compare the various schools and decide which ones you wish to investigate further. This investigation can include a visit to their campuses and interviews with their admissions officers, financial aid counselors, and placement directors. The interview at the admissions office can include questions regarding the academic quality of the programs offered and the student-to-faculty ratio. See Chapter 5, "Where Do You Want to Go, Kid?" for more on this subject.

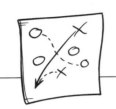

Action Plan

The more you know about the financial aid system, the better prepared you will be to pay for college. Start with Financial Aid Facts (www.ais.fsu.edu/drafts/facts/newdesign3/fa.asp) and Twenty Things You Need to Know (www.collegeboard.org/finaid/fastud/twent...tml/phase1.html), which are just two of the Web sites you'll find in the "Financial Aid Resources" section of Appendix B.

Ask Questions

The questions you ask the FAA (financial aid administrator) should be about the type of financial assistance programs available, application deadlines, the awarding process, the financial aid appeal process, special aid programs, and the average indebtedness of recent graduates. This last statistic is critical because it can reveal several things, such as how rich the average student's family is, how expensive the college is, how generous their scholarship programs are, and how closely the financial aid office monitors its students' debt burden. If this information is not available at the time of your meeting, ask when it will be made available. If the FAA can't tell you, scratch that college off your list.

What's the Best College for Your Kid?

Meet with the college placement director and ask what placement services are available. Questions to ask the placement director are covered in Chapter 5.

Here are some suggestions for subjects to discuss with an FAA or admissions officer:

Cost competitiveness with other comparable schools

Academic programs offered

The faculty-per-student ratio

Number of faculty with Ph.D. degrees

Special programs offered

Library facilities

Research opportunities

Financial aid policies

Work-study opportunities

Student body profile

Athletic opportunities

Extracurricular activities

Housing options

Crime rate in the area

Graduation rate

Average student indebtedness

College placement rate for graduates

Help

If it's not possible for you to visit all the colleges on your kid's preferred list, obtain answers to your questions about admission, financial aid, and placement over the telephone.

Get Colleges to Tell You What the Cost Is

Before you can think about how you're going to pay for your kid's college education, you need to know what it will cost. In this section, we discuss the different types of expenses that you should expect and how to get colleges to disclose their costs.

The *cost of attendance* is the total amount it will cost your son or daughter to go to school, which is usually expressed as a yearly figure. Each college is responsible for determining the annual average cost of attendance for its students by using a standard definition established by the U.S. Congress.

Action Plan

Some expenses will depend on the choices that you make, such as whether it's a public or private college, its location, and your kid's decision to live on or off campus or at home. Other expenses, such as the total cost of books, stay relatively constant from college to college.

Call every college that's on your child's "preferred" list, and ask them to send you an estimate of what it costs to attend their institution annually. This figure is used to calculate your financial aid eligibility. Remember, once your kid is in school, the actual expenses will vary based on his or her lifestyle.

Direct Cost

The *direct cost* typically includes tuition, fees, and room and board. You pay the money directly to the college. Tuition and fees vary by college, and if you've selected a state college or university, your tuition will depend on your residency status. The difference between in-state and out-of-state tuition can amount to thousands of dollars per year.

Tuition

Some colleges base their *tuition,* which is the cost of the student's classes, on the number of credit hours taken during an academic period. Others rely on enrollment status (full-time versus half-time). These details are easy to find out from the financial aid or admissions officer or from school brochures.

Fees

Colleges often charge additional *fees* for other services, activities, or facilities. For example, they may charge for health insurance or class labs or for use of a gymnasium or recreational center. Usually, these fees appear on your tuition bill and are not charged on a per-use basis.

Room and Board

Students may choose to live on campus and eat in campus dining facilities. A variety of meal plans may be offered, and costs may vary significantly based on the particular plan selected. Housing may be in a dorm or in an off-campus rental, which may or may not be associated with the college. In either case, off-campus housing usually involves utilities charges for electricity, gas, and water, in addition to phone and possibly Internet access. In a dorm, all of these expenses are typically included.

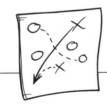

Action Plan

Look into the total cost of each college your kid is applying to. Once you know how much it will cost for tuition, housing, food, books and supplies, travel, and personal expenses, you'll have a better idea of the financial aid you'll need.

Variable Costs

Variable costs are costs that you, the student, have some control over, since they tend to vary based on what you buy and how much you use it. For example, do your really *need* a laptop as opposed to a less-expensive desktop PC? Is it necessary to have a car on campus, or would a bike do instead? In short, you have more control over variable costs than you do over direct costs.

Books and Supplies

Individual *book costs* vary greatly, depending on the courses you're taking. You may be able to purchase used books to lower these costs, but for planning purposes it's best to assume that you will be paying full cost. Some classes also require more supplies than others, such as course materials or equipment, printing, copying, and computer costs.

Computers

Many colleges require each student to have a PC. Check the school's admissions requirements to determine whether you need a basic PC or a more-expensive laptop model. And, don't forget additional expenses, such as software and a printer. If you live off-campus, you may have fees for hookup to the school network.

Transportation

Transportation costs cover gas, parking, public transportation, auto insurance, and maintenance. These costs depend on your school's location. If you commute, be sure to factor in the cost of public transportation or gas, car insurance, and parking fees. Some schools provide free parking, while others may require you to pay for a permit. Don't forget the cost of breaks and holiday travel! For example, think about how many times you'll want to go home. You can lower these costs by carpooling or shopping around for student rates on airfare.

Personal Expenses

Lifestyle can have a big impact on the *personal expenses* category. Consider such living expenses as clothing, laundry, haircuts, phone bills, recreation, and entertainment. When kids live at home, their allowance can for the most part be spent on fun stuff. When they get to college, that same allowance may have to fund more essentials than fun. Parents should work with their kids to reevaluate their priorities so their expenses stay within your budget. Maybe that long-distance call that they want to make to their girl- or boyfriend for a half-hour a pop can be replaced with an e-mail message.

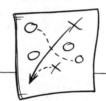

Action Plan

Some expenses will depend on the basic choices you and your student make: a public or private school; an in-state versus out-of-state college at a local or long-distance location; housing that is on-campus, off-campus, or at home? Other expenses, such as the total cost of books, stay relatively constant regardless of the school.

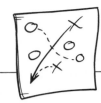

Other Costs

Other costs may be unexpected, such as drop-and-add fees to change a course schedule. And don't forget athletic, sorority or fraternity, or other organizational expenses! Always try to keep a little extra money in your budget to cover emergencies. Other costs that your kid may want to include on his or her checklist are ...

➤ Clothing, laundry, and cleaning.

➤ Food costs covering meal plans, groceries, and eating out.

➤ Loan payments for education loans, credit cards, and banking fees.

➤ Personal expenses, including toiletries, haircuts, and so on.

➤ Medical, dental, and vision care expenses and insurance.

➤ Entertainment, covering movies, cable television, music CDs, and cultural and sporting events.

➤ Miscellaneous gifts and cleaning supplies.

Breaking Down the Expenses

Breaking down college expenses can show you where you can economize, such as by buying secondhand books or living at home and commuting to classes.

You can break down costs into the following categories: (1) tuition; (2) books, fees, and miscellaneous expenses; (3) living expenses. Assuming that financial assistance will not meet all of these expenses, let's further assume that some combination of student, family, and school resources will meet the educational costs of attendance.

Students and their families have the primary responsibility to finance their education. Schools have a responsibility to assist families in this process. Careful planning, creative resourcefulness, and hard work are the key ingredients, but one other factor is essential: determination. It's important that families and students approach student financial planning with a positive attitude. The earlier you plan, the more information and options you will have.

Create an Effective Action Plan

Prior to admission, you should know the institution's financial aid policies and understand their financial aid application and awarding process.

In addition to federal and state programs administered through the school's financial aid office, private or corporate programs can be investigated. Local unions, churches, civic organizations, and charitable institutions often will sponsor needy students. The objective in exploring the various avenues of financial assistance is to attempt to meet tuition costs through a combination of federal, state, and private sources.

No source should be eliminated from consideration. Scholarship assistance should have priority over loan sources, but you should be prepared to borrow a portion of tuition expenses if necessary. This early process of financial planning to meet tuition expenses allows you and your family to organize your finances. The search for financial aid funds can follow immediately after the career analysis and school search have been completed (see Chapter 5) and before you enroll in any post-secondary institution.

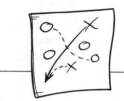

Action Plan

High school kids can work during the summer months to save money to pay a portion of the cost of books, fees, and other expenses. These costs can be estimated. A resourceful student can plan ahead and find employment that will fulfill the objectives of achieving financial survival.

Dividing Up the Money

One suggested method of meeting living expenses during the academic year is for parents to apportion the monthly living costs of the family members. By figuring out the average amount of money spent on your kid's food and miscellaneous expenses, you can calculate the amount of money you could contribute to meet your kid's monthly college living expenses. The money can be set aside and added to the student's monthly income while at college.

Let's say that you determined it cost an average of $250 a month to support your kid when he or she was living at home, and this included housing, food, clothing, and miscellaneous. If the kid's monthly living budget is $500 at college, and he or she is contributing $250 per month from summer job earnings, you could provide the rest and break even.

If you can't afford to contribute anything to meet living expenses, investigate housing alternatives. Many housing offices list low-cost or no-cost housing. Check with the housing officer at the college your son or daughter has chosen to attend.

If low-cost housing is not an option at the school, maybe a high-paying job is possible. The average student can work approximately 10 hours per week without jeopardizing academic studies. A resourceful student can expect to earn about $200 or more a month. Over the course of an academic year, this represents approximately $2,000 that can be used to meet expenses.

Students can seek help in locating employment from the financial aid administrator's office. Most students participate either in the Federal Work-Study Program (FWS) or in the school's employment program. Both programs can assist in employment placement.

Parents who can should help their kids find jobs that pay more than the minimum wage. You can encourage them to capitalize on any particular job skills they may possess. Can they tutor, paint, or offer specific computer skills that are in demand? Meeting some expenses through employment is useful in keeping debt levels manageable.

Action Plan

If you're a student, not long after you were born, your parents may have started putting money away for your education. And if you've been working or saving money on your own, you have something to contribute as well. Maybe those savings won't completely cover all costs, but chances are they're going to be a big help. Stay in your savings plan, but don't stop there. Keep searching for other investment options.

If you know beforehand that working is an essential part of your financial plan, you'll be better prepared to incorporate employment into your kid's academic schedule. Over the course of four years, the money your student earns can go a long way toward reducing the amount of money you as parents need to borrow to meet college costs.

What about the student who, for academic reasons, cannot work while attending classes? Your financial plan must consider academic success a first priority. Special arrangements can be made for students who cannot maintain an acceptable academic grade point average while they're working. Consult with your school's financial aid counselor and academic dean to find a solution to the problem. Some schools have scholarship funds set aside for these situations.

Help

Check out the "Financial Planning" section in Appendix B for financial issues that college-bound students should consider, including how to manage college costs. Check out the College Cost site at www.nationalguardian.com/solu/calc.html, which breaks down college expenses, reduces sticker shock, and answers frequently asked questions. Also check out College Cost Press Release at www.expan.com/ to see recent trends in college tuition and financial aid.

Homework for Your Kid

College is an investment in your kid's future. But it doesn't come cheap. Whether your son or daughter chooses a low-cost community college or a high-priced private institution, his or her education will cost you money. As high as the prices may seem, your family can finance the education that your child deserves. Creating a plan to pay for college takes effort, so you'll need some help and guidance. Financial aid is limited. It's important to start early and investigate all your options. Make sure you have an in-depth discussion with your college-bound kid and other family members about how to go about financing his or her education.

The Least You Need to Know

➤ Know how much college is going to cost before you start putting together a financial plan.

➤ Understand all of the hidden costs it takes to go to college so that you are financially well prepared.

➤ Know what the difference is between fixed versus variable costs, so you can accurately project what the total cost of going to college will be.

➤ Involve your college-bound kids as well as other family members in plans for financing college expenses.

Chapter 8

My Plan
1. work
2. Beg
3. Plead
4. Cry
5. Go To college

Develop a College Financial Plan

In This Chapter

➤ Learning what every college financial plan must include

➤ Knowing how to establish short- and long-term plan objectives

➤ Pulling it all together into a consolidated plan

The key to being able to pay for your son's or daughter's education is not necessarily having a lot of money to invest. Most parents don't have it. What is needed is a financial plan. Planning is the first step in taking control of your kids' future—their college education. Your plan should be flexible but firm, and, most important, you must agree to stick to it. Planning is not difficult if you adhere to the fundamentals.

Remember the old saying, "Watch your pennies and the dollars will take care of themselves"? It's still true today. The fundamentals of financial planning are so simple and obvious; yet many parents spend all their free time looking for an easier way to finance their kids' education, only to find out when their kids are ready to go to college that it's too late to plan. Had they done even some basic planning in the beginning, they could have been in great financial shape when the time came.

The very least that colleges expect from students is that they make contributions to their education from their summer earnings. It makes sense for parents and students to begin saving long before the summer after graduation. Parents should also encourage their kids to earmark a portion of any gift money they receive over the years as a contribution toward their college savings.

Having a college financial plan means starting as early as possible and involving the whole family in setting priorities and in saving and investing wisely.

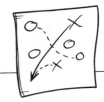

Action Plan

To develop a successful college savings program, you first must decide what you want to accomplish financially and how you're going to get there. You and your family should collectively review what you want to achieve. What are your family goals for your children's education? The important thing is to spell them out clearly so every member has a clear view of where the family is going.

Getting Started

Reputable financial planners can provide advice for families exploring the various savings vehicles currently available. However, be aware of others who are not as helpful. In recent years, some people engaged in what might more accurately be described as financial *aid* planning have typically been claiming that they can help a family increase its eligibility for financial assistance. Many of these planners seem to suggest methods that keep a family's assets hidden. This undermines a system designed to help families who most need financial aid. It can also freeze assets that you had counted on to pay college costs, putting your child's education in jeopardy.

Good financial aid consultants can help families develop sound financial-planning strategies, assist in filling out forms, negotiate better offers, and so on. If you want to engage a financial aid consultant and avoid problems down the line, just be sure the "expert" you hire is reputable. See Chapter 17, "Financial Aid Consulting Services," for information on how to choose a consultant who can greatly increase your chances of receiving the most financial aid possible.

Setting Priorities

If your family is like most families, you'll often spend money on things that you really don't need or, somehow, the money you make always seems to be just enough to cover expenses. Your first short-term plan should be to get control over your family's spending habits. Budgeting is an excellent way to get started. You may be amazed at how a budget can help you save on little things that can add up to big dollars.

Let's take a simple example. Suppose that you, your spouse, and two children attend a baseball game once a week. If it costs $35 for the four of you to eat at the game, you're spending about $400 on food during the season. Suppose you made sandwiches and carried them to the game, along with your own soft drinks. If you invest this $400 savings at 10 percent over a 10-year period, you'd find that your $400 had grown to $6,500 by the time your kids were ready to go to college (assuming their average age is eight years old today). And you would not have deprived yourself or your family of anything. Okay, we didn't take into consideration that it still cost you something to make your own sandwiches. That's because we wanted to keep the math simple and focus on the concept!

By making one minor adjustment to your family's priorities, you can have instant money available to invest in long-term planning for your kids' future. If you're serious about controlling your money, you've got to set priorities and recognize that you can't have everything right now. If you want to have money set aside for their education, you must be prepared to make sacrifices over a period of time.

Part of the budget-prioritizing process is distinguishing between what you need and what you want. For example, you might need a car, but you want a Mercedes. Or, you may have to cut your vacation plans back, and that's tough. But in many cases, it simply has to be done.

Emergency Funds

Many families start a program to save money, then withdraw the money when emergencies arise. They lose not only their initial savings, but also a part of their investment program because they were forced to terminate their plan prematurely. An emergency fund should be considered a critical part of your overall financial plan. As a rule, your emergency fund should be equivalent to at least three times the size of your family's monthly income, enough to cover job losses, medical problems, or unexpected major repairs.

Money market funds are an excellent place to invest emergency dollars. Your money is readily accessible when it's needed, and it's earning interest at rates considerably higher than traditional savings accounts. Money market funds have become extremely popular in recent years as a way to gain ground in inflationary periods. They are widely advertised and available through savings and loan associations, banks, and brokerage firms.

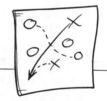

Action Plan

We often make purchases on the basis of impulse and wants, rather than reality. If you want to get serious about planning for your kids' education, you must be prepared to postpone some of your desires. The trade-off is that you're doing without something now so that you can afford to send your kids to college.

Use Time Wisely

It's a common misconception that to save a lot of money you have to make a lot of money. In reality, acquiring a substantial sum of money requires only time and discipline. The importance of long-term planning cannot be underestimated. It's a major factor in your overall planning for college expenses. Most families fail to use time to their advantage, because they allow procrastination to delay the start of their financial plan. Don't make that mistake: Start early, and make long-term plans.

Suppose that you and your spouse are 25 years old and you've set a goal to accumulate $50,000 for your kid's college education in 10 years. You could accomplish it by saving only $10 per month at 12 percent! However, if you are 35 and have the same goal, you would have to save $445 a month, or 44 times as much as you needed to amass the same sum at age 25.

In addition to time, the only other factor you need to make money is discipline. Suppose you want to start saving $100 per month over a long period of time and you are able to earn a 12 percent return on it. The following table dramatically illustrates how much you can earn with enough time and discipline.

The Rewards of Discipline (Investing $100 a Month at 12%)

5 Years	10 Years	15 Years	20 Years	30 Years
$14,015	$32,940	$58,455	$92,870	$201,910

The Magic of Compound Interest

One of the most exciting facets of financial management and also one of the simplest to understand is what successful investors call "the magic of compound interest." You've just seen how even a small amount of money ($100 a month), saved systematically over a period of time, multiplies dramatically through the compound interest formula.

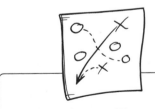

Action Plan

Think of your money as your work force, and put it to work now!

No amount is too small or insignificant to save for your kids' college education. The important thing is to take advantage of the time portion of the formula and start to invest now. Look at yourselves as employers of your income. The dollars you earn are your "employees." If the two of you own a business, you can't afford to let your employees sit around doing nothing. In today's economy, you can't let that happen to your money, either. Your money is your work force. Get it working now, for your kids' future.

Making a long-term investment with a fair rate of return, you can take advantage of compound interest. The illustration that follows shows what happens when you invest $100 each month at 5, 10, and 12 percent, respectively. Again, the difference in the total amount of money you accumulate at the different rates illustrates just how important a few percentage points can be.

Another important concept to understand about compound interest is what is known as the "Rule of 72." If you divide 72 by the rate of interest you're receiving, you can determine when your money will double. For example, if you're lucky enough to find an investment that's earning 18 percent a year, you'll double your money over four years (72 divided by 18 percent is 4).

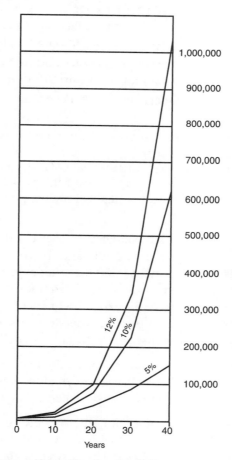

Compound interest from investing $100 per month

Putting It All Together

Understanding your benefits and knowing how to use them will help you lay out the foundation of your financial plan. You can see how that's done in this simple example. Let's assume that you and your spouse are both 30 years old and earn a combined yearly income of $75,000. Both of your incomes are covered by pension plans. Your intent is to save enough money over the next 10 years to put your kid through college. What do you need to do to get there? For starters, review the following checklist:

➤ Estimate the annual rate of inflation over the next 10 years.

➤ Determine as best you can whether your kid will go to a state college or a private college. Find out what the tuition rates are today and, using your projected inflation rate, determine what the tuition rates will be 10 years from now.

➤ Contact one of the colleges of your choice and find out what it costs to attend their institution for everything except tuition (room, board, books, etc.).

➤ Estimate how much financial aid you believe your family will be able to qualify for.

➤ Project the rate of return you expect from your investment program.

This example assumes an average inflation rate of 3 percent and a 5 percent average annual increase in college tuition per year over the next 10 years. The return on investments is projected at 10 percent. Here is how the plan comes together in three simple steps:

Step 1: You believe your kid will want to attend a state college as a state resident. Current tuition rates are $2,500, and the college estimates that the average student spends an additional $6,500 for other expenses. The total cost in today's dollars is $9,000. Ten years from now, based upon a 5 percent annual increase, you can expect tuition to be $4,070. Other expenses will be $8,735 if the average inflation rate holds at 3 percent. Therefore, you can expect to pay $12,805 ($4,070 + $8,735) for the first year your kid is in college.

Step 2: You've had a conversation with a financial aid person who, based on the information you provided, believes you would be responsible for about 20 percent of your kid's total annual college expenses, or about $2,560 ($12,805 × .20).

Step 3: Your expected cost for your kid's first year of college 10 years from now is $10,245 ($12,805 − $2,560). How much would you have to start saving now to cover that first year of college? The answer is, about $50 a month if you assume a 10 percent return on your money.

Don't concern yourself now with whether or not these numbers and assumptions are realistic. You can establish your own assumptions, based on your personal requirements and earnings. For the time being, follow the progress of this couple of 30-year-olds who are doing some long-term financial planning.

In order to support their retirement program and their kids' college education, they need to initiate a $6,000-per-year savings and investment program. Up to this point, all that the family in our example has done is determine where they are today and where they want to be in 10 years when their oldest kid will reach college age. The next step is to map out a way to get there.

Choosing an Investment Program

Before you start to plan your kid's college savings program, you'll need to become familiar with the various aspects and varieties of investment vehicles that are available to you. You can reach your savings goal, one payday at a time, by developing a savings habit.

> **Help**
>
> The importance of saving to meet college costs can't be overemphasized. The College Savings Calculator at www.embark.wiredscholar.com/paying/lt_financial_planning/ltfp_monthbud.jsp is a calculator that you can use to estimate the amount of money you need to save by the time your kid enters college.

As explained earlier, you need to do short-term budgeting in order to have the funds to invest in long-term financial planning. Budget for savings each month, just as you budget for food or loan payments. Once you've decided to save a percentage of your incomes, stick to your decision. If your employers offer payroll deduction plans, you can arrange to have money deducted from your paycheck and automatically deposited into a savings account every payday. You could also make regular contributions to an education IRA (tax-deferred earnings), or better yet, a 529 plan, which is a state college plan with tax-deferred growth and estate tax advantages. (See Chapter 16, "Tax-Saving Strategies," for more on this subject.)

Here are several investment points to consider:

➤ **Return**   The amount your money can earn in interest.

➤ **Security**   The more secure your account is, the less risk you face of losing your investment.

➤ **Liquidity**   The speed with which you can obtain your money.

➤ **Convenience**   The ease with which you can manage your investment plan. Take into account the location of the financial institution where you save, Web access to your account, and the quality of service that you receive.

In choosing investments that are right for you, you'll need to think realistically about your financial situation, your educational goals for your kids, and the period of time in which you want to reach them. Since no single investment is likely to satisfy all of your financial requirements, you might want to consider using a combination of investment vehicles to achieve your goals. You could invest a portion of your money in a passbook savings account and the rest in mutual funds.

Investing and Savings Options

In planning for college, it may be a good idea to sit down with your accountant, financial advisor, banker, investment broker, or insurance agent to assess your child's pending long-term educational needs. Even though many financial plans specifically designed to pay for future college costs are of value, in some cases parents may be better off dealing with traditional financial investments earmarked for future college plans. For example, if your kids are young (under 10 years old), you may want to invest in the stock market, which has traditionally earned higher returns than conventional savings programs over the long term.

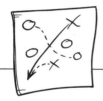

Action Plan

No matter how young your kids are, it's better to learn what options you have now and begin figuring college expenses into your long-term financial plan.

Investing for Your Preteen

Some financial analysts recommend investing in higher risk, higher-income-producing vehicles during a kid's preteen years, then moving into more secure and conservative investments as the kid approaches college age.

When you're looking into taxable or nontaxable investments, consider your kids' ages. If they're under 14, consider investing in more aggressive nontaxable investments, such as stocks or mutual funds. When they become 14, you may want to switch over to a more-conservative investment, such as municipal bonds, to protect your principal as each kid begins to approach college age.

College Savings Plans

A growing number of colleges and universities offer *savings plans* in which parents or guardians can invest a certain amount of money that is placed in a certificate of deposit. The interest earned on the investment is based on the anticipated level of that college's inflation rate. The amount to be invested is determined by the age of your child, the type of school (public or private) he or she will be entering, and its cost.

Theoretically, the investment will grow at a rate to pay for all education-related costs when your child is ready to enter college. The downside is that many of these investments may not produce as high a rate of return as your money might have earned on the open market. Additionally, in some cases, if the child for one reason or another does not attend college, the parent may recoup only the initial investment with less than the full amount of interest earned.

Prepaid Tuition Plans

Similarly, some state governments offer *prepaid college tuition plans.* One state, for example, allows parents or guardians to invest a lump sum for tuition, room, board, and other academic fees; thereby ensuring that the student will be entitled to a prepaid education (provided the youth qualifies for admission). Consult your state department of education (see Appendix C, "Alphabetical State Financial Aid Listings") or the financial aid offices at your state colleges and/or universities for information about any prepaid college tuition programs.

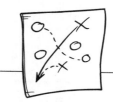

Action Plan

Take advantage of tuition prepayment discounts. Many colleges offer up to a 10 percent discount for early payment.

Where to Invest

A wide range of savings programs are available through savings and loan institutions and commercial banks. Programs include savings and time deposit accounts, interest-bearing checking accounts, and money market deposit accounts. Credit unions also offer various savings programs of their own.

Deposits in federal and state chartered credit unions are insured for up to $100,000 through the National Credit Union Administration. Brokerage houses and mutual fund companies offer a wide variety of financial services, including time deposit and money market accounts. The terms and security of these accounts can vary substantially from those of more traditional savings institutions.

Passbook Accounts

Sometimes called a *passbook account,* a regular savings account is the most basic and flexible account available. In some cases, you're required to deposit a minimum amount to open an account. You can make deposits to your account in any amount and are allowed to withdraw funds at any time. Some institutions limit the number of withdrawals that you can make in a given period of time without incurring a separate service charge.

Although passbook accounts are extremely safe investments that also offer liquidity and convenience, they typically pay one of the lowest rates of return of any of the alternative investment vehicles.

If your kid has a passbook account, don't be tempted to put your own savings there. It may offer tax advantages, but you'll later find that it reduces his or her eligibility for financial aid. It would be foolish to have a demonstrated need for assistance lowered because parents placed savings in their child's account. On the other hand, it would not be ethical to transfer a student's savings to a parent's account.

Warning

Money a student earns or receives as a gift should be placed in a savings account in the student's name. Parents should not put their own savings in the student's account. This is because a maximum of 6 percent of a parent's savings will be included in the family contribution. But 35 percent of the student's assets and savings are considered available for each academic year and are deducted from financial aid offers.

Money Market Accounts

If you can meet the minimum deposit requirement, you may want to consider investing in a *money market account* that combines high yields and liquidity with the safety of federal insurance. They're like regular savings accounts in that you can withdraw your money at any time without paying a penalty. They differ in that they offer a variable rate of interest comparable to money market rates. However, if your balance drops below a specified minimum (usually $2,500), interest rates are reduced accordingly.

Savings Bonds

U.S. Savings Bonds are among the most convenient bonds to purchase and redeem. They're extremely safe, and the interest isn't subject to state or local taxes. The government offers two types of bonds: Series EE and Series HH. Series EE bonds are available in denominations of from $50 to $10,000 and are sold at less than their face value (discounted). Bonds are purchased at 50 percent of the face value printed on the bond and redeemed for their full value at maturity. The maturity period is determined by how long it takes enough interest to accumulate to double the issue value of the bond.

Bonds that you purchase now earn interest at a fixed rate that increases on a graduated scale for the first five years, to a maximum of 7$^1/_2$ percent interest compounded annually.

Bonds held for a minimum of five years earn interest at a rate tied to the money market rates. When you redeem a bond, the interest rate you'll receive will be based on the average rate earned for the term. You are guaranteed a minimum of 7$^1/_2$ percent interest compounded annually. Series EE bonds can be purchased through most financial institutions.

Series HH bonds are no longer available for direct purchase. The only way to get an HH bond is in exchange for an EE bond. They are obtained at face value. Every six months, the U.S. Treasury sends you a check for your interest earnings. Although the maturity period for HH bonds is 10 years, they may be redeemed six months after their issue date.

Mutual Funds and Stocks

The decade of the 1990s was one of the best ever for both stock market and mutual fund investors. Parents continue to draw on mutual funds as a viable investment vehicle to finance their kids' education, and they do so for several good reasons.

Mutual funds are professionally managed by experienced investment managers who provide instant diversification by investing in a broad range of stocks if you invest in the right fund. The triple AAA funds have provided stellar performance over the last 10 years. Available investment funds range all the way from super conservative to extremely aggressive. Almost all of them will outperform the rates of return in savings accounts, bonds, or Treasury bills.

This chapter began with a discussion about the magic of compound interest. A relatively small amount of money, if properly invested, will accumulate into substantial dollars over a period of time. An example illustrated how to determine the amount of savings needed to meet your financial goals. The importance of budget planning was also emphasized.

Help

If you're interested in learning more about the high rate of return on mutual funds, check out "Mutual Funds" in Appendix B.

As your financial situation and goals change, you'll need to make adjustments to your savings and investment programs. When you're just starting out, you may need the liquidity and relatively high yield of a money market account to help provide for a growing family. When your kid approaches college age, you may choose to shift to short-term secured investments to make sure the money is there when you start paying your share of college expenses.

Whichever savings strategy you adopt, you'll see the rewards of your effort as you reach each of your savings goals.

The Least You Need to Know

➤ Your financial plan for your kids' college educations should include both your short- and long-term financial objectives.

➤ Make sure you have an alternate emergency fund set aside so that you will not have to rely on the savings that are in your kids' college savings plans.

➤ Know how the "magic of compound interest" works so that you can meet college expenses when the time comes.

Part 3

Seek and You Shall Find—Money

Remember when you were a kid, or an adult for that matter, and you went to a treasure hunt party? You and your team were given a list of seemingly impossible items to find, and you eagerly struck out to knock on your neighbors' doors to see if they had anything on your list. You didn't know where to look, which was part of the fun of the game. Whoever returned to party headquarters with all the items on the list won at least a sack of candy.

Finding financial aid isn't that much different from a treasure hunt. There's money to be had out there if you know where to look for it. Fortunately, you have this book: Think of it as a financial aid treasure map. Whatever is on your list of needs, these chapters can point you in the right direction to meet them.

Chapter 9

Grant Me
a Grant

> ## In This Chapter
>
> ➤ Distinguishing between merit-based and need-based grants
>
> ➤ Searching for grant money
>
> ➤ Writing a winning grant proposal
>
> ➤ Learning the guidelines for submitting grants

Grants are a type of need-based aid awarded to students who demonstrate the most financial need. Both federal and state governments provide grant programs.

Pell Grants are the largest source of need-based gift aid and are available to undergraduate students who demonstrate financial need. If you apply by the deadline and meet the eligibility criteria, you receive Pell Grant funds. The amount you receive is partly determined by the total funding approved by the U.S. Congress.

The *Federal Supplemental Educational Opportunity Grants (FSEOG)* program is administered by the financial aid office at your college and is available to Pell Grant recipients. Each school has a limited amount of funding for this program, so it's important to file early for financial aid. You could receive up to $4,000 a year in FSEOG grants. You'll find more about Pell Grants and the FSEOG program in this chapter.

The Various Types of Grants

According to a survey conducted by Gallup and Robinson, most parents of college-bound students have saved only 25 percent or less of college costs. Before we begin our discussion about how grants can help ease the burden of meeting college expenses, it's important to distinguish between the various types of financial aid for college.

Almost all aid comes in one of two varieties: grants or loans. Both *grants* and loans can be paid directly to the student, to the student's school, or to the student's parents. The key distinction is that loans have to be paid back, whereas grants do not.

There are several problems, however, for a student who relies solely on need-based aid to finance an education. The major ones are:

➤ There just aren't enough need-based funds to go around. Most colleges have strict financial aid budgets, restricting the amount of need-based grants they can award. The majority of families soon discover that a financial aid office's estimate of need is very different (usually lower) from the realities of a family's cash flow and bank accounts.

➤ Even though a college may claim that a significant percentage of its student body receives financial aid, such statements can be misleading. When loans carry an interest rate below the current market level and don't have to be paid back until after graduation, they're classified as "financial aid." What college students and their families soon discover is that these types of low-interest loans make up the bulk of most financial aid packages. And although such loans are helpful in delaying payment, they still have one overwhelmingly undesirable feature: They eventually have to be repaid.

➤ Students from middle-income families often find themselves caught "between a rock and a hard place." Such families aren't wealthy enough to cover all of the costs on their own, but they don't have low-enough incomes to qualify for substantial levels of need-based aid. Having to send more than one child to college further aggravates the situation.

Insight

A **grant** is a type of financial aid that does not have to be repaid. Grants are usually awarded on the basis of need, but they can also be awarded for a student's special skills.

Winning grants can help students and their families substantially lower their debt burden, or even avoid borrowing money altogether. This is especially important in a debt-ridden era where increasing numbers of parents resist taking out new loans for college expenses, opting instead for less expensive schools. Grants allow students to take control of their educational destinies by empowering them to choose the right college, regardless of the financial situation of their families.

Grants generally come in two flavors: merit-based and need-based:

➤ **Merit-based grants** are awarded on the basis of student achievement. The judging criteria used to evaluate achievement vary substantially among grant programs, which frequently take into account a wide range of student talents and interests.

➤ **Need-based grants** are awarded solely on the basis of financial need, as determined by formulas that weigh financial resources against living expenses, parental assets, income, and expenses (if the student is a dependent).

Merit-Based Grants

A *merit-based grant* is what most people generally mean when they use the word "scholarship." Grants, or scholarships, are awarded by corporations, nonprofit groups, foundations, service clubs, state and federal governments, and other organizations. Some colleges also offer merit-based grants to students who enroll at their institutions, although this is rare at the more-competitive schools, which don't have to offer this type of financial incentive to attract students.

An example of a merit-based grant, or scholarship, is the Tylenol Scholarship program. It requires that students submit 100- to 200-word essays describing their goals and aspirations, including two or three sentences about their experiences, or about people who have contributed to their achievements. Basically, the program's creators expect the student to summarize his or her entire future in less than 200 words.

The program's creators are looking for how precise someone can be while writing his or her essay. For example, is the theme of your essay clearly identified in the opening paragraph?

Applying for Merit-Based Grants

If you apply for a merit-based grant (scholarship) and the sponsors ask you for information about your extracurricular activities, they basically want a summary of everything you do outside of class time. This includes school clubs, sports, jobs, independent projects, volunteer activities, and everything in between. Sometimes, scholarship applications will distinguish between different types of extracurricular activities. In the Tylenol scholarship example, the application requests information about two separate categories of extracurricular activities: (1) school-related activities and (2) community and volunteer service activities.

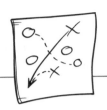

Action Plan

Make sure you can validate all of your extracurricular activities. For example, if you participated as a volunteer in a United Way program, make sure you keep all of the documentation that confirms your part in the program.

Most applications request information about extracurricular activities in some type of list format. Some contests will limit you to the space provided on the physical application, while others will let you attach additional sheets. In addition to requesting a brief description of the activity itself, contest applications may also ask for information about the time commitment devoted to the activity, any leadership positions or offices held, and any awards or honors received from the endeavor.

Although not all scholarships request information about a student's academic record, a substantial number do make it part of the judging criteria. The way in which this is taken into account can vary tremendously. For scholarships such as the All-USA Academic Team sponsored by *USA Today,* grades are an important part of the judging criteria. On the other hand, many scholarship contests use only activity accomplishments.

Need-Based Grants

The largest *need-based grant* program is the *Pell Grant,* which is sponsored by the federal government. The program awards money to students from lower-income families. A relatively small number of grant programs use both merit-based and need-based criteria in making awards.

Institutional aid is also awarded by colleges and universities from their own coffers. The majority of this aid comes in the form of discounts on published sticker prices of, for example, tuition, and it's distributed according to financial need.

Need-based grants are sometimes offered by foundations and other organizations, but such programs are less common.

Federal Grant Programs

The rising costs of higher education, combined with only minimal relief from college financial aid offices, has made federal need- and merit-based grants an even more critical source of funding in recent years.

Quite simply, merit-based grants are monetary prizes awarded on the basis of some measure of achievement. What constitutes achievement depends on who is awarding the money, but you'll soon discover that merit-based grants are targeted at virtually every type of student. An enterprising student can exert tremendous influence over the amount of merit-based grants he or she receives; this is not the case with need-based grants.

Pell Grants

Last year, the *Federal Pell Grant Program* awarded gift money to nearly four million students in amounts ranging from $400 to $3,000 yearly. Unfortunately, the grants are off-limits to graduate students and to students who have already received a bachelor's degree.

The amount you get depends on your demonstrated need, the costs of education at the particular college you want to attend, the length of the program in which you are enrolled, whether your enrollment is full- or part-time, and the amount of money Congress approves, divided by the number of qualifying students. You apply for a Pell Grant by filling out and submitting the FAFSA form.

Insight

The **Federal Pell Grant Program** is for undergraduate students who have not completed a first baccalaureate degree. It is designed to financially assist students who are the least able to contribute toward their basic education expenses.

Supplemental Education Grants

Do you have exceptional demonstrated need? If your answer is "yes", then the *Federal Supplemental Educational Opportunity Grant Program,* fondly known as *SEOG,* is for you. To qualify, you must be enrolled at least half-time in an undergraduate program at an accredited institution. Grants in the neighborhood of $4,000 are possible on the basis of pure, unadulterated need. However, most colleges don't receive enough SEOG funds to pay out maximum eligibility, and $1,000 to $1,500 is considered a good award. Roughly a million students are awarded this crucial funding, which is designed to equalize college opportunity.

The SEOG program is campus-based, which means that, although the money comes from the federal government, the colleges hand it out to students who show exceptional need. Typically, students eligible for Pell Grant awards are also eligible for SEOG funds.

If you're turned down for a SEOG grant, you're allowed to borrow an additional unsubsidized Federal Stafford or Direct loan, as long as you submit your parents' rejection letter with your application. Through this process, you can borrow $4,000 for each of the first two years and $5,000 for each of the last two years. Although your parents' interest rate for the new loan can increase, your repayment of the principal begins after graduation or when you're no longer attending college at least half-time. By contrast, your parents' repayment of the principal begins 60 days after they receive their final installment. In short, this type of borrowing is great for your cash flow.

Work-Study Programs

Work-study programs are campus-based programs in which federal dollars are distributed by colleges. To qualify for these jobs, you must have demonstrated need and be enrolled for at least half-time study at either the undergraduate or graduate level. Employment is almost always on campus, although jobs are also arranged off-campus in community service programs.

The pay is at least the current federal minimum wage, usually higher. Compensation for off-campus jobs is left to the discretion of the employer and may be greater than for campus jobs. The military offers a cornucopia of financial aid opportunities, described in Chapter 12, "Military and Veteran Scholarship Programs."

The federal government tries hard to help your education money numbers add up to an affordable year of college.

Five Ways to Begin Your Grant Search

The grants game is an ever-changing field that requires hard work, persistence, and a little luck. Finding an *appropriate* grant source takes a lot of work; writing the proposal is actually easier than finding the right grant source.

Unfortunately, there is no master list or 800 number to call for the information you need. Nevertheless, let's get started with some basic resources to find out what's available.

Help

For more information about grants, check out the "Scholarship, Grants, and Fellowship Sources" section in Appendix B, and the listings by state in Appendix C.

Community Services

Check with your high school, local school district, and county or state agency to see if they have a grants listing service or a grants assistance office (see Appendix C, "Alphabetical State Financial Aid Listings," for resources listed alphabetically by state). Since these lists are not all-inclusive, you'll still have to monitor grant awards and announcements in other print or online media. Find out if your school district or county office has a reference center where you can go to use their reference materials.

The key to finding a grant locally is that you have to take the initiative! Corporations and privately endowed organizations frequently are open to grant proposals from students in their community.

Library Resources and School Districts

Check with your local, regional, and university libraries to see what grant research resources are available to you. Some of the reference materials are very expensive, but they are usually available in a collection that you can use, rather than buy. Some school districts have their own professional development libraries, which contain grant research resources. Some of this information is also available on the Internet.

Subscription Services

Consider subscribing to one of the national services that sends subscribers timely grant information. These services can cost anywhere from $80 to $300 a year. The people who write grant newsletters read through the federal register and check with other sources to provide you with leads to grants and the federal agencies that are offering them.

Subscription services are expensive, and you can often find the materials they provide on your own with a little digging. However, if you're busy, the time saved could be worth the money.

The News Media

There are several newspapers and magazines that contain grant proposal notices. Some publications print short articles about who was funded for which grant. These are fascinating to read. For example, check out a copy of *Education Week* or the *Chronicle of Philanthropy* for grant information. You'll also find many leads in such magazines as *Electronic Learning* and *Technology and Learning,* and in vendor advertisements, mailings, and your local newspaper.

Help

Check out Eschool News at www.ais.cs.sandia.gov/~jwallace/eschool_ais/eschool_ais.html to learn more about grant subscription services. This Web site and others are listed under "Scholarships, Grants, and Fellowships" in Appendix B, "Directory of General Financial Aid Resources."

Online Services

The major online services have grant areas that are worth a look.

On AmericaOnline you'll find useful information in the National Education Association's (NEA) files, the Association for Supervision and Curriculum Development (ASCD) area, and the Reference Service Press (RSP) Funding Focus section.

Help

There are many ERIC Web sites, all linked by a system-wide site run by ACCESS ERIC. Internet users visit ERIC sites at www. aspensys.com/eric more than 500,000 times each week.

For background research, use the *Educational Resources Information Center (ERIC)* on the Net. ERIC is a federally funded national information system that provides access to an extensive body of education-related resources. These resources will help you find current information about educational issues. Write your projects based on the latest research in the field.

Federal Grants

In the old days, just a few years ago, grant-seekers had two options: live in a big city with a great library system or go to a university library to manually research grant leads. Today, with telecommunications common in schools, many of the traditional library resources for finding grant opportunities are available online. Finding them does, however, take some persistence.

These resources are the cornerstones of any funding program. When searching for federal or national corporate funds, books such as *Barron's Complete College Financial Guide* and Web sites like finaid.com will help you identify which programs are available. In some resources, you simply read all programs available nationwide. In others, the resources are listed alphabetically by state. Federal programs are targeted nationwide.

Corporate and foundation programs often provide funds for areas of the country where their businesses are physically located. Private foundations and nonprofits often fund specific kinds of programs, such as technology or professional development.

Resources such as John Schwartz's book *College Scholarships and Financial Aid* include a CD that will give you the details you need on just about every scholarship available. For practical, up-to-date information on federal, state, and individual college financial aid programs, get a copy of *Barron's Complete College Financing Guide* at your local bookstore.

Federal Register

The *Federal Register* is the official publication in which all regulations must be published in order to notify the public of federal agency actions. The United States government has committed itself to maintaining a full-text digital database of the *Federal Register* and the *Code of Federal Regulations*. You can find out more about the different ways of accessing the *Federal Register* if you visit the U.S. Government Printing Office site at www.access.gpo.gov/aboutgpo/whatsnew.html.

Catalog of Federal Domestic Assistance

The *Catalog of Federal Domestic Assistance (CFDA)* is the federal government's guide to all funding programs. The *Catalog* is a good place to start a grants search for Federal funding.

The CFDA number consists of two digits that identify the agency. For example, the Educational Department is 84 and the Health and Human Services Department is 93. A decimal point followed by three digits identifies the specific program. Some CFDA numbers, such as those in the Education Department section, end in letters to indicate multiple grant competitions under a single program.

Programs with numbers ending in 999 have not yet been assigned permanent CFDA numbers.

You can order a free copy of the CFDA from the Superintendent of Documents, U.S. Government Printing Office, Washington, DC 20402 or through their Web site at www.access.gpo.gov/aboutgpo/whatsnew.html.

Action Plan

To see what's available from the federal government for the current fiscal year, check out the Department of Education's site at www.fafsa.ed.gov/ and the Federal Register's site at www.fsa.usda.gov/pas/fedreg.html. These sites and others are listed under Scholarships, Grants, and Fellowships in Appendix B. They have links to the latest funding programs and information about future programs.

Making the Grant Process Work for You

The *Office of Management and Budget* (OMB) provides grant management guidelines to help grantees follow the rules and limitations for how the money may be spent and how it must be accounted for.

The OMB, the main overseer of federal grant administration, has set standards and processes for managing federal funds, covering such issues as dealing with audits, cost principles, and indirect cost rates.

The agency publishes a book entitled *OBM Grant Programs and Guidelines,* which includes the text of OMB's circulars, as well as other circulars, texts, and points of contact. This book is available at Federal bookstores or by writing to the Superintendent of Documents, U.S. Government Printing Office, Washington, DC 20402. Write for current pricing or check their Web site at www.access.gpo.gov/aboutgpo/whatsnew.html.

Education Department General Administration Regulations

In its entirety, *Education Department General Administrative Regulations (EDGAR)* applies only to programs of the U.S. Department of Education. Other federal programs described in the *Guide to Federal Assistance* may be affected by some of the regulations included in EDGAR regarding intergovernmental review, lobbying activities, and the provision of a drug-free workplace.

The *United States Government Manual* describes every agency, commission, and federal department. It lists addresses, telephone numbers, and key personnel. Revised annually, the *Manual* is useful in identifying names and addresses for programs described in the *Catalog of Federal Domestic Assistance*. Order from the Superintendent of Documents, U.S. Government Printing Office, Washington, DC 20402 or through their Web site at www.access.gpo.gov/aboutgpo/whatsnew.html.

Private Funding Sources

The *Foundation Directory* is an annual reference source for information about private and community grant-making foundations in the United States. It provides basic descriptions and current fiscal data for the nation's largest foundations. Check the Foundation Center's Web site at www.fdncenter.org/ for a catalogue of products, or call 1-800-478-4661 for a free catalogue.

The *Foundation Center* is a national nonprofit organization established in 1956. Its mission is to collect, organize, and disseminate factual data on foundation and corporate philanthropy.

The Center offers free public access to this information by means of four Center-operated libraries and a nationwide network of more than 180 cooperating collections. In addition, the Center's publications program features over 50 titles on philanthropic giving and other nonprofit sector concerns. The latest edition is in two volumes and can be found at many cooperating collections around the United States. For more information, check out the Center's Web site.

The *Foundation Grants Index* is an annual source for determining the current funding priorities of the nation's largest foundations. It is useful to develop an initial list of potential funding sources based on a foundation's giving program and its application procedures before submitting grant requests.

The *National Guide to Funding for Elementary & Secondary Education* is a starting point for grant-seekers looking for foundation and corporate support for

Warning

Proofread! Spelling and grammar errors do not convey a positive image. Great grant ideas, when they're submitted laced with spelling and grammar errors, are automatically rejected.

organizations serving elementary and secondary education. This resource is also available from the Foundation Center. The *National Guide* is aimed at grant-seekers looking for foundation and corporate support for libraries and information services.

Grant-Writing Tips

The most important thing for grant-writers to remember is that they might submit a perfect application and still receive a rejection. Most foundations have limited resources with which to fund projects. Do not get discouraged if you get a rejection from a possible funding source.

Understand the Guidelines

Read the grantor's guidelines and instructions carefully. Do not try to make the grantor's program fit what you want to do; your program must be in line with the funding agency's priorities. Follow the grantor's instructions to the letter. Applications are turned away when they do not exactly meet the funding agency's requirements.

Be Innovative

Grant ideas should be innovative, creative, and educational. Grantors will rarely fund operating expenses. They usually invest in supplemental programs. Private foundations often seek creative solutions to problems or needs of the community, but they usually do not wish to fund risky projects. Try proposing a project that puts a fresh spin on a controversial, but popular topic, such as controlling wildfires through increased logging activities.

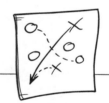

Action Plan

Clarity in communicating the ideas in your grant request is very important. Have someone who is not involved in the project read and critique your draft application.

Don't assume that you can't qualify for a grant even if you're a freshman. Many corporations are eager to offer grants to freshmen on subjects that address issues that are unique to freshmen students. For example, I was awarded a grant from Computech Corporation to write an essay entitled "What Every Freshman Must Learn in the First 30 Days at College." Computech wanted to offer this advice to their employees who had kids who were about to enter college.

Back Up Your Goals with a Budget

Keep your goals realistic! It's important to have an evaluation plan. Grantors want to know if the projects they fund are viable. They also want to know if your project is meeting its goals.

Have a reasonable and detailed budget. Do your homework on costs prior to submitting your application, and be sure to explain your budget even if there are no requirements to do so.

If your project is rejected, ask the grantor for reviewer comments. The comments can offer invaluable tips for improving your future grant applications. Never forget to write thank-you notes, even if your project is not funded.

The Least You Need to Know

➤ Be prepared to work hard to find grants made to students for specific projects.

➤ The most common federal government grants are the Pell and FSEOG grants.

➤ There are numerous private funding sources for grants if you know where to find them.

Chapter 10

State Aid Programs

In This Chapter

➤ Taking advantage of your state's aid programs if you can't get federal aid

➤ Learning about types of state aid and how they differ from federal aid programs

➤ Finding out about special programs available in your state

States are usually more generous than the federal government in determining whether you qualify for financial aid. Federal awards are based on your adjusted gross income and your asset base at the time of your application for aid. In contrast, most states consider only your adjusted gross income. That means that if you have a relatively low gross income but live in a posh home and own expensive assets, you may still be able to qualify for state aid if your income falls within your state's guidelines.

Last year, total state aid was more than $50 billion. Savvy students who took the initiative to obtain as much information as possible about state financial aid programs were the ones who benefited the most from state-directed financial aid programs.

This chapter gives you an overview and a sampling of the types of programs available in individual states. It covers the basics, and points you to Appendix C, "Alphabetical State Financial Aid Listings," where you can get information about specific programs in all the states of the U.S. Programs are constantly changing, so be sure to ask your state aid office for its most recent information on financial aid opportunities.

Overview of State Aid Programs

All state educational agencies provide need-based financial assistance, and all states award merit-based scholarship assistance. Most states have created a guaranteed tuition plan or educational savings program for their residents. About a quarter of the states have adopted the Taylor Plan, which guarantees that the state will pay the tuition costs of eligible moderate- and low-income students who meet the state's minimum academic qualifications to attend college.

Unfortunately, only about 30 percent of the states are currently offering work-study programs, though the number of states endorsing the programs increases every year.

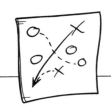

Many states offer loan-forgiveness programs for specific professions, such as education- or health-related careers. Under this program, the state will pay off your loan if you graduate in a certain profession and reside in the state for a specified period of time after you graduate.

Action Plan

Tuition and fees are still a bargain at most state colleges. About 16 percent of the actual cost of a public college education comes from tuition. The state and federal governments make up the rest.

A Sampling of State Aid Programs

Several federally funded aid programs are administered by individual states. This gives a little more consistency to the crazy quilt of state aid programs and gives you some program names to look out for when going over state aid information.

Student Incentive Grants

Although the states administer the program and decide individually whether the grants apply to full- or part-time students, the *Student Incentive Grants program* is partially funded by the federal government. It awards an annual maximum amount of $2,500.

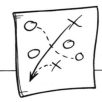

Action Plan

Find out whether you can take a state grant with you if you enroll in an out-of-state college or university. Many states have reciprocal agreements with other states.

Robert C. Byrd Honors Scholarships

The *Robert C. Byrd Honors Scholarship* program recognizes 10 students from each congressional district for outstanding academic achievement and provides $1,500 for the first year of higher education.

Paul Douglas Teacher Scholarship Program

The *Paul Douglas Teacher Scholarships* are a merit-based, state-administered program. This program is intended to encourage students who graduate in the top 10 percent of their classes to enter the field of teaching. States may give each student up to $5,000 a year for up to four years. Participating students are then obligated to teach for two years.

Help

The addresses and telephone numbers of all the state aid offices can be found listed by state in Appendix C.

State Aid Offices

State aid offices are the central clearinghouses for the aid programs provided within the state. Since even programs that sound similar vary in their particulars from state to state, these offices can help you sort out the differences. You can get current information from counselors at your high school or at the college financial aid office. However, if the world isn't working as well as you would like and local sources aren't helpful, the state financial aid agencies have the most up-to-date and comprehensive information.

Insight

According to the National Association of State Student Grant and Aid Programs, the top 10 spenders of need-based grant aid per full-time undergraduate student in 1999 were ...

New York $850

Illinois $815

New Jersey $790

Pennsylvania $710

Minnesota $685

Vermont $570

Indiana $410

Washington $380

Iowa $370

Virginia $355

How Much Aid Comes from the States?

Our states vary widely in the amount of aid that each gives to education, according to the authoritative New York State Higher Education Services Corporation, which keeps track of state financial aid expenditures on students.

Last year, states awarded over $3 billion in aid to more than two million students. About 85 percent of that amount went to need-based aid. The New York State Higher Education group predicts that the numbers will continue to rise.

Some states spend more than others on their students. Last year, five states (California, Illinois, New Jersey, New York, and Pennsylvania) dispersed a total of $1.5 billion in need-based awards to undergraduates—a whopping 50 percent of the total for that category.

The less-populous states will argue that citing the raw dollar amounts spent overall is misleading, because they end up spending more per capita on their smaller numbers of students. They'll also tell you that the full extent of their aid doesn't show up in the standard measures used by the federal government. Here's their argument: If their schools are relatively inexpensive, then students don't need as much financial aid as they do in the more expensive schools in other, larger states. Thus, they say, the less-populated states are to some degree penalized in the rankings for helping students out with lower tuitions.

Types of Programs Administered by the States

The range of state aid is broad and shows the political process at work. Along with the standard varieties of need-based aid, states are now moving heavily into non-need-based aid programs that reward students for outstanding academic achievement, regardless of their need for funds.

State legislatures also try to influence future careers by offering money to students who pursue certain areas of study or professions that are in demand within a respective state, just as the federal government rewards students entering certain professions. Many states push math and science studies for students who intend to go into teaching, whereas others boost a wide array of professions, ranging from physical therapy to teaching.

Other state programs try to reward people less for what they do than for who they are. Minority group programs and programs to aid the dependents of prisoners of war or children of police officers killed in active duty all fall under this broad heading.

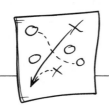

Action Plan

Most state financial aid programs apply only to state residents. Check the residency and transfer requirements of each program, and find out if your state has any reciprocal financial aid agreements with other states.

Many states also offer low-interest loan programs, which are similar to federal loan aid. To make their private colleges more attractive, several states now offer "equalization" money to help the tuition grants of private colleges match those of the state's public institutions.

The best benefit a state offers is the protection it gives its own citizens in the form of in-state tuition at its public institutions. Resident status also provides eligibility for certain aid programs.

If you plan to attend an out-of-state public college, it may be worth your while to take the time to establish residency in that state first. Before you take this action, make sure you understand the particular state's residency requirements. In some states, it takes two years to establish residency. If you're attracted to an academic program offered in another state, but don't want to give up possible aid from your own state, check in Appendix C to see if your state has an established agreement with the other state to allow you to take advantage of your home state's aid while studying elsewhere.

The Non-Need Aid Trend

There's a growing trend toward non-need-based aid. Last year, 37 states had such programs and they paid out over $425 million. Those programs have been growing, though over 90 percent of the grant dollars awarded to undergraduates by states are need-based, according to the National Association of State Scholarship and Grant Programs.

Of the non-need pool, the biggest chunk of cash went into academic scholarships, so maintaining good grades still pays big dividends. Non-need-based aid is broken down into three categories:

➤ **Tuition equalization programs**   These programs help reduce the difference in tuition costs between public and private schools.

➤ **Scholarship programs or merit awards**   This category rewards academic achievement and is largely aimed at charming academic talent into staying in-state.

➤ **Categorical aid programs**   This type of aid encourages students to go into particular fields of study, such as math and science. It also helps special constituencies like veterans and police officers.

As with all state programs, some states award a lot more in non-need aid than others. Last year, for example, most of the growth in non–need-based programs was attributed to Florida and Georgia, which increased their spending by more than $26 million. The spurt in non-need monies is still minor compared with the massive $2 billion in need-based funds that goes to undergraduates annually, but non-need aid is out there if you're willing to go after it.

Starting new non-need programs makes good political sense. Giving non-need programs enough money to make a difference makes state legislators look decidedly good to their affluent constituents. As a result, if you deduct the expenditures for such behemoth programs as New York's Part-Time Student Grant Program and Ohio's Student Choice Program, the remaining allotment for less visible non-need programs drops off dramatically.

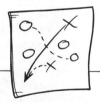

Action Plan

According to the National Association of State Scholarship and Grant Programs, adding new non-need programs has contributed little to the growth of state financial aid. Of course, a million dollars here and there is not pocket change, and any student would be very happy with just a fraction of that money.

Where Do States Get Their Money?

Several federally funded aid programs are administered by individual states. This gives a little more consistency to the overall state financial aid programs. Here are several examples of federal programs that are administered by the states:

➤ **State Student Incentive Grants**   Although the states administer the program and decide individually whether the grants apply to full- or half-time students, the program is partially funded by the federal government. The annual maximum is $2,500 and is based primarily on the financial need of the student.

➤ **Robert C. Byrd Honors Scholarship Program**   This program recognizes 10 students from each congressional district for outstanding academic achievement, providing $1,500 for the first year of higher education.

➤ **Paul Douglas Teacher Scholarship Program**   A merit-based, state-administered program intended to encourage students who graduate in the top 10 percent of their classes to enter the field of teaching. The states may give each student up to $5,000 a year for up to four years. Recipient students are then obligated to teach within the states for two years.

State Guaranty Agencies

A *state guaranty agency* is a nonprofit organization that administers the FFEL (Federal Family Education Loan) and Stafford PLUS (Parent Loans for Undergraduate Students) loans that are covered in detail in Chapter 15, "The Inside Scoop on Student Loans."

The federal government sets the loan limits and interest rates for these programs, but the states set their own limitations and conditions. You'll want to contact your state guaranty agency for the latest information on loan availability, and repayment and deferment conditions; the agency can also put you in touch with willing lenders.

Help

The address and phone number of each state's guaranty office is listed in Appendix C.

Special State Programs to Consider

All state educational agencies provide need-based financial assistance, and many state agencies award merit-based scholarship assistance. Over 60 percent of all states have created some kind of guaranteed tuition plan or educational savings program for their state residents.

Prepaid Tuition Plans

Prepaid tuition plans allow parents to pay a certain sum of money, years in advance, for their children's education; *tuition savings plans* are usually in the form of tax-exempt bonds or zero coupon bonds. The following states offer prepaid tuition plans or tuition savings plans:

> Alabama, Arkansas, Colorado, Connecticut, Delaware, Georgia, Hawaii, Illinois, Indiana, Iowa, Kentucky, Louisiana, Maine, Maryland, Massachusetts, Michigan, Minnesota, Missouri, New Hampshire, New Jersey, New York, North Carolina, North Dakota, Ohio, Oklahoma, Oregon, Pennsylvania, Rhode Island, Tennessee, Texas, Virginia, Washington, West Virginia, Wisconsin, and Wyoming

Guaranteed Tuition Plans

The *Taylor Plan*, which guarantees that the state will pay the tuition costs of eligible moderate- and low-income students who meet the academic qualifications to attend college, has been adopted by these states:

> Louisiana, Florida, Texas, and Ohio

Work-Study Programs

The following states offer *work-study programs:*

> California, Colorado, Connecticut, Florida, Iowa, Indiana, Kansas, Louisiana, Massachusetts, Michigan, Minnesota, Nevada, New Mexico, North Carolina, Pennsylvania, Rhode Island, South Carolina, Texas, Vermont, and Washington

Loan Forgiveness Programs

The following states offer *loan forgiveness programs* for specific professions such as education or health-related careers:

> Alabama, Arkansas, California, Connecticut, Delaware, Florida, Georgia, Hawaii, Illinois, Indiana, Iowa, Kentucky, Louisiana, Maryland, Massachusetts, Mississippi, Missouri, New Jersey, New Mexico, New York, North Carolina, Ohio, Oklahoma, Oregon, Pennsylvania, South Carolina, Tennessee, Texas, Utah, Vermont, Virginia, Washington, West Virginia, and Wisconsin

Western Student Exchange Program

Fourteen states participate in the *Western Undergraduate Exchange Program* administered by the Western Interstate Commission for Higher Education (WICHE). This program allows students to participate in tuition reciprocity agreements. The following states participate in the WICHE program:

Alaska, Arizona, Colorado, Hawaii, Idaho, Montana, Nevada, New Mexico, North Dakota, Oregon, South Dakota, Utah, Washington, and Wyoming

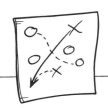

Action Plan

The amount of state aid for academically talented students is growing faster than aid for financially needy students. However, the competition for academic scholarships is tough.

Highlights of State Financial Aid Programs

Each state offers a wide variety of scholarship, grant, work-study, and loan programs. In Appendix C, you will find selected programs in each state described to give you a better idea of the different types of state aid that might be available to you.

Keep in mind that states are constantly adding and deleting programs. Contact your state's financial aid office to get the latest list of state aid programs.

The Least You Need to Know

➤ State agencies may be able to offer you financial aid even if you don't qualify for federal aid.

➤ Because state aid programs are dynamic and change rapidly, check with your state's financial aid office for the latest information on what is available.

➤ Contact your state's financial aid office to apply for a grant or scholarship. See your state's guaranty office to apply for a student loan. In some states, the two offices are combined.

Chapter 11

Playing the Scholarship Game

> ## In This Chapter
>
> ➤ Learning what scholarships are all about and how to get one
>
> ➤ Finding out how to increase your odds of getting a scholarship
>
> ➤ Knowing how to spot and avoid scholarship scams

A *scholarship* is a form of financial assistance that doesn't require repayment. This type of award is usually given to students who demonstrate potential for distinction in academic performance or who show special talents in other areas.

Scholarship dollars can come from many sources: federal and state governments; the school you'll attend; or private sources, such as corporations, fraternal organizations, local professional associations, unions, and high school or college alumni associations, to name a few. They can also come from your parents' employers or, if you're working, your own employer.

Scholarship awards are either need-based or merit-based, and do not have to be repaid. Many scholarships are awarded for one academic year but are renewable if you continue to meet their requirements.

Need-based scholarships are awarded to those who need more help paying for school. Merit-based scholarships typically are awarded to students who excel in academics, the arts, or sports, so don't give up on those violin lessons! Merit scholarships typically have qualifiers attached to them, such as religious affiliation, intended field of study, ethnic background, or leadership skills. To renew these scholarships annually, you may be expected to maintain a specific grade-point average or pursue a specific major.

Surfing the Web for Scholarships

The best way to search for a scholarship is to use personalized search tools on the Web that will compare your background with a database of available scholarships. Only scholarships that fit your profile are identified in the matches.

With more than $1 billion in scholarships available annually, *FastWeb* at www.fastweb.com/ is the largest, most accurate, and most frequently updated scholarship database. If you supply an e-mail address, FastWeb will notify you when new awards that match your profile are added to its database. You can even submit an electronic application to some of the scholarships listed on FastWeb, saving you time and money. The site also includes college Web sites and numerous other student resources that are available on the Web.

Insight

FastWeb is able to offer its free services, in part, based on the willingness of its users to be reached by FastWeb's marketing partners. The information you supply to FastWeb may be made available to leading companies, so you'll receive free information on college financing and admissions, and offers and promotions designed just for students, including coupons from campus bookstores, retail store freebies, and more. It doesn't take much time to search, and it's free.

To find small local awards that aren't listed in any book or database, look for notices posted on bulletin boards at your school's guidance office, the public library, and outside the financial aid offices at nearby colleges and universities.

Don't waste your money on scholarship matching services that charge you a fee. You won't get any better information than you can get from the free services available on the Web.

Scholarships that sound too good to be true usually are. Learn how to recognize and protect yourself from the most common scholarship scams. The number one tip is that if you have to pay to get scholarship money, it's probably a scam.

Scholarship Databases

In addition to searching FastWeb, you should also search at least one of the other large scholarship databases, such as www.scholarships.kachinatech.com/scholarships/scholars.html or www.college-scholarships.com/. Search each database to make certain that you've found all the awards for which you qualify.

You'll notice a significant amount of overlap among the databases in that they all use similar methods to compile their listings. Each database usually includes a few awards not listed in others.

Peterson's Scholarship Search

Peterson's Award Search makes it quick and easy to find the right scholarships for you. The database covers over 2,000 scholarship sources in 70 academic subject areas.

Peterson's is one of the most trusted names in education and careers publishing. Their dedication to providing the best possible information guided the design of their scholarship database.

Help

Students who are awarded scholarships often need additional financial assistance. See the "Lenders of College Loans" section of Appendix B for Web sites and information on student and parent loans.

College Board's Fund Finder

The *College Board's FUND FINDER* scholarship database, also known as ExPAN Scholarship Search, lists scholarships and other types of financial aid programs from over 3,000 national, state, public, and private sources. The database is updated annually. You'll find its Web site at www.collegeboard.org/fundfinder/html/ssrchtop.html. Also check the "Scholarships" section in Appendix B "Directory of General Financial Aid Resources."

SRN Express

SRN Express at www.finder.ru/ is a free Web version of the Scholarship Resource Network (SRN) database. The SRN database focuses on private sector, non–need-based aid and includes information about awards from more than 1,500 organizations. The database is updated annually.

CollegeNET MACH25

CollegeNET MACH25 at www.collegenet.com/ is a free Web version of the Wintergreen Scholarship Finder database. The database lists awards from over 1,500 sponsors and is updated annually.

In addition to the scholarship databases listed in this section, there are several other free scholarship databases listed in Appendix B. These databases are smaller but more tightly focused, providing information for specific majors or career interests, such as art, computer science, journalism, or nursing.

Searching for scholarships does take time, but this book makes it easy. Spend about 30 minutes on the Web completing a profile, and let computer technology begin working for you. You can also use the Web to quickly send away for scholarship applications that you're interested in. Soon your mailbox will be filled with scholarship applications, and you'll be well on your way to applying for a scholarship. Here's a sampling of some of the great scholarships that are out there:

➤ **American Chemical Society (ACS)**   Better education through chemistry is the motto of the ACS. They offer science scholarships to minorities. Their Web site at www.acs.org/ also lists many other sources of academic scholarships.

➤ **American Indian College Fund**   The American Indian College Fund supports over 30 tribal colleges and helps thousands of Native Americans get scholarships.

➤ **America's Junior Miss Scholarship Program**   The country's largest and oldest scholarship program for high school girls offers academic scholarships to young women.

➤ **AmeriCorp Scholarships**   Do some good for others, like build homes or clear hiking trails, and qualify for a college scholarship or loans through AmeriCorp.

➤ **Army ROTC**   Learn all that you can learn and let the Army help pay for it through their generous ROTC scholarship program, which I cover in detail in Chapter 12, "Military and Veteran Scholarship Programs."

➤ **Coca-Cola Scholars Foundation**   Coca-Cola awards thousands of dollars in college scholarships each year to over 250 high school seniors.

➤ **Discover Card Tribute Awards**   The Discover Card folks have teamed with the American Association of School Administrators for a scholarship program. Apply when you're a high school junior.

➤ **Easley National Scholarship Program**   The Easley Foundation offers academic scholarships. They also publish a newsletter about the other forms of financial aid they offer.

➤ **Elks National Foundation**   The Elks give away over $3 million a year in college scholarships to top high school seniors.

➤ **Fulbright Scholarship Program**   Teachers, students, and scholars in a wide array of fields can apply for these academic grants to study overseas.

➤ **Harry Truman Scholarship Foundation**   The bucks start here for college students looking to enter public service. The Truman scholarship program will help you get there.

➤ **Hispanic College Fund** This minority scholarship program is looking for Hispanic business leaders of the future, and they're willing to offer you a scholarship to help you get there.

➤ **Hispanic Scholarship Fund** Hispanic students in high school, community college, or four-year colleges can apply to the Hispanic Scholarship Funds program for awards.

➤ **Imagine America Scholarships** The Career Training Foundation's program for technical schools offers numerous scholarships.

➤ **Intel Foundation** Each year, the Intel Foundation provides undergraduate scholarships and graduate fellowships to outstanding engineering and computer science students at colleges and universities around the world.

➤ **Jackie Robinson Foundation** The Robinson Foundation offers college scholarships for talented minority youths.

➤ **National Action Council for Minorities in Engineering** The Council offers scholarships for African-Americans, Latinos, and American Indians majoring in engineering.

➤ **National Collegiate Athletic Association (NCAA) Scholarships** Student athletes in college can continue their education with the support of athletic scholarships that are sponsored by the NCAA.

➤ **Rhodes Scholarships** The best and brightest college students apply to spend a couple of years at Oxford. The Rhodes scholarship is one of the premier scholarships to win.

➤ **Rotary Foundation Ambassadorial Scholarship** The Rotary Foundation gives out more than a thousand academic scholarships a year worldwide. It's the biggest program of its kind.

➤ **United Negro College Fund** A mind is a terrible thing to waste and so is an opportunity like this for African-American students who can qualify for United Negro College scholarships.

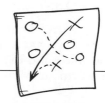

Action Plan

Scholarships are a great way to finance your education. Because they are gifts, these funds do not have to be repaid.

Help

The Web site addresses for all of the scholarships covered in this section are listed under "Scholarships, Grants, and Fellowships" in Appendix B.

Scholarship Programs for Minorities

In addition to the preceding scholarships focusing on minority students, literally thousands of additional opportunities are out there for both minorities and non-minorities. This section covers just a few of them in order to give you an idea of what's available.

Project Excellence

Founded in 1987 by syndicated columnist Carl T. Rowan, *Project Excellence* is a college scholarship program for black high school seniors who display outstanding writing and speaking skills. Mr. Rowan founded Project Excellence to reward black students who excel academically. The program rewards students who rise above stereotypes and negative peer influence, and who want to succeed.

Mr. Rowan's committee of journalists, community leaders, and school officials over-sees the program. Their mission is to help make youngsters realize that approval of the know-nothings is worth next to nothing, whereas hard work and good grades can be worth an awful lot. Participants are African-American students in their senior year of high school in the metropolitan Washington, D.C., area, including those portions in Virginia and Maryland.

Help

If you'd like more information about Project Excellence, write to Project Excellence, 3251 C Sutton Place NW, Washington, D.C. 20016.

Since the founding of Project Excellence, 3,000 scholarships have been awarded for a total of over $76 million dollars. Last year, Project Excellence provided $21 million in scholarships to over 700 high school seniors. African-American students who compete for Project Excellence scholarships must be nominated by their schools and must be able to demonstrate outstanding oral and written command of the English language and possess a cumulative grade-point average of at least 3.5.

Every public, private, and parochial high school in the Washington, D.C., metropolitan area is eligible to nominate four students. They must submit all application information to Project Excellence by February.

Children's Scholarship Fund

The *Children's Scholarship Fund* helps provide educational opportunities for low-income children. Siebel Systems, which is a California-based software company, has donated over $3 million toward the mission of providing more students with access to colleges. Their Children's Scholarship Fund has awarded over $160 million in scholarships to about 40,000 such children around the country since 1998. The scholarships pay up to 75 percent of their tuition.

Educational Opportunity Programs (EOP)

EOP programs are administered through California State University (CSU), the University of California (UC), and California's community colleges. They provide grants, counseling, and tutorial services to low-income disadvantaged students. At UC and some CSU campuses, counseling and tutorial services are provided through the campus Equal Opportunity Programs (EOP), but grants come from the financial aid office.

To be eligible for the EOP program, a student must be disadvantaged according to criteria established by California regulations and be enrolled fulltime at a community college or at a CSU or UC campus.

William Simon Foundation

The *William Simon Foundation* provides support for scholarships and fellowships for academically qualified students in need of financial assistance. These awards, which support a portion of the expenses of tuition and room and board, are made through grants.

How to Win a Scholarship

When requesting information on a particular scholarship, send a personalized letter to the scholarship provider with a self-addressed, stamped envelope. When you get the application, make sure you follow the instructions—to the letter—for completing the form! The biggest mistake you can make when applying for scholarships is to overlook the fine print. If the provider requests your high school transcripts, send them! If the application says to include an essay on how to live "La Vida Loca," do it! And, most important, don't miss the deadline: There are no exceptions for late applications.

If you are asked to send a letter of recommendation, ask the person writing it to take the time to personalize it on letterhead, since presentation is very important. Scholarship providers do not like to see generic recommendation letters. If at all possible, submit only word-processed applications. Make copies of everything you submit to scholarship providers.

Warning

Follow the instructions for application forms to the letter. Use a word processor to write the applications, or if you still have a typewriter, type them out. Handwritten applications don't cut it!

If you're a school leader, president of your class, for example, then there are a bunch of scholarship opportunities for you to explore. The William Randolph Hearst Foundation has a scholarship program that acknowledges students who have been elected to leadership offices in their high school's school government. The program distributes $2,000 each to over 100 students a year. Tylenol (the headache company) offers a similar program to high school leaders. The awards are based on leadership credentials, academic records, and extracurricular activities. Each year, 500 students receive $1,000 awards and 10 get whopping ones of $10,000.

Help

Send your completed scholarship application packet via certified mail to ensure that the scholarship provider receives it.

Can Average Students Get Scholarships?

Of course, average students can get scholarships. Not all scholarships are based on grades or test scores. For example, you can get a scholarship because you were born in New York or just because your dad works at US Airways. You'd be surprised to know just how many awards exist for all types of students.

Scholarship searching is an ongoing process, not a one-time project. Just as your academic status, qualifications, and interests change, so will the scholarships in the databases. In any scholarship database you use, be sure to update your profile and search for new awards frequently to increase your chances of obtaining one.

Scholarship Scams

Every year, several hundred thousand students and parents are defrauded by scholarship scams. The victims of these scams lose more than $100 million annually.

Scam operations often imitate legitimate government agencies, grant-giving foundations, education lenders, and scholarship matching services, using official-sounding names containing words like "National," "Federal," "Foundation," or "Administration." If you have to pay money to get a scholarship, it's probably a scam.

Fellowships

Fellowships are like scholarships in that they require no repayment of service in return for the reward. Fellowships provide money to cover the cost of tuition, books, fees, and even nondiscretionary expenses. They can be awarded based on a student's demonstrated need, academic merit, or any combination of variables that meet the objectives of specific fellows. Fellowships are primarily for graduate and postdoctoral students. To learn more about them, see Chapter 14, "Adult, Graduate, and International Programs."

Private School Scholarships

Parents seeking assistance with private school tuition for their children might get help from the school your son or daughter would like to attend. They may have scholarships available or be able to direct you to local sources of assistance.

The Least You Need to Know

➤ Scholarships are everywhere if you know where to look.

➤ Routinely search the scholarship databases that are listed in Appendix B to find new and exciting scholarship and grant opportunities.

➤ You will win a scholarship only if you follow the application instructions to the letter.

Chapter 12

Military and Veteran Scholarship Programs

> ## In This Chapter
>
> ➤ Learning about the many financial aid opportunities available through ROTC and other military programs
>
> ➤ Finding out how you can qualify for a military scholarship
>
> ➤ Discovering the educational options that are available to you as a veteran

The GI Bill, which was passed after World War II, has helped to finance the education of millions of military personnel and veterans. If you qualify, financial assistance programs offered by the military services are a way to reduce your college costs. This chapter examines the numerous scholarship and tuition programs offered by the military financial assistance programs for their personnel and their dependents.

Reserve Officers Training Corps (ROTC) Scholarships

The *ROTC Scholarships* are offered to qualified men and women who are enrolled in either two-year community colleges or four-year undergraduate college programs. Candidates must be U.S. citizens between the ages of 17 and 21 when they apply for a scholarship. There are physical requirements for acceptance into the program, and applicants must take either the ACT or SAT test. A personal interview is required.

ROTC scholarships pay for up to $8,000 or 80 percent of college expenses and provide a monthly living stipend. Tuition and fees are paid directly to the school and are considered financial aid. The monthly stipend paid to the student is considered income, and it's taxable.

Recipients are required to study military science while in college, participate in summer training sessions, and maintain satisfactory academic progress as determined by their schools. Upon successful completion of the program and graduation, a recipient is awarded a military commission. Scholarship recipients must enlist in the Army, Navy, Air Force, or Marines and must agree to serve for four years on active duty and two years on reserve status after graduation.

Over 600 colleges and universities participate in this program. Speak with the school's ROTC representative to obtain specific information, program obligations, and application materials. Contact the following for additional information:

Air Force
Air Force ROTC Scholarship Program, JQ Recruiting Division
Maxwell Air Force Base
Maxwell, Alabama 36112-6106
205-953-2091

Army
Army ROTC Scholarship Program
Gold QUEST Center Box 3279
Warminster, Pennsylvania 18794-0128
1-800-USA-ROTC (872-7682)

Marine Corps
Command General
Marine Corps Recruiting Consul Code MRON, 2 Navy Annex
Washington, D.C. 20380-1775
703-614-8541

Navy
Navy Opportunity
Information Center, P.O. Box 9406
Gaithersburg, Maryland 20898-9979
1-800-327-NAVY (327-6289)

Military Academy Scholarships

Military Academy scholarships are awarded each year to qualified students for attendance at the Air Force Academy, the Army Academy, the Naval Academy, the Merchant Marine Academy, and the Coast Guard Academy. Nominations are usually made by the applicant's U.S. senator or congressional representative. The scholarships are competitive and are based upon a number of factors, including high school grades, SAT or ACT test scores, leadership qualities, and athletic ability.

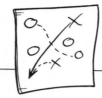

Action Plan

All of the U.S. military academies offer "Ivy League"–quality educational programs that will serve you well throughout your career. The trick is figuring out a way to get into an academy. It starts with your congressman or congresswoman, who must first nominate you for entrance. Get to know these people well, and be prepared to network your way through the political system. If you can find out from those in the know exactly how the entrance system works and what you need to do to crack it, you'll be miles ahead of your competition.

Applicants must apply separately for each academy. Students enrolled in this program receive their undergraduate education at the respective academies. Begin the process very early, especially the securing of a nomination from a senator or congressperson. Contact the following military offices for further information:

Air Force
Director of Admissions HQ USAFNRRS
U.S. Air Force Academy
2304 Cadet Drive, Suite 200
Colorado Springs, Colorado 80840-5025
719-472-2520

Army
Director of Admissions West Point
600 Thayer Road
West Point, New York 10996-1797
914-938-4041

Coast Guard
Director of Admissions
U.S. Coast Guard Academy
15 Mohegan Avenue
New London, Connecticut 06320-4195
203-444-8501
1-800-883-8724

Merchant Marine
Director of Admissions
U.S. Merchant Marine Academy
300 Steamboat Road
Kings Point, New York 11024
516-773-5391
1-800-732-6267

Navy
Candidate Guidance Office, U.S. Naval Academy
117 Decatur Road
Annapolis, Maryland 21402-5018
410-293-4361
1-800-638-9156

Military Financial Assistance Programs

Each branch of the Armed Services offers numerous programs for both enlisted and officer personnel interested in continuing their educations. Most military bases have education officers who can provide information on specific programs offered during your period of service and after active duty is completed.

Service programs pay a portion of the cost of college attendance, which usually ranges from 75 to 90 percent of undergraduate or graduate school expenses. At the graduate level, commissioned officers are selected to attend a graduate school, where all of the educational expenses are paid.

As an incentive for enlistment, certain branches of the Armed Forces will repay a borrower's student loan. Under the Veterans' Educational Assistance Program, the government will double the monthly education contribution of the service person. The military services offer excellent opportunities to learn new skills and save for higher education at the same time. Follow these procedures if you're interested in learning more about the educational benefits offered by the Armed Services:

1. Speak to a local recruiting officer. He or she can provide specific information on the educational benefits offered by each branch of the Armed Services.

2. If possible, contact the local military base education officer to obtain more information on specific programs.

3. Determine whether the education benefits offered by the military match your long-term career plans and objectives.

There are so many military college financial aid programs to consider that this chapter can't possibly cover all of them. Check out the "Military and Veteran Programs" section in Appendix B, "Directory of General Financial Aid Resources," for additional programs and options. Military aid programs are constantly changing, so you may discover options that were not available at the time this book went to press.

Here are some examples of what you'll find when you visit the Web sites listed in Appendix B in the "Military and Veteran Programs" section.

Air Force Aid Society

The *Air Force Aid Society* provides educational loan assistance to the children of qualified Air Force personnel. Candidates for the program must be enrolled or accepted for enrollment as full-time students in an approved college. Contact the National Headquarters, Air Force Aid Society, 1745 Jefferson Davis Highway, Arlington, Virginia 22202, or call 703-607-3072 for further information.

Air Force Sergeants Association/Airmen Memorial Foundation

The *Air Force Sergeants/Airmen Memorial* program offers approximately 40 academic and technical grants ranging from $1,000 to $3,000. Applicants must have a cumulative GPA of 3.5 to qualify and are accepted between November and March. To apply, send a self-addressed, stamped 9-by-12-inch envelope to: AFSAIAMF Scholarship Program, P.O. Box 50, Temple Hills, Maryland 20757-0050.

Help

If you contact the Air Force Sergeants Association, make sure you ask about special scholarship programs that are available to dependents of Air Force personnel.

Army College Fund

The *Army College Fund* provides a way for Army personnel to finance their college educations while still on active duty. Under the plan, army personnel on active duty contribute $100 per month for the first 12 months to their education fund. The Army also contributes to the fund based on the length of enlistment. If you serve for four years, the Army will give you its maximum benefit of $18,000. Contact your local Army recruiter for further details.

Army Continuing Education System

The *Army Continuing Education System* provides numerous educational programs for Army personnel. A variety of academic and nonacademic educational opportunities are available. The following programs are offered: Basic Skills Education Program,

High School Completion Program, English as a Second Language Program, Advanced Skills Education Program, Army Apprenticeship Program, and Defense Activity for Nontraditional Education Support. Contact your local Army recruiter for further information.

Army ROTC

The *Army ROTC Four-Year Program* provides college-trained officers for the Army, Army Reserve, and Army National Guard. The Army ROTC program is offered at more than 600 colleges and universities throughout the nation. As the largest single source of Army officers, the ROTC program fulfills a vital role in providing mature young men and women for leadership and management positions in an increasingly technical Army. Even though the Army is getting smaller, it still needs thousands of new officers each year.

Army Nurse Corps

The *Army Nurse Corps* program enables nursing students interested in careers as Army nurses to participate in Army ROTC while in college. Nursing cadets who meet all of the professional requirements and successfully complete the program are commissioned as second lieutenants upon graduation from college. Contact your local Army recruiter for further information.

Army Loan Repayment Program

The *Army Loan Repayment Program* offers special financial incentives to regular and reserve Army enlisted persons. Under the program, the Army will repay the Stafford Federal Loans and Federal Perkins Loans (see Chapter 15, "The Inside Scoop on Student Loans") of persons who enlist in areas specified as critical by the Army. Contact your local Army recruiter or military base education officer for further details.

Service Members Opportunity Colleges

Colleges that are members of the *Service Members Opportunity Colleges* allow service people to transfer credits and pursue programs of study, regardless of location, in a coordinated network of junior colleges, community colleges, and four-year colleges. Flexible course hours and entrance requirements make it possible for military personnel to continue their educations and obtain college degrees wherever they may be stationed. Contact your local recruiter for further details.

Broadened Opportunity for Officer Selection and Training Program (BOOST)

The *BOOST* program is designed for high school seniors who have good academic grades but not the required College Board test scores for the four-year Navy ROTC Scholarship Program. Students selected for the BOOST Program attend a training school. After graduation, a student either is granted a four-year Navy ROTC Scholarship or receives an appointment to the Naval Academy. Contact your local Navy recruiting office for further information.

Navy's Dependents Scholarship Program

The *Navy's Dependents Scholarship Program* offers scholarship assistance to the dependent children of Navy, Marine, and Coast Guard personnel. Recipients must be enrolled as full-time students in accredited programs. Write to the Naval Military Personnel Command, Department of the Navy, Washington, D.C. 20370-5121 for additional information.

Navy Student Loans

The *Navy Federal Credit Union Student Loans* offer Federal Stafford Loans and Federal Parent Loans for Undergraduate Students (PLUS) to qualified Navy personnel. For information and application forms, contact Navy Federal Credit Union facilities or write to the Navy Federal Credit Union, Security Place, P.O. Box 3350, Merrifield, Virginia 22119-3350.

The Marine Corps Scholarship Foundation

The *Marine Corps Scholarship Foundation* provides scholarship assistance to the dependent children of active service Marines, as well as to the children of discharged and reserve status Marines. The awards are based on financial need, and the amounts of the scholarships vary. Contact the Marine Corps Scholarship Foundation, P.O. Box 3008, Princeton, New Jersey 08543, for further information on this program. The application deadline is February 1.

Montgomery GI Bill

The *Montgomery GI Bill* is a federal program that provides financial assistance to all military personnel who joined one of the Armed Services after June 30, 1985. Under the terms of the program, the government contributes to the serviceperson's education fund in the amount of $275 a month after two years of service and $350 a month after three years of service. The college fund for some military persons can

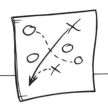

exceed $10,000. For further information, contact your local recruiter, base education officer, or local Veterans Administration Office. The following opportunities are available under the Montgomery GI Bill:

➤ Courses at colleges and universities leading to associate, bachelor, or graduate degrees, and independent study or cooperative training programs.

➤ Courses leading to a certificate or diploma from a business, technical, or vocational school, or an apprenticeship or on-the-job training program.

➤ Flight training programs for qualified veterans. Before beginning training, a veteran must have a private pilot's license and meet the physical requirements for a commercial license.

Action Plan

The Montgomery GI Bill applies to those who entered active duty after June 30, 1985. To receive the maximum benefits the program offers, you must serve on active duty for three years.

Veterans Programs

The *Office of Student Financial Assistance (OSFA)* provides information and special services specific to the needs of veterans, servicepersons, and eligible dependents in the community. The OSFA office will help you apply for educational assistance benefits under the provisions of the GI Bill and other programs of the Veterans Administration, as well as state veterans programs. Contact the OSFA office for further information and assistance.

Veterans Education Assistance Program (VEAP)

The *Veterans Education Assistance Program (VEAP)* allows enlisted men and women as well as officers to contribute from $25 to $100 per month to an educational fund. When the person enrolls in a postsecondary program, the federal government matches the contribution with $2 for every $1 contributed by the military person. The Tuition Assistance Program pays the serviceperson up to 75 percent for undergraduate courses and 90 percent for job-related courses. Contact your local recruiter or military base education officer for further details.

Disabled American Veterans Auxiliary National Education Loan Fund

The *Disabled American Veterans Auxiliary Education* fund provides interest-free loans to undergraduate students. Academic achievement and financial need are considered when making the awards. Children of fully paid life members of the Disabled American Veterans Auxiliary are eligible to apply. Loans of up to $12,000 can be awarded to students during each year of college. Repayment begins 90 days after graduation or immediately upon withdrawal from school. The application deadline is March 1. Write to the National Education Loan Fund Director, National Headquarters, Disabled American Veterans Auxiliary, 3725 Alexandria Pike, Cold Spring, Kentucky 41076.

Veterans Administration Dependents Education Assistance Act

Through the *Veterans Administration Dependents Education Assistance Act*, the federal government provides financial assistance to the dependent children and spouses of veterans who have died or who are totally disabled as a result of service-related injuries, as well as to the spouses and children of living veterans. Survivors of deceased veterans, spouses of living veterans, and their children between the ages of 18 and 26 are also eligible for benefits. For application forms, contact any Veterans Administration Center (see Appendix C, "Alphabetical State Financial Aid Listings"). For further information, write to the Division of Student Services and Veterans Programs, 400 Maryland Avenue, SW, Room 4010, Washington, D.C. 20202.

Knights of Columbus Educational Fund

The *Knights of Columbus* Supreme Council offers financial assistance to the children of veterans who were members of the Knights of Columbus, and were either killed in action or permanently disabled as a result of military service. For further information, write to the Director of Scholarship Aid, Knights of Columbus, P.O. Box 1670, New Haven, Connecticut 06507.

Noncommissioned Officers Association Scholarship Foundation

The *Noncommissioned Officers Association Scholarship Foundation* awards renewable scholarships to the children and spouses of noncommissioned officers who are members of the association. For further information, write to the NCOA Scholarship Foundation, P.O. Box 33610, San Antonio, Texas 78265, or phone 512-653-6161. The application deadline is March 31.

Retired Officers Association Scholarship Loan Program

Children of active duty or retired members of the military can receive financial assistance from the *Retired Officers Association Scholarship Loan Program*. Loans are made for up to five years of full-time undergraduate study at accredited colleges or technical schools. For applications, write to the Administrator, Scholarship Loan Program, 201 N. Washington Street, Alexandria, Virginia 22314. The application deadline is March 1.

Warning

If you contact one of the Veterans Administration Centers, don't limit your questions to just a few specific subjects. There's a wealth of VA programs out there that you may not be aware of, so ask general questions like: "I want to go to college. Can you provide me with information that shows me all of the financial aid that might be available to me through the VA?"

Veterans Administration Centers

For a complete list of state addresses for Veterans Administration Centers that can provide information on all programs for veterans and their dependents, look under your state in Appendix C.

Help

The military offers a series of examinations that can help service personnel receive credit for life experiences. Ask for information on DANTES (Defense Activity for Nontraditional Educational Support) from your local recruiter. DANTES also offers correspondence courses and certificate programs that range from high school level through postgraduate study.

Publications

Many excellent publications provide information on programs offered by the Armed Services and Veterans Administration. And best of all, most of them are free. The following publications can be used to obtain further information:

Army ROTC Scholarship Program   Army ROTC Department of Military Science, 73 Harmon Gym, University of California at Berkeley, Berkeley, California 94720. Free.

Federal Benefits for Veterans and Dependents Veterans Administration, Government Printing Office, Washington, D.C. 20402.

Financial Aid for Veterans, Military Personnel, and Their Dependents   Reference Service Press, 1100 Industrial Road, Suite 9, San Carlos, California 94070.

How the Military Will Help You Pay for College   Don M. Betterton, P.O. Box 2123, Princeton, New Jersey 08543-2123.

Need a Lift?   The American Legion, P.O. Box 1055, Indianapolis, Indiana 46206.

Scholarship Pamphlet for USN-USM-USCG Dependent Children   Naval Military Personnel Command, NMPC-121D, Navy Department, Washington, D.C. 20370-5121. Free.

Some of the best education in the nation is available to those who qualify for admission to a military academy. However, enrollment is limited, and full-time military careers are not necessarily for everyone. Nonetheless, if you are willing to devote a part of your life to military service, there are many ways in which the federal government can help pay your way through college. The four branches of military service—the Army, Navy, Air Force, and Marines—provide in-service educational assistance. Ask your local military recruiter about these and other programs. Your high school's guidance counselor should have information on these programs as well.

The Least You Need to Know

➤ Each branch of the military offers its own unique financial aid program.

➤ ROTC programs offer you a way to go to college and get paid at the same time.

➤ Dependents of military personnel are eligible for many types of assistance.

➤ The Office of Veterans Affairs offers numerous educational assistance programs.

Chapter 13

Minority and Other Special Programs

> ## In This Chapter
>
> ➤ Discovering some of the excellent financial aid programs available to minorities
>
> ➤ Finding out about special aid programs for women, adult students, and part-time or handicapped students
>
> ➤ Learning where to look for the kinds of scholarship programs you could qualify for
>
> ➤ Finding out how to tap into private sources to get the funds you need

Over the past several years, it has become apparent that the "traditional" college student, defined as white, 18 years old, and middle class, has changed. Minority students, women, adult students, and part-time students who were previously classified as "nontraditional" are fast becoming the majority on many college campuses. Federal legislation now includes these students as eligible to receive financial aid. This chapter looks at programs targeted for nontraditional and handicapped students.

Financial Aid for Minority Students

Unfortunately, minority students looking for financial aid will not find much support at the federal level. Federal monies are concentrated in counseling for minority students or are transferred to the states for administration. All of the states therefore have minority financial aid programs and can direct you to funds available at the schools you're most interested in attending. State financial aid offices are listed in Appendix C, "Alphabetical State Financial Aid Listings." For a list of reference guides to the more prominent scholarships for minority students, look under "Minority Programs" in Appendix B, "Directory of General Financial Aid Resources."

To enhance the opportunities of minority students, several states have funded various programs ranging from the California Grant B program to the Florida Seminole-Miccosukee Indian Scholarship Program. Contact your state's Department of Education for more information. The offices are listed by state in Appendix C. Colleges are trying to fulfill their federal commitment to affirmative action programs by working harder to recruit and retain qualified minority students.

There's a category of minority student aid you should know about that often doesn't get publicized. There are broad areas of minority financial aid contributions kicked in from many financial aid sources, including the federal and state governments, the schools themselves, and private groups.

Another area of minority aid involves programs that are attempting to correct a different type of imbalance: the lack of minority students entering certain professions, such as teaching or health care. To get more minority students into these areas, government and private organizations are offering lucrative scholarships. Minority students with the right qualifications may find that they can't afford to pass up the opportunities these programs offer.

We obviously can't list every minority program offered, or the many programs would fill the entire book. Instead, we will concentrate on the state level, where much of the money is. We will also cover scholarships offered by religious organizations, civic groups, and professional associations, which provide many of these awards. The best-known program sponsored by a professional association, the National Action Council for Minorities in Engineering, aids minority students interested in engineering careers. Most nongovernmental programs are funded through the schools.

For more programs, review the minority scholarship programs covered in Appendix B and in Chapter 11, "Playing the Scholarship Game." Also check in with your high school counselor or college financial aid office for more information.

Action Plan

For a list of schools that offer scholarships to minorities interested in pursuing degrees in engineering, write to the National Action Council for Minorities in Engineering, The Empire State Building, 350 Fifth Avenue, Suite 2212, New York, New York 10118–2299, or call 212–279–2626.

Nontraditional Students

Colleges and universities are required to allocate a minimum of 5 percent of their campus-based aid to their nontraditional student population. Institutions are also required to use a reasonable amount of their administrative funds to provide financial aid services to part-time and adult learners. These services are to be provided at times and in places that are convenient to this cohort of students.

Federal Pell Grant eligibility is extended to students who are enrolled in less than half-time programs. An allowance for childcare or for disability-related expenses might be added to the cost of school attendance.

Financial Aid Programs for Women

There are many financial aid programs for qualifying women. Some of them are:

➤ **The Verda White Barnes Memorial Scholarship Fund**   This program provides scholarships to qualified junior and senior students at Idaho State University. Applicants must be Idaho residents and must be full-time students. Preference will be given to students majoring in political science. Awards are based on academic merit, financial need, and feminist views. For further information, write to the Scholarship Office, Idaho State University, P.O. Box 8391, Pocatello, Idaho 83209.

➤ **The Business and Professional Women's Foundation (BPWF)**   Various scholarship and loan programs focus on women enrolled in health professions, engineering, and graduate business schools. Applicants must be at least 25 years old, U.S. citizens, and enrolled at least half-time at an approved school. The amounts of the awards vary and are based upon financial need.

The BPWF sponsors several financial aid programs, including:

➤ New York Life Foundation Scholarship for Women in Health Careers

➤ Loan Fund for Women in Engineering Studies

➤ Sally Butler Memorial Fund for Latina Research

➤ Lena Lake Forrest Fellowship Program

➤ Clairol Loving Care Scholarship Program

➤ The Avon Foundation Scholarship Program for Women in Business Studies:

For further information, write to the Business and Professional Women's Foundation, Attn: Scholarships and Loans, 2012 Massachusetts Avenue NW, Washington, D.C. 20036, or call 202-293-1200. Fax: 202-861-0298.

➤ **Ada Comstock Scholars Program**   Affiliated with Smith College, this program provides need-based financial assistance to students of nontraditional age admitted to Smith. Applicants should complete at least one year of

Help

In addition to the regular federal, state, and institutional financial assistance programs that are available to women students, many financial aid programs are funded specifically for women. Women needing financial assistance should seek the advice of their school's financial aid director.

liberal arts work before applying. An interview is required, and the application deadline is February 10. For more information, write to the Ada Comstock Scholars Program, Smith College, Northampton, Massachusetts 01063. Fax: 413-585-2123. E-mail: comstock@smith.edu.

➤ **Daughters of the American Revolution (DAR)**   The DAR sponsors financial assistance programs for qualified women students. Most of the scholarships are administered by individual state societies, which have their own requirements, deadlines, and application procedures. There are several scholarships offered to graduating high school seniors as well as to students already enrolled in college or university degree programs. Scholarships are offered for certain subjects, and eligibility will depend on the student's declared major.

➤ **The Society of Women Engineers**   This professional organization offers scholarships and loans to women students. They can also provide you with a list of scholarships for women that are not widely publicized. For more information, write to United Engineering Center, 120 Wall Street, New York, New York 10005; 212-509-9577.

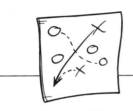

Action Plan

The money for women in higher education comes almost exclusively from colleges and private sources. College money most often takes the form of athletic scholarships; for an up-to-date listing of such awards, write for general information to: Women's Sports Foundation, Eisenhower Park, East Meadow, New York 11554; 1-800-227-3988.

If you're a female student with small children, you should find out whether your college offers day care for free or at low cost. In any case, the expenses associated with raising kids should be reflected in your financial need, which could get you more aid.

Handicapped Students

Handicapped students will find financial assistance programs offered by both the federal government and the individual states.

Federal legislation forbids discrimination on the basis of handicap and encourages handicapped persons to enroll in postsecondary institutions. Colleges and universities must meet the needs of their handicapped students or risk losing their federal financial aid funds.

The U.S. Department of Education Rehabilitation Services Administration administers the Rehabilitation Act, which determines financial eligibility for handicapped persons. However, each state has its own programs for the handicapped. Addresses for state rehabilitation services are listed in Appendix C.

Handicapped students have expenses not usually incurred by other students, and these should be considered when calculating financial need. These costs include special equipment needs, transportation, interpreters, note takers, and personal attendants. The student's financial aid director should be informed of any additional expenses, and information should be coordinated with the institution's director for handicapped or disabled persons. Here are three programs that offer financial assistance to handicapped students:

➤ **AMBUCS Resource Center (AMBUCS)**   This organization offers scholarships to U.S. citizens in their junior or senior year of college. Applicants must be accepted into an accredited program by the appropriate health/therapy profession authority in physical therapy, occupational therapy, music therapy, speech language pathology, hearing audiology, or recreational therapy. Awards are based on financial need and a GPA of 3.0 or above. The deadline for applications is April 15. Awards are announced in June. For further information, contact AMBUCS Scholarship Committee, P.O. Box 5121, High Point, North Carolina 27262, or call 910-869-2166. Fax: 910-881-8451.

Help

The U.S. Department of Education is ultimately responsible for the overall administration and disbursement of financial aid funds to the states. Their Web site is www.irs.ustreas.gov.

➤ **American Foundation for the Blind**   Scholarship assistance to blind women is the focus. Awards range from $1,000 to $3,000 per academic year. Contact the American Foundation for the Blind, 15 W. 16th Street, New York, New York 10011, for additional information and application forms.

➤ **Alexander Graham Bell Association for the Deaf**   This association funds scholarships to deaf students who use speech and speech reading to communicate, and who are attending or planning to attend a regular university or college for students with normal hearing. Applicants must use speech and residual hearing and/or speech reading as their primary form of communication. Applications are mailed in November, and the deadline is April 1. For further information, write to the Alexander Graham Bell Association for the Deaf, 3417 Volta Place NW, Washington, D.C. 20007-2778.

A Sampling of Minority Aid Programs

Many organizations provide financial assistance to minority students. Seek advice from high school counselors and college financial aid officers in locating sources of funds. There are many church-sponsored minority programs. Ask church officials to help you locate these funding sources.

American Institute of Certified Public Accountants

The *American Institute of Certified Public Accountants* provides scholarships to undergraduate minority accounting majors. To be eligible for the scholarships, minority students must be citizens of the United States and must be enrolled in an undergraduate accounting program. For further information, write to the Manager of Minority Recruitment, American Institute of Certified Public Accountants, 1211 Avenue of the Americas, New York, New York 10036-3775.

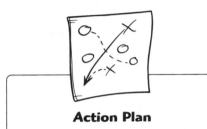

Action Plan

If you're a minority student and you file for financial aid correctly and on time, you'll receive some kind of financial aid. It's almost guaranteed!

Association of University Programs in Health Administration

Qualified African American, Native American, Asian American, Mexican American, and Puerto Rican students can participate in internship programs offered by the *Association of University Programs in Health Administration*. Recipients must be either second- or third-year undergraduate students. Academic ability is considered in awarding the internship. For further information, write to the Association of University Programs in Health Administration, 1911 N. Fort Myer Drive, Arlington, Virginia 22209.

Bureau of Indian Affairs Higher Education Grant Program

Grants from the *Bureau of Indian Affairs Higher Education* program provide financial aid to eligible Native American students. The awards are based upon financial need. For further information, write to the Bureau of Indian Affairs Higher Education Grant Program, Bureau of Indian Affairs, 18th and C Street NW, Washington, D.C. 20245.

Congressional Hispanic Caucus

The *Congressional Hispanic Caucus* provides qualified Hispanic students with fellowships to work with members of Congress. The fellowships are for one academic term. For further information on this program, write to the Congressional Hispanic Caucus, 504 C Street NE, Washington, D.C. 20002.

General Motors Scholarship Program

The *GM Corporation* provides scholarship assistance to qualified minority undergraduate students through several colleges and universities throughout the United States.

For more information, write to the General Motors Scholarship Program, General Motors Corporation, 8-163 General Motors Building, Detroit, Michigan 48202.

Indian Education and Psychology Fellowship Program

The *Indian Education and Psychology Fellowship Program,* which is supported by the U.S. Department of Education, provides scholarship assistance to Native American or Alaskan Native students who are enrolled in accredited undergraduate or graduate school programs in education, psychology, or related fields. Contact the U.S. Department of Education, Indian Education and Psychology Fellowship Program, 400 Maryland Avenue SW, Washington, D.C. 20202, for additional information.

Action Plan

Most of the Fortune 100 companies offer scholarship programs for minorities. Contact their public relations department to find out how to apply. The research librarian at any good public library can provide you with a directory of Fortune 100 companies, giving addresses and telephone numbers.

Indian Fellowship Program

The *Indian Fellowship Program* awards fellowships to Native American students enrolled in undergraduate and graduate degree programs in business administration, engineering, education, law, medicine, and related fields. The awards are based on financial need. For further information, write to the Indian Fellowship Program, Office of Indian Education Programs, 1849 C Street NW, MS-Room 3525, Washington, D.C. 20242.

National Achievement Scholarship Program

Outstanding African-American high school students can receive assistance from the *National Achievement Scholarship Program.* Over 800 scholarships are awarded each year. For further information, write to the National Achievement Scholarship Program, One Rotary Center, 1560 Shennan Avenue, Suite 200, Evanston, Illinois 60201-4897.

National Action Council for Minorities in Engineering (NACME)

The *NACME* organization provides financial assistance to qualified undergraduate minority students pursuing degrees in engineering. The major funding is directed through corporate scholarships that are administered by NACME. For more information, write to the National Action Council for Minorities in Engineering, 3 West 35th Street, New York, New York 10001, or call 212-279-2644.

151

National Merit Scholarship Program

The *National Merit Scholarship Program* is the largest academically competitive scholarship program in the United States. Each year, more than 3,000 scholarships are awarded among 5,000 finalists, and an additional 650 scholarships go to African-American students. Fifteen hundred of these awards are one-timers of $1,000, and 1,500 are four-year awards for the same amount.

Competition is abundant, but if you win, your harvest is more abundant than the $1,000 award. Schools that value lustrous reputations lure National Merit winners with additional financial aid awards.

To qualify, take the Preliminary Scholastic Aptitude Test (PSAT) or the National Merit Scholarship Qualifying Test (NMSQT), usually given in your junior year of high school. Ask your high school guidance counselor for details. Finalists are chosen based on scores. Write to the National Merit Scholarship Corporation, One Rotary Center, 1560 Sherman Avenue, Evanston, Illinois 60201-4897, for additional information and application forms.

Action Plan

If you want to win merit or sports scholarships, keep your nose in the books. The people handing them out love to give them to athletes who have great GPAs and devour SAT and ACT tests. You have to be able to leap over a high bar if you want to win a sports scholarship. Both talent and academic achievement must be stellar to win one.

United Methodist Church

The Board of Higher Education and Ministry of the *United Methodist Church* awards scholarships to qualified undergraduate and graduate minority students. Applicants must be U.S. citizens or permanent residents; must be Hispanic, Asian, or Native American; and must be active members of the Methodist church. The United Methodist Church also sponsors several scholarship and loan programs for graduate students. Church-sponsored loan programs are available to undergraduate and graduate students. For additional information, write to the United Methodist Church, Board of Higher Education and Ministry, Box 871, Nashville, Tennessee 37202.

United Negro College Fund Schools

Over a thousand scholarships a year are given to students attending *United Negro College Fund* schools. The awards are based on financial need and academic merit. For more information, write to the United Negro College Fund, 8260 Willow Oaks Corporate Drive, Fairfax, Virginia 22031. If you're interested in a specific school, contact the school for more information. Here's a listing of United Negro College Fund schools:

Paine College
Augusta, Georgia 30901

Paul Quinn College
Dallas, Texas 75241

Philander Smith College
Little Rock, Arkansas 72202

Rust College
Holly Springs, Mississippi 38635

Saint Augustine's College
Raleigh, North Carolina 27610

Saint Paul's College
Lawrenceville, Virginia 23805

Shaw University
Raleigh, North Carolina 27601

Spelman College
Atlanta, Georgia 30314

Stillman College
Tuscaloosa, Alabama 35403

Talladega College
Talladega, Alabama 35160

Texas College
Tyler, Texas 75702

Tougaloo College
Tougaloo, Mississippi 39174

Tuskegee University
Tuskegee, Alabama 36088

Virginia Union University
Richmond, Virginia 23220

Voorhees College
Denmark, South Carolina 29042

Wilberforce University
Wilberforce, Ohio 45384

Wiley College
Marshall, Texas 75670

Xavier University of Louisiana
New Orleans, Louisiana 70125

Financial Aid Publications for Minority Students

A number of excellent publications are available to minorities who are interested in applying for financial aid. This section introduces you to what we believe are some of the better publications that you may want to check out at your local library or purchase outright.

Directory of Financial Aid for Minorities, Reference Service Press, 1100 Industrial Road, San Carlos, California 94070

Garrett Park Press Publications, Garrett Park Press, P.O. Box 190, Garrett Park, Maryland 20896

Hispanic Financial Resource Handbook, Ohio State University, Hispanic Student Programs, 347 Ohio Union, 1739 N. High Street, Columbus, Ohio 43210

Minority Student Opportunities in U.S. Medical Schools, Association of American Medical Colleges, Office of Minority Affairs, Division of Student Programs, One Dupont Circle, Washington, D.C. 20036.

The following titles are available from the Superintendent of Documents, U.S. Government Printing Office, Washington, D.C. 20402:

Financial Aid for Minority Students in Allied Health

Financial Aid for Minority Students in Business

Financial Aid for Minority Students in Education

Financial Aid for Minority Students in Engineering

Financial Aid for Minority Students in Law

Financial Aid for Minority Students in Mass Communications and Journalism

Financial Aid for Minority Students in Medicine

Financial Aid for Minority Students in Science

Minority Organizations: A National Directory

The Big Book of Minority Opportunities

Higher Education Opportunities for Minorities and Women

To be honest with you, if you're a minority student with outstanding qualifications, you have an outstanding chance of getting an excellent scholarship. That's because most scholarship programs favor awarding minorities money for college. Although this chapter discusses specific programs directed at minorities, don't ignore all of the other "nonminority" scholarship programs, such as those in Chapter 11. Our advice to you is to apply for every scholarship that you have a chance of getting.

The Least You Need To Know

➤ Know where to apply for specially targeted scholarships for which you are qualified.

➤ Many professional organizations offer financial aid for minorities and women studying in specific professional fields.

➤ Federal aid programs grant special allowances for such expenses as child care for children of adult students and special equipment for handicapped students.

➤ Don't overlook church-sponsored minority programs. Seek the advice of church officials to help you locate these opportunities.

➤ In general, scholarship programs favor minorities, so go after every one with a vengeance.

Chapter 14

Adult, Graduate, and International Programs

In This Chapter

➤ Finding the few adult financial aid sources and options that are out there

➤ Learning how to dig for hidden aid opportunities for graduate students

➤ Discovering unique financial aid opportunities to study abroad

➤ Getting the details on employee tuition assistance and learning how to get some from your employer

➤ Understanding why you must have a plan to spend less and save more for college

---

The nontraditional student, as the previous chapter pointed out, is either one of, or some combination of, the following: an adult student, a graduate student, and/or a student who wants to study abroad. If you fall into any of these categories and are seeking financial aid to help you get the education you want, you have one thing in common with your peers. It's going to be tough to get aid.

Why is it so tough? Because, unfortunately, most financial aid programs have been designed to help the under-24-year-old age groups. They also cater to students trying to earn baccalaureate degrees rather than master's degrees. In the case of foreign study, the various agencies that administer funds are very selfish about using taxpayer dollars to fund educational institutions that are located outside the United States.

We don't want to discourage you from pursuing a degree as an adult or a graduate student, whether you study stateside or in another country. We just want you to be aware of the facts before you start your search for financial aid.

Adult Student Programs

Let's take a step backward and review what the Fed's original intentions were when, in all its wisdom, it created financial aid programs for colleges. Quite simply, the program was constructed to help parents pay for their kids' education if they could show that they truly needed supplemental funds.

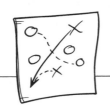

Action Plan

If you think the task of getting financial aid for a foreign university is overwhelming, remember the words of the poet Henry Wadsworth Longfellow: "Perseverance is a great element of success. If you only knock long enough and loud enough at the gate, you are sure to wake up somebody."

With rare exceptions, you won't find the words "adult aid" listed anywhere in program brochures. Why is that? Well, for one thing, the Feds have another program for adults that they call "welfare."

Federal welfare programs cost the government substantially more than the college aid program, and its funds are awarded primarily to adults. Welfare grants are made to adults who qualify for welfare and want to attend college or technical, vocational, or trade schools. The clear intent of the program is to help people find viable employment that will take them off the welfare rolls.

If you're on welfare or can qualify for being on welfare, contact your state's welfare office to discover the educational opportunities they may be able to offer you.

Graduate Student Programs

Graduate study means study that follows a Bachelor's degree in a given academic field, such as chemistry or business. The Doctor of Philosophy (Ph.D.) is a graduate degree, as is the Master of Business Administration (MBA). On average, only about 20 percent of the graduate students in the United States are receiving any kind of financial aid. Most of the available aid money is flowing into the scientific and engineering disciplines.

The admissions requirements for most graduate programs include at least one exam. See the "Postgraduate Tests" section in Chapter 6, "Take the Tests," and "Graduate Tests" in Appendix B, "Directory of General Financial Aid Resources."

Graduate Student Loans

Unfortunately, loans are the chief source of funding for most students who pursue graduate and professional studies. Graduate student loans are acquired from the same places that are open to undergraduate students (see Chapter 15, "The Inside Scoop on Student Loans"). Some colleges will award money for fellowships and teaching assistantships, which carry teaching and research responsibilities (see Chapter 9, "Grant Me a Grant").

Fellowships

Fortunately, if you're a graduate or postdoctoral student, you have a chance at getting a *fellowship*. Most fellowships are issued by universities and private foundations, and are typically based on merit. The reason is clear: The school or foundation wants the student to accomplish something that contributes to the prestige of the sponsoring institution. If you have a sterling academic record and are pursuing research projects that are attractive to a particular school or foundation, you have a good shot at a fellowship.

The National Service Fellows Scholarship Program was announced in 1997, and 12 fellowships were awarded that year after a competitive selection process. The fellows who have been selected annually since then contract with the Corporation for National Service to produce a product or outcome of value to the Corporation, or, broadly, to the field of service.

Although fellows are not employees, they are attached to an office of the Corporation or an affiliated state organization. In addition to producing the outcomes specified in their proposals, the fellows comprise a self-managed team that assesses progress, considers synergies among projects, and promotes further individual development.

The mission of the Corporation for National Service is to improve the quality of service through the talents of a diverse, self-managed team that will learn with the Corporation and will contribute to the future of national service. The National Service Fellows Program has become a high-quality

Help

Several institutions offer special loan programs for graduate students. You'll find them listed under "Graduate and Professional Student Loans" in Appendix B.

Insight

Fellowships are grants of money to a student from private and public organizations that generally require something in return, such as conducting research or teaching. Fellowships are usually awarded to post-graduate students, but there are an increasing number of them that are being awarded to undergraduates.

program, which has strengthened national service through continuous learning, new models, stronger networks, and professional growth. You can contact them at their Web site (www.cns.gov/jobs/fellowships/overview.html) to learn more about the program.

International Student Programs

As mentioned in the beginning of this chapter, finding financial aid to supplement your education abroad will be difficult. Most of the financial aid funds have been allocated to stateside programs, and there is a disproportionate number of students trying to get at the crumbs left over for international study, so competition is stiff. However, don't allow yourself to get discouraged: You'll find some suggestions in the following sections.

International Co-Op Programs

If you want to study abroad and you're looking for some financial support to get there, the deepest pockets can often be found in the college or university you're already attending. Many institutions across the country have established student co-op programs with international schools that allow their students to attend foreign colleges at substantially discounted rates.

Unfortunately, these programs are generally not available to you until you've completed your sophomore college year. The exchange periods are typically limited to one or two semesters, when you'll be required to return to your home-base college. If you take courses that have been preapproved by your sponsoring college while you are on your international tour, you'll receive full credit. Here's a partial list of colleges that award significant aid to international students:

Harvard University

Radcliffe University

University of Miami

Massachusetts Institute of Technology

University of Pennsylvania

Princeton University

Brown University

Stanford University

Arizona State University

Help

Check out the International Financial Aid Directory in Appendix B for key agencies that may be able to help you get financial aid to study abroad. For a comprehensive list of federal financial programs for study abroad check out: http://cnsearch.collegenet.com/cgi-bin/CN/index.

U.S. students who attend accredited U.S. institutions overseas that are an extension of their stateside institution are eligible for the full range of federal financial aid programs.

How International Co-Op Programs Are Administered

Colleges set their own policies for institutional aid abroad.

U.S. students who attend an international institution overseas are eligible for federal and private loan programs only, but not for any gift aid.

Students from other countries can find out about U.S.-sponsored aid that may be available to them by contacting the United States embassy or consulate in their home country.

NAFSA, previously called the National Association of Foreign Student Affairs, has a membership of international educators who promote international educational exchange between the United States and the rest of the world. However, the organization offers virtually no direct grants to international students. They do provide links to international financial aid through their Web site, along with online searches you can do to find other sources of potential aid www.nafsa.org/. Also see the International Financial Aid Directory in Appendix B for relevant addresses and Web sites.

Support from Abroad Does Happen

Eleven American college students recently were awarded scholarships by the Winston Churchill Foundation for graduate study in mathematics, engineering, and the sciences. The students are drawn from the 50 accredited institutions participating in the program. They study for one year at Churchill College, Cambridge University, in Great Britain, receiving $23,000 toward tuition, travel, and living expenses there. The Churchill awards come from the Winston Churchill Foundation of the United States, which is located in New York City.

International Student Loans

Loans are difficult to come by for students who want to study in other countries. That's probably because lenders are afraid the students won't come back to pay off their debts. But if you have an excellent credit history, you have a fair chance of getting a loan. The International Education Finance Corporation is a unique private firm that specializes in global student loans. If you want more

Warning

Don't expect the governments or private funding sources of other nations to be too generous with study money for noncitizens (with a few exceptions, such as Japan, Germany, and Canada). Get your cash at home before you take off to schools abroad.

information, contact them at International Finance Corporation, 424 Adams Street, Milton, MA 02186; 617-696-7840.

They May Want You

Believe it or not, there are a lot of colleges out there that want adult students in the same classroom with the younger students. It adds a level of maturity to classes because adults tend to ask tougher questions, a fact that was so elegantly demonstrated by Rodney Dangerfield in the movie classic *Back to School*. If you're an older student, the experience you can offer gives you a potential negotiating edge that you may not have known you had.

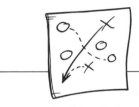

Action Plan

You never know what the answer will be until you ask the question! If you never ask the question, you are wrongfully assuming that the answer would have been "no."

Walk into the admissions office of the college of your choice, and ask to speak to the director of admissions or whatever title the college uses for the person who manages that office. Better yet, make an appointment with this person. When you meet with him or her, briefly explain why you want to go to that college, why you need financial support, and what you can contribute on your own in return for the favor.

For example, let's suppose you have some expertise in counseling young people on how to find jobs, or on how to do difficult searches on the Web, or whatever. Bring up these offerings when you talk to the admissions officer, and you could solicit a very favorable response. The officer may ask you to chair a discussion group with students in one or more fields of your expertise in return for a substantial reduction in tuition and fees.

Employee Educational Assistance Packages (EAP)

Can you get your boss to pay the bills while you attend college part-time? That's an easy question if you're working for a company that offers its employees an EAP (educational assistance package), complete with reimbursement of tuition, books, and fees. You simply sign up for the program through your personnel office, and your financial aid package is a reality. You're on your way! Who cares if federal and state financial aid funds are scarce for adult students when you have an employer-sponsored financial aid package available to you?

Where Do You Find EAP Funding?

EAPs are more commonly found among sizable companies than at small firms. Among the companies that offer the most generous EAPs, according to an annual survey by the Chamber of Commerce of the United States, are those engaged in industries such as insurance, hospital care, and public utilities. Less than half of all retailers offer EAPs, and manufacturing plants aren't high on education benefits either.

Do You Pay Taxes on EAP Funds?

There are two kinds of EAPs typically offered by employers: those that are specifically job-related and those that are for general self-improvement purposes.

Funds provided to employees for job-related education and training are tax-free to employees and are tax-deductible to employers.

Education for the general self-improvement of the employee is more ambiguous. For the past two decades, companies have been able to deduct their educational expenses from their tax returns and employees were not taxed on the educational assistance money they received. However, this has been a controversial issue in Congress, so make sure you know what the latest tax regulations are when you apply for EAP funds.

Action Plan

Studies by the National Association of Independent Colleges and Universities show that, of employees who go to college on the employer's nickel: 33 percent pursue associate (two-year) degrees, 23 percent pursue bachelor's degrees, 22 percent pursue master's degrees, and 13 percent pursue professional certificates.

Do You Have to Pay Back EAPs?

Twenty years ago, employers weren't fussy if you didn't stick around after you completed your schooling. That's changed, says Cynthia Pintails, senior government relations associate for the American Society of Training and Development: "Increasingly, employers want to be sure they get a return on their educational investments." Don't be surprised if you're asked to sign an agreement stating that you'll repay the company if you depart the premises before a specific period of time.

Negotiate, Negotiate, and Negotiate Some More

What are your options if you work for a company that doesn't offer educational assistance for its employees? For starters, it doesn't hurt to ask for help anyway! Walk into your boss's office and simply ask him or her if there's any way the company can assist you in getting a college degree. The way you phrase the questions and your subsequent conversation will clearly have to depend on your position in the company.

It's time to negotiate! Let's suppose you're an accountant and you have a burning desire to get a degree in accounting. You can remind your boss that if the company is

Action Plan

Most employers that do have educational reimbursement plans reimburse employees for tuition, rather than paying the college outright. About half of them pay 100 percent of the tuition, and 30 percent pay below 50 percent. The other 20 percent pay somewhere between 50 and 90 percent. In almost all instances, you must get a C or above before you can be reimbursed.

willing to invest a few bucks in your education, with what you'll learn you'll be able to return a whole lot more to the company. You may get a very favorable response.

What If You Get a "No"?

Let's suppose you're working for a company that flat out rejects any notion of helping you or any other employee meet his or her respective educational expenses. Maybe it's time to look for an employer that offers a generous educational reimbursement plan to its employees. Here's a classic example of what we're talking about.

Dan was working for a company, which we'll call XYZ Corporation. Although he liked his job and the people, he did not enjoy the fact that XYZ Corporation had limited employee benefits and no employee educational program. Dan believed that if he didn't get a college degree, he would be relegated to doing the same job for the rest of his life—not a very exciting option to him.

Dan started looking for other job opportunities and found a position with a company that was willing to offer him a salary that was $2,000 a year less than what he was currently earning, but their employee education program would pay him up to $6,000 a year for educational expenses. In effect, Dan was getting a $4,000 increase in salary ($6,000 – $2,000) because he intended to take full advantage of the company's educational program. He took the job.

Making It All Happen with an Action Plan

The key to going to college as an adult student, a graduate student, an international student, or any combination thereof is not necessarily having a lot of money. Most of us don't have a lot of money. What we need is a plan. Planning is the first step in taking control of your educational future. Your plan should be flexible, but structured, and most important, you must decide to stick to it.

Planning for college is not difficult if you stick to the fundamentals, which are simple and obvious. Yet many adult students spend a disproportionate amount of time trying to find an easy way to get there by relying on others, rather than on themselves. Had they done even some basic planning in the beginning, they could have been in great shape to enhance their educational objectives.

Watch Your Pennies

Remember the old saying: "Watch your pennies and the dollars will take care of themselves"? It's still true today. If you're like most people, you spend money on things you don't really need and, somehow, the money you make is just enough to cover your expenses. Your first challenge will be to get control over your spending habits and establish a monthly budget. You'll be amazed at how it will help you save, and how those little things add up to big dollars over a relatively short period of time.

Here's how you can do it. Let's say you get paid twice a month like most people. The first thing you do is run to the bank to deposit your paycheck so that you can start paying off all of those ugly bills. Before you pay off any bill, pay yourself first. Write a check out for a hundred dollars and de-posit it into a savings account, and then forget about it. Over a period of one year, you will have deposited $2,600 into your savings account and earned interest on top of that.

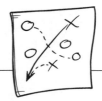

Action Plan

Collectively, the majority of American graduate and under-graduate students now fit non-traditional descriptions. They're not in the bloom of their youth and are not full-time students, according to the University of Phoenix, which caters strictly to nontraditional students. Over 74,000 students have attended this nationally based university.

Set Priorities with a Spending Plan

If you want to get serious about going to college, you have to set priorities and recog-nize that you can't have everything right now.

A *spending plan* is an active strategy you use to control your spending so you can af-ford to go to college. It starts with a commitment to yourself: "I want to save more of my money." Why? "Because I want to have enough money to go to college so that I can expand my career opportunities."

When you activate your plan, it will capture the cash that slips through your fingers every day, unnoticed. It will help you discern the difference between what you need and what you want. Here are 10 reasons why you need a good spending plan:

1. You can use your plan to get out of debt. Without a spending plan, it'll never happen.
2. It helps you prepare for the really big expenses, such as college.
3. You eliminate spending on the frivolous things you might otherwise buy.
4. More money will go into your savings account for college every month.
5. It shows you how much money you're spending on stuff you don't really need.

Action Plan

Be sure to review the financial planning material in Chapter 8, "Develop a College Financial Plan." It supplements the money-saving tips in this section.

6. You get used to living on what you make.

7. Money won't slip through your fingers anymore.

8. It sets the groundwork for developing a financial plan, your road map to financial independence.

9. You, your spouse, and your kids will be pulling in the same direction so that you can meet your goal of going to college.

10. You will have a clear vision about what you really want: a college degree, an advanced college degree, or an opportunity to study abroad.

Painless Money-Saving Tips

What you really need is a savings account that you can count on to pay for college. You can do this only if you're willing to pay yourself first:

➤ Make up a savings bill in the form of a card or envelope labeled "savings bill" that you keep with your other monthly bills. When it comes time to pay the bills, make sure it's the first bill that gets paid, in the form of a deposit to your college expenses savings account.

Help

If you're looking for more advice on how to save money, get a copy of Larry Roth's book *The Best of Living Cheap Views* (NTC/Contemporary Publishing, 1996). It's a collection of great money-saving articles and tips from a newsletter that Larry Roth publishes.

➤ Whenever you pay off all your bills and discover that you have some money left over, make another deposit to your savings account.

➤ Find out if your employer's payroll system allows you to make direct deposits into a savings account. If it does, sign up for a direct deposit tomorrow. In a short period of time, you won't even miss the money that's deducted from your paycheck.

➤ When you get a raise, deposit the extra amount of the raise directly into your savings account so you won't miss it.

➤ Take lunches to work instead of eating out. You'll be amazed at how much you'll save.

➤ When you get your income tax refund, use it to pay off credit cards. Then cut up the cards, and deposit the money you previously spent on monthly credit card payments into your savings account.

➤ Deposit all overtime and bonus checks in your savings account.

➤ When you get your college bills you'll be glad you had an action plan, and have money in the bank to pay them.

The Least You Need to Know

➤ If you're an adult, a pending graduate student, or a student who is interested in studying outside of the United States, you'll soon discover that financial aid funds are relatively scarce.

➤ International college co-op programs are one of the easiest ways to study abroad at discounted rates.

➤ The admissions officer of the college of your choice may be willing to help you create a financial aid program that benefits both you and the school.

➤ Try hitting up your employer for tuition assistance—whether the company has a formal program or not.

➤ To make it all happen, you must have an action plan to cut spending and increase savings earmarked for college expenses.

Chapter 15

The Inside Scoop on Student Loans

In This Chapter

➤ Learning about the various low-interest student loans that you can apply for

➤ Discovering how to find the best lender for you

➤ Learning how to compare different loan offers to pick the one that best meets your needs

---

A *student loan* is money you borrow to help meet the cost of your education. Applying for a loan, whether from government or private sources, is not something to be afraid of, and you should not let it prohibit you from going to the school of your choice. You should research all your options and clearly understand the terms of any loans you're considering.

Loans are part of the self-help portion of any financial aid award you might receive from a school. There are several types of loan programs available to you, including Federal Perkins Loans, Subsidized Federal Stafford Loans, Subsidized Federal Direct Loans, Unsubsidized Federal Stafford Loans, and Direct Loans, to name a few.

Subsidized and Unsubsidized Loans

Subsidized student loans have lower interest rates than commercial or unsubsidized loans. Federal Perkins Loans, Subsidized Federal Stafford Loans, and Subsidized Federal Direct Loans are all need-based subsidized loans. No payments are made while a student is in school, but six months after leaving school, students must begin to make regular monthly payments.

Unsubsidized Federal Stafford Loans and Federal Direct Loans are awarded without regard to need. Interest payments begin immediately, and regular payments start six months after the borrower ceases to be at least a half-time student. The amount you may borrow is fixed and is dependent on your year in school.

Warning

Before you sign any loan documents, ask the lender every question you can think of regarding your repayment options. If you don't get a clear answer, ask the same question again until you fully understand what all of your options are. Get it in writing.

Parent Loans

Federal Parent Loans for Undergraduate Students, also known as *PLUS Loans,* are for creditworthy parents. These loans have annually adjusted variable interest rates. Repayment begins within 60 days after the loan has been fully disbursed. Interest begins to accrue on the day the loan is disbursed. Parents may borrow up to all school costs not covered by estimated financial assistance. For help with loan application procedures, contact your high school's guidance counselor, the college's financial aid officer, your congressional representatives, and see the federal financial aid listings in Appendix B, "Directory of General Financial Aid Resources," and the listings of financial aid offices by state in Appendix C, "Alphabetical State Financial Aid Listings."

Stafford Loans

All *Stafford Loans* are either subsidized, which means the government pays the interest while you're in school, or unsubsidized, in which case you pay all the interest. If you pay the interest on an unsubsidized loan, you can have the payments deferred until after graduation.

To receive a subsidized Stafford Loan, you must be able to demonstrate financial need. With an unsubsidized Stafford Loan, you can defer the payments until after graduation by capitalizing the interest. *Capitalizing* means the interest payments are added to the loan balance, increasing the size and cost of the loan. All students, regardless of need, are eligible for the unsubsidized Stafford Loans.

Stafford Loans allow dependent undergraduates to borrow up to $2,625 for their freshman year, $3,500 for their sophomore year, and $5,500 for each remaining year. Independent students can borrow an additional unsubsidized $4,000 the first two years and $5,000 the remaining years. Graduate students can borrow $18,500 per year, although only $8,500 of the loan is subsidized. Many students combine subsidized loans with unsubsidized loans to borrow the maximum amount permitted each year.

To apply for a Stafford Loan, you must submit the Free Application for Federal Aid (FAFSA) form. Even though the unsubsidized Stafford Loan is available to all students regardless of financial need, you must still submit the FASFA to be eligible. You can receive a subsidized loan and an unsubsidized loan for the same period.

Perkins Loans

The *Perkins Loan* is the best student loan available. Perkins Loans are awarded to undergraduate and graduate students with exceptional financial need. This is a campus-based loan program in which the school acts as the lender, using a limited pool of funds provided by the federal government. It's a subsidized loan, with the interest paid by the federal government during the in-school and nine-month grace periods. There are no origination or guarantee fees, and the interest rate is very competitive with other loan alternatives. There is a 10-year repayment period.

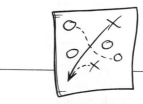

Action Plan

Commercial lenders offer varying loan policies. If possible, stick with one lender for all of your loans so that you have a single point of contact to simplify your life.

The amount of a Perkins Loan is determined by the financial aid office. The program limits are $3,000 per year for undergraduate students and $5,000 per year for graduate students, with cumulative limits of $15,000 for undergraduate loans and $30,000 for undergraduate and graduate loans combined.

Institutions participating in the *Expanded Lending Option (ELO)* may offer higher loan limits for the Perkins Loan. To participate in the ELO, a school must have a default rate no higher than 15 percent. The annual loan limits are increased by $1,000 each and the cumulative limits increased by $5,000 and $10,000, respectively. Perkins Loans offer better cancellation provisions than the Stafford or PLUS loans.

Signature Education Loans

Sallie Mae's Signature Education Loan Program offers all the money you need to pay for school through low-cost loan alternatives. The Sallie Mae (officially known as the Student Loan Marketing Association) program works hand-in-hand with federal loan programs such as FFELP and FDLP loans and helps with costs not covered by traditional programs, such as grants and scholarships. You can read more about Sallie Mae later in the chapter.

You may be eligible for a Signature Loan if you're an undergraduate or graduate student about to attend, or already attending, an eligible school at least half-time. Submit a FAFSA when you apply for this credit-based loan. Your credit history will be reviewed by the lender. The better your credit score or your coborrower's score (if you have one), the lower your interest rate and, generally, the lower the fees, and the greater the possibility of loan approval.

Help

To order the Sallie Mae application by mail call Sallie Mae at 1-800-543-7562. For more information, look under "Graduate and Professional Student Loans" in Appendix B, or visit the Sallie Mae Web site at www.salliemae.com/.

Private Loans

Private loans, also known as alternative loans, help parents bridge the gap between the actual cost of their kids' education and the limited amount the government allows them to borrow in its loan programs.

Private loans are offered by private lenders, and there are no federal forms to complete. Some families turn to private loans when the federal loans don't provide enough money or when they need different repayment options. For example, a parent might want to defer repayment until the student graduates, an option that is not available from the government parent-loan program. Lenders provide different types of private loans, depending on the student's level of study.

Institutional Loans

An *institutional loan* means the school is the lender. Eligibility and loan characteristics will be different at each school you consider. Talk to someone in the Financial Aid Office to find out whether your school offers these loans. If you pay on time or have your payments automatically deducted from your checking or savings account, you can receive interest-rate reductions worth hundreds or even thousands of dollars in savings over the life of your loan.

Sallie Mae Loans

Sallie Mae is one of the biggest student loan producers in the system. It is responsible for most student loans because it buys them back from banks and other financial institutions. A little background about Sallie Mae can help you understand how this all works.

Congress established Sallie Mae as a quasi profit/nonprofit agency to buy student loan paper from lenders, thus replenishing the supply of money to make new student loans available.

Here's how the Sallie Mae program works. Suppose a bank starts out with $10 million to lend to students. The bank has the students sign all of the promissory notes and related statements, and then it sells the loan paper to Sallie Mae and gets another $10 million to circulate.

Sallie Mae, as well as all its commercial customers who lent the money in the first place, receives a cost allowance referred to as a special allowance. This fee adds up to substantial profits for the banks and other financial institutions.

Perhaps because the student loan-banking complex wants you to borrow, borrow, borrow, it's not surprising that neither Sallie Mae nor its participating lenders have developed a program for loan forgiveness. But other nonprofit entities, including government agencies, have discovered that it pays to reward graduates for putting their education to use to serve society by granting partial-to-full loan forgiveness.

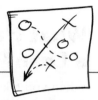

Action Plan

Some programs provide partial or complete loan forgiveness for people who volunteer to help others or who work under special circumstances. AmeriCorps is a program of volunteer service in return for help with college tuition. Participating states have programs that reward 12 months' volunteer service with up to $7,400 in stipends plus $4,725 that can be used to pay college costs. See "Loan Consolidation and Forgiveness Programs" in Appendix B for more details.

Applying for a Loan

Although your financial aid package may indicate that you are eligible for an educational loan, you can't receive a loan without completing a loan application. Complete the FAFSA to determine the types of loans you might be eligible to receive.

The FAFSA form is required for all students who seek consideration for federal financial aid programs. Before completing the form, compile all tax information, both student's and parents'. For most federal student aid programs, the FAFSA is the only form you'll need to file. To receive a Federal Family Education Loan (FFEL), Stafford Loan, or a FFEL Plus Loan, you'll have to complete additional forms.

Check with your high school or your college's financial aid office for a loan application, or download one from the Internet at www.ed.gov/.

Submit the forms in January. (Also see Chapter 2, "Staking Out Your Financial Aid Claim," for FAFSA information, and Chapter 19, "Decoding the Forms," for line-by-line guidance in filling out the forms.)

About a month after you submit your application, you'll receive your *Student Aid Report (SAR)*, which you should check for accuracy. This report will identify the amount you're expected to contribute toward your education, called the *Expected Family Contribution (EFC)*. At about the same time, the school you plan to attend will send you a financial aid award letter summarizing the grants and loans you're eligible for. (See Chapter 2 for more information on the *SAR* and the *EFC*.)

Warning

Financial aid loan dollars are distributed on a first-come basis. If you're last on the list because you were late in filing your application, there may be no more funds available, and you'll be out of luck.

What Happens When You Get a Loan?

When you take out a student loan, you have certain responsibilities.

You're required to sign a promissory note, agreeing to repay the loan according to the terms of the note. The note is a binding legal document and states that you must repay the loan even if you don't complete your education, except in cases of discharge where your loan is forgiven (that is, you don't have to pay it back).

Loan funds are either distributed by check or sent electronically to your college in installments. The money is first applied to your college costs, and then you receive any remaining amount for additional expenses.

Think about what this obligation means before you take out a loan. If you don't repay your loan on time or according to the terms in your promissory note (that is, your promise to pay back a loan), you may go into *default,* which has very serious consequences. You must make payments on your loan even if you don't receive a bill or repayment notice. Billing statements or coupon books are sent to you as a convenience, but you're obligated to make payments even if you don't receive any reminders.

If you apply for a *deferment* or *forbearance* that allows you to delay payment, you must continue to make payments until you're notified that the request has been granted. If you don't continue, you may end up in default. You should keep a copy of any request form you submit, and you should document all contacts with the organization that holds your loan.

Insight

Default is a legal term that lending institutions use to declare that a borrower has failed to make payments on a loan in accordance with the loan's terms and conditions. It authorizes the lender to initiate aggressive collection procedures and to submit a "bad debt" report on the borrower's credit status. **Deferment** of a loan is a period of postponement during which repaying the loan principal is suspended because the borrower has met one or more of a number of deferment requirements established by law. **Forbearance** on a loan allows a temporary cessation of payments or a reduction of payment amounts for subsidized or unsubsidized federal loans.

If you find yourself in any of the following circumstances, you must notify the appropriate representative who manages your loan.

Notify the loan representative when you:

➤ Graduate.

➤ Withdraw from school.

➤ Drop below half-time status.

➤ Change your name, address, or Social Security Number.

➤ Transfer to another school.

How Are Loans Administered?

How your loan is administered depends on the type of loan it is.

If you borrow a Perkins Loan, your loan will be managed by the school that lends you the money or by an agency that the school assigns to service the loan.

If you borrow a direct loan, it will be managed by the Direct Loan Servicing Center.

If you borrow a Federal Family Education Loan (FFEL), your lender or its servicing agent will manage it. During your loan counseling session, you'll be given the name of the representative who manages your loan.

Regardless of the type of loan you borrow, you must receive entrance counseling before you're given your first loan disbursement, and you must receive exit counseling before you leave school. These counseling sessions will be administered by your school and will explain important information about your loan. Your lender or the Direct Loan Servicing Center will provide you with additional information.

What Happens If You Default?

If you default on your loan, your school or the agency that holds your loan may take action to recover the money, including notifying national credit bureaus of your default. This may affect your credit rating for a long time. If that happens, you may find it very difficult to borrow from a bank to buy a car or a house.

In addition, if you default:

➤ The agency holding your loan may ask your employer to deduct payments from your paycheck.

➤ You may be held liable for expenses incurred in collecting the loan.

➤ If you decide to return to school, you won't be entitled to receive any more federal student aid.

➤ The U.S. Department of Education may ask the Internal Revenue Service to withhold your income tax refund and apply it toward the amount you owe.

Warning

If loan defaults and poor payment records get on your credit report, you may find it difficult or impossible to get future loans unless you're willing to pay exorbitant loan fees and interest rates. Paying your debts, and paying them on time, however, will help you build a solid credit record for the future.

Loan Terms and Conditions

Whenever your school credits your account with funds from a Stafford Loan, PLUS Loan, or Perkins Loan, it must notify you or your parents in writing. This notification must be sent no earlier than 30 days before and no later than 30 days after the school credits your account. If you or your parents want to cancel all or a portion of a PLUS loan, you can do so by informing your school within 14 days after the date of the notification, or by the first day of the payment period, whichever is later. Your school can tell you what the first day of your payment period is.

If you receive loan funds directly by check, you may refuse the funds simply by not depositing the check, or by returning it with "cancel" written on the face of the check.

Before you graduate and leave school, you'll receive information about your loan from your school, lender, or the Direct Loan Servicing Center. For example, they'll tell you the amount of your total debt, including principal and the estimated interest payments over the term of the loan.

If you borrow a Federal Perkins Loan, your school will provide this same information to you.

If you borrow a Direct Loan or an FFEL Program Loan, the Direct Loan Servicing Center or your lender will provide this information to you, as appropriate.

If you have Direct or FFEL Stafford loans, your school will provide you with a current description of your loans, including average monthly-anticipated payments. You'll also get a description of applicable deferment, forbearance, and discharge provisions, and repayment options.

Repayment Plans

When you contact a lending organization, you'll discover that they offer several types of loans and a number of options for reducing your monthly payments. Make sure you compare the options to see which ones best fit with both your short- and long-term career plans. Don't assume that you're doomed to giant payments for as far as the eye can see. Before you jump into repayment waves that may be over your head, test the water. If your income can support standard plan payments, you'll save interest over the term of the loan. Although a standard plan carries the highest monthly payment, you can overcome your debt faster and pay less in interest. You may pay a fixed amount for up to 10 years; payments on loans with variable interest rates may fluctuate.

The following sections describe the kinds of plans you may want to consider.

Graduated Payment Plans

If your starting income is relatively low or next to zero, but expected to increase on a regular basis as you get closer to graduating, then a *graduated payment plan* is a more graceful method that may ease your payment pangs. Payments start low and increase every two to three years for the next 10 to 30 years. Interest charges, which are based on the outstanding principal, will remain high for the first few years, so you'll pay more total interest over the life of your loan.

Help

Check out the Web sites listed under "Lenders of College Loans" (Web Sites) in Appendix B to help you find a lender who can meet your exacting requirements.

Federal education loans, including Stafford, SLS, PLUS, HEAL, and Federal Consolidation Loans, as well as some private loans, offer graduated repayment terms, which can vary from lender to lender. Some lenders, including Sallie Mae, let you make interest-only payments for the first two to four years; after that period, you must pay principal and interest.

Long-Term Payment Plans

If all you can afford is a tiny monthly payment, an extended *long-term repayment plan* may be your best option. The Feds and other lenders allow you to extend payments from 12 to 30 years and even offer plans that combine graduated repayments with an extended schedule. Although your monthly payments may be low, you could end up paying twice the original amount of your loan over the long term.

As mentioned earlier in this chapter, AmeriCorps is a program of providing help with college tuition in return for volunteer service. Participating states have programs that reward 12 months' volunteer service with up to $7,400 in stipends plus $4,725 that can be used to pay off long-term loans.

Grace Periods

Students have the right to a *grace period* before their repayment period begins. Parents do not receive a grace period for a PLUS Loan. Your grace period begins when you leave school or drop below half-time status. During exit counseling, your school, lender, and/or the Direct Loan Servicing Center, as appropriate, must give you a loan repayment schedule that states when your first payment is due, the number and frequency of payments, and the amount of each payment.

If you or your parents borrow an FFEL Loan, you must be notified when the loan is sold if the results of the sale mean that you will be making payments to a new lender or agency. Both the old and new lenders or agencies must notify the borrower of the sale. Further, they must state the identity of the new lender or agency holding the loan, the address to which the borrower must make payments, and the telephone numbers of both the old and the new lenders or agencies.

Insight

Six out of ten college students go to college on borrowed money. The average student will owe $20,000 when he or she graduates and will face monthly payments of $250 for 10 years thereafter.

Finding the Right Lender

Your neighborhood bank, savings and loan association, or credit union may offer special loan programs for college-bound students. Unless you the student have a record of regular income and a credit history, these financial institutions will examine your parents' ability to repay loans.

Although the rates offered on these loans may not be much different from those for any other form of commercial credit, the repayment schedules may be more liberal. We recommend that you apply for federally subsidized loans through your college financial aid office before pursuing other lenders.

Many student loan borrowers do not give much consideration to choosing a lender. They often rely totally on the lender list provided by the school, thinking that, because loan terms and benefits programs are very similar, the lender decision is not that important. There are, however, subtle differences, and they could save you time and money.

Some lenders may offer to simplify and shorten the application process. Don't underestimate what some lenders offer over the life of the loan. Since you're entering into a relationship with a lender that could last for many years, you should learn more about these differences. This section gives you the information you need to make a more informed decision.

Ask the financial aid office at your school for its list of preferred lenders for FFELP and private loan programs. Your school's preferred lender list should include lenders that are trustworthy and reliable, with proven track records, and that offer attractive loan terms to borrowers.

Preferred lenders offer excellent service to the borrower. You don't have to pick a lender from the list, but it's a good idea to do so if you want to ensure that your application is processed in a timely and accurate manner. Remember, you do not have a choice of lenders for loans under the FDLP and federal Perkins Loan programs.

The services of some preferred lenders to consider are outlined in the following list. To learn more about any of them, visit their Web sites. See "Lenders of College Loans," "Loan Programs," and also "Financial Aid Resources," all in Appendix B.

Action Plan

Consider all available financial loan options, including federal, state, and local loan programs; institutional loan plans; home equity loans; and any other loan program you can find to help you get through college. The money you spend today will reward you with big dividends in the future.

➤ **Chase Bank** This site at www.chase.com/chase/gx.cgi/FTcs?pagename=Chase/ Href&urlname=personal/prodservs/studentloan offers information about the financial aid process, as well as a planning calendar for high school students, need-estimation and budgeting calculators, and an online application.

➤ **Academic Management Services** Academic Management Services at www.amsWeb.com makes education financing more manageable by coupling flexible payment options with innovative customer service. In addition to offering Stafford, PLUS, and private alternative loans, they are the nation's largest provider of monthly tuition payment plans.

➤ **Bank of America (BOA)** Bank of America offers Federal Stafford and PLUS loans, as well as a private loan program for students and their parents. The bank's Student Maximizer is an alternative source of funding that supplements federal loans at competitive rates. BOA also offers Guaranteed Access to Education (GATE) loans, home equity loans, and lines of credit loans. Visit www.bankofamerica.com/studentbanking.

➤ **Bank One** In addition to providing an overview of the financial aid process, this site at www.bankofamerica.com/studentbanking includes a college planning calendar, a guide to managing finances, loan calculators, debt counseling tools, and a discussion of different loan types.

Action Plan

Build a budget and stick to it! Using the budget calculator on the Web, you can quickly get an overview of where your money goes. And you may be able to cut expenses or increase your income to avoid having to borrow. The site address is http:// embark.wiredscholar.com/ paying/lt_financial_planning/ ltfp_monthbud.jsp, listed under "Budgeting" and "Adult Financial Aid Programs," both in Appendix B.

➤ **Fleet Bank** Fleet Bank at www.fleet.com/bref. html is the number-one student loan lender in New England. Fleet offers Federal Stafford Loans, Federal PLUS loans, home equity loans, and lines of credit to help pay for education.

➤ **Key Bank** Key Bank has been helping families achieve their education goals for more than 40 years. Key provides students and parents with convenient access to quality educational finance products, payment plans, and support services. Key offers both federal and private loans for undergraduate students. Check them out at www.key.com/templates/t-le1.5.jhtml? nodeID=H-5.

➤ **PNC Bank** PNC Bank's site at www.finaid.org/loans/lenders/pncbank.html provides details about their financing options and scholarship program. It also includes several loan calculators.

Before you borrow, calculate how much you'll be expected to repay on education loans each month and how that amount compares with what you think you'll earn after graduation. What percentage of your monthly income is the monthly loan payment? If it's more than 10 percent, then either you've already borrowed too much or you're getting ready to!

Remember, even if you don't finish school or can't find a job, you'll still have to repay your loans with interest.

Comparing Loan Offers

It seems simple enough when your loan is approved! You borrow money, and as long as you repay it, everything is okay. But as you begin to read the fine print, you realize it's not so simple. There's lots of small print and it's confusing. And that's only for one loan. What happens when you have more than one loan to consider?

First of all, don't panic. The writing on each application or brochure may seem different, but all loans have the same basic characteristics. The following list will help you decide which loan is best for you.

Warning

Borrow only what you absolutely need to cover the cost of your education. Be conservative. If you have to borrow, accept only what's necessary to cover your college costs.

➤ **Compare interest rates and terms.** For federal programs, they're generally very similar. However, some lenders offer discounts for early payments. Private programs can vary significantly.

➤ **Compare borrower benefits,** including those for paying on time and for making loan payments electronically.

➤ **Compare repayment plans.**

➤ **Compare loan application processes.** Lenders are beginning to offer online applications and instant loan approvals.

➤ **Compare levels of customer service.**

Interest Rates and Fees

Some loans have a *variable rate and an interest rate cap,* which means that the cost of borrowing the money can fluctuate up to a specific percentage while you're repaying it. Your goal as you look at the various loans is to find the lowest interest rate with the lowest cap.

➤ **Look for fixed interest rate loans where the payment amount will be constant.** If the interest rate is variable, find out how often the rate could change.

➤ **If the interest rate is variable, find out if the payments start low but balloon later** to unmanageable monthly payments.

➤ **Determine whether the rate is linked to a published rate, such as the prime rate.** This could tell you how often it might change.

➤ **Ask for estimates of total interest charges, and find out if there are any interest-free periods.**

Most private loans have a variety of fees associated with them. Fees for originating the loan and fees for insuring loans are the most common. Make sure you understand all of the fees; if you don't understand one, ask the lender to explain it.

➤ **Ask how the fees are handled.** Are they deducted from the amount you're borrowing, are they in addition to that amount, or are they "out of pocket"? If the fees are not "out of pocket," you'll probably have to pay interest on the fee amounts.

➤ **Find out if the fees are based on a percentage of your loan or are flat fees** regardless of the amount you're borrowing.

➤ **Ask how late fees are assessed and whether there are any service charges** that you're required to pay over the life of the loan.

Warning

Restrict your use of credit cards, or they'll eat you up. Restrict yourself to one or two credit cards, because owning multiple cards will only compound your problem. Balancing your debt across many cards can lull you into believing that you don't have a problem because each card's balance looks small in comparison with the total debt.

Loan Terms

Each private loan may give you a different length of time, or term, in which to repay the loan. Understand that you'll pay more in interest on a longer-term loan. A 20-year loan with low payments may look very enticing, but it will cost you much more over the long haul than the 10-year loan with slightly higher payments.

When you take out a student loan, you sign a promissory note. This is your promise to repay the loan with interest, on time, and in full. Responsible management of your student loans can be easy. It can help you establish a good credit rating and can protect you from experiencing the negative impact of too much debt. Even if you don't complete your education or are unsatisfied with your schooling, you still have to pay back your loan.

Failing to pay back a loan will put you in default, which can scar your credit rating for years. If you ever have trouble paying back a loan, call your lender or service right away. They can help you explore different repayment options that will work with your particular financial situation.

The Least You Need to Know

➤ Low-interest subsidized loans are need-based; unsubsidized loans are not, and interest payments begin while the student is still in school.

➤ You can balance your future with loan repayment plans that won't get in your way.

➤ Interpret and compare different loan terms and conditions to determine which loan is best for you.

Chapter 16

Tax-Saving Strategies

In This Chapter

➤ Learning how to take advantage of savings plans that offer tax credits

➤ Discovering savings plans that earn tax-free interest if the money is used for your kid's education

➤ Finding out about college savings plans that let you have the money when you need it

Smart parents know how much a college degree can improve job and income prospects, so they begin saving up for their kids' education while the kids are still young. Like most college-minded families, they're planning on how they're going to pay for it! What will college cost when your kids are ready? How much should you start saving, and when? Where's the money going to come from?

Most families' answers lie in long-term savings, where they start socking away money in stocks and bonds even before their children utter their first words. Financial wizards call this *long-term planning*. They also recommend all kinds of detailed financial asset reshuffling about two years before anyone goes to college, which they call *short-term planning*.

College costs are high enough to discourage most parents before they even begin the long run. Use the tips in this chapter to start a fund for your kids' education. There are several ways to save money to pay for college, and some programs include tax-deferred or even tax-free incentives. Be sure to explore all of the options in this chapter, and start saving today. Remember, it's never too late to start!

Tax Credits

A *tax credit* is an amount you can subtract from your federal income tax to reduce your taxable income. Tax credits can help finance school and offer a way to recover some of the costs of college expenses. For example, the HOPE Scholarship and the Lifetime Learning Tax Credit offer students and their families credit on their federal income tax bill for tuition and fees incurred at eligible schools.

HOPE Scholarship Tax Credits

Tax credits for the *HOPE (Helping Outstanding Pupils Educationally) Scholarship* cover 100 percent of the first $1,000 in payments for qualified tuition and fees, and 50 percent of the second $1,000. Expenses that qualify for the HOPE Scholarship include school tuition and required fees minus any tax-free grants or scholarships. The costs of books and supplies are usually not covered, but you should check with your school. This tax credit does not cover room and board, insurance, transportation, or medical fees.

Help

If you need more information about HOPE scholarships, see "Tax Deductions" in Appendix B, "Directory of General Financial Aid Resources."

The HOPE Scholarship provides a family with a maximum tax credit of $1,500 a year per student. You may claim it for two years if your kid is a freshman or sophomore, and is enrolled in a program that leads to a degree, certificate, or other recognized educational credential. Students also must be taking at least half the normal full-time course load for their major, and they must be doing so for at least one academic period that begins during the calendar year. They must be free of any felony conviction for possessing or distributing a controlled substance. If you have questions, your school's financial aid office should be able to help you determine whether you meet the requirements.

Lifetime Learning Tax Credits

Lifetime Learning Tax Credits allow up to a $1,000 tax credit per family for postsecondary education courses. You may claim only one credit per tax year. To get this credit, parents have to file a tax return. They may claim the Lifetime Learning Tax Credit if their kids are enrolled at eligible institutions. Lifetime credits are not based on the student's workload and are allowed for one or more courses. They are not limited to students in the first two years of postsecondary education and can be claimed for expenses for graduate-level degree work.

Lifetime credits have no limits on the number of years for which the credit can be claimed for each student and do not increase based on the number of students receiving qualified expenses.

Tax-Exempt Bonds

Tax-exempt bonds are basically IOUs that you purchase from local, state, or federal government agencies in a financial instrument that is known as a bond. Otherwise known as municipal bonds, government-issued bonds earn you tax-exempt interest. U.S. government-issued bonds or Treasury Bonds are both state and federal tax-exempt investments and are relatively risk-free.

City, county, and state governments and agencies with a public purpose, such as funding public utility companies, hospitals, and schools, issue *municipal bonds,* which are often called munis. Interest rates are lower than for other investments because you don't have to pay taxes on the interest you make on your investment. Munis and tax-sheltered retirement accounts generally help parents in tax brackets higher than 30 percent to cover college expenses far better than bonds that require taxable interest. Interest is exempt from federal and state taxes. Munis are low risk as long as the credit rating on the bond is good. They are redeemable before their maturity date.

Although nothing is totally risk-free, most bonds are about as low risk as you can get. However, there are some high-risk government bonds that offer no guarantees that they'll grow or survive. Check with your broker or banker before you buy any bonds to find out the bond rating (that is, high-, medium-, or low-risk). All bonds normally pay more in returns than bank savings or money market mutual funds, but they tend to carry a greater risk of investment money. Consider the following college savings options.

U.S. Series EE Bonds

If you have little to invest, *EE bonds* may be your best strategy because they can cost as little as $25 or as much as $5,000 each. The most you can buy in any one year is $15,000 worth. U.S. bonds guarantee earnings with their fixed interest rate, but on the downside they return less than other savings tools. Nevertheless, U.S. savings bonds do have some advantages over other types of long-range savings.

➤ Bonds are purchased for half their worth. For example, if you want to buy a $1,000 savings bond, you'll pay $500 for it.

➤ Bonds can be redeemed after six months in return for the exact purchase price plus any interest earned. The coupon rate is reset every six months, resulting in little risk of losing interest and no risk of losing the capital investment.

➤ The original purchase price or capital outlay will never go down, and its interest will always be positive.

➤ Taxes on the interest earned are deferred until the bond is cashed, as long as the bond is held for a minimum of five years.

➤ If you cash in the bonds to pay for college fees and tuition, taxes on the interest earned are forgiven.

U.S. Treasury Bonds

Just as secure as savings bonds, *U.S. Treasury Bonds,* or T-bills, require you to accept the Feds' IOU for a longer period of time. But the longer you sit on T-bills, the more they're worth. Don't buy Treasury bonds that exceed five years because other investments will probably earn you more over the same period of time. To purchase Treasury bonds, contact your nearest Federal Reserve Bank branch or call 202-377-7715 for more information.

Although Treasury bonds may not be your lifelong best buddies, they have redeeming qualities worth considering for college financing, such as

Warning

T-bills normally have lower returns than other investments, and there are limits on how much you can invest in them at any one time.

➤ Earnings are exempt from state and local taxes.

➤ T-bills have virtually no credit risk. As long as the U.S. government is sound, these bills are sound.

➤ T-bills are more liquid than some other investments, such as CDs, and T-bills can be cashed in anytime after the maturity date without penalty.

➤ T-bills can be purchased at maturity dates that coincide with college bills. They can be withdrawn anytime before maturity to pay for college without penalty fees. However, if interest rates rise, you will get less money back if you sell before maturity.

State Tuition Bonds

More than 20 states sponsor programs modeled after Illinois' College Bonds to finance higher education. Parents can buy *state-sponsored college bonds* at extremely high discounts. Because the bonds serve as a college savings vehicle, they are sometimes referred to as baccalaureate bonds. States issue these bonds as a way for families to save for future education expenses. These instruments are known as zero-coupon bonds, and they allow you to buy a heavily discounted bond with high interest and begin collecting interest when the bond reaches maturity, instead of gradually collecting lower interest.

Like U.S. savings bonds, state-sponsored college (or baccalaureate) bonds sell for less than their face value and pay no interest until maturity. States use the proceeds from these bonds to meet the cost of their targeted building projects. State college savings bonds cost from $1,000 to $5,000, with maturities between 5 and 20 years. For college planning, bonds should mature the same year your kid goes to college.

Insight

Zero-coupon bonds are debt securities that are issued at substantial discounts from face value, offer no periodic interest payments, and pay the principal amount or face value at maturity. They may be obligations of the U.S. Treasury, governmental agencies, municipalities, or corporations. For example, on January 1, 2000, Mr. Smith purchases a $15,000, 8 percent, five-year, zero-coupon bond issued by XYZ Company for $10,000. He will not receive any cash payments until December 31, 2005, when the bond matures and XYZ Company pays him $15,000.

In some states, college savings bonds can't be included in the college financial aid assessment (covered in Chapter 10, "State Aid Programs"). Although baccalaureate bonds are marketed as a means of saving for college, no requirements obligate you to use them for college tuition. You don't even have to designate a beneficiary, such as a college.

Although savings in the student's name typically subtract from financial aid eligibility, some tax breaks and earned interest plans may make up for the loss. For example, if the parent or grandparent deposits the money into a trust account for the student under the UGMA (Uniform Gifts to Minors Act) or the UTMA (Uniform Transfers to Minors Act), the IRS provides some tax breaks on the earned interest.

Some advantages of state college savings bonds include

➤ First $650 in earned interest is exempt from federal income tax.

➤ Second $650 in earned interest gets taxed at the student's tax rate, which could be next to nothing if the student earns nearly zilch.

➤ Earned interest above $1,300 gets taxed at the parents' rate until the student turns age 14.

➤ Funds can be withdrawn only for education and specific reasons until the student reaches an age between 18 and 21 (it varies with the state).

➤ Interest earned is tax-exempt from federal taxes and from state taxes for residents of the issuing state.

➤ Funds can be used at any time for any college expense, even out-of-state college expenses.

187

Some disadvantages of state tuition bonds include

➤ Funds can be withdrawn for any use, but only after the student reaches an age between 18 and 21, depending on the state.

➤ The money belongs to the student, and until the designated age, it can be used to cover only education costs, health, security, and welfare.

➤ The funds saved in your kid's name do subtract heavily (to the tune of 35 percent of the amount saved annually) from the student's financial aid eligibility.

➤ Minimum bond purchase amount is $1,000 at high-discount, low credit risk.

Baccalaureate Bonds

Baccalaureate bonds are special tax-exempt municipal savings bonds, sold in $1,000 units. They are often sold by state agencies as zero-coupon bonds. About 50 percent of states already offer these college savings bonds, and others have passed legislation authorizing this type of financial plan. With "baccalaureate" bonds, as their nickname implies, parents know how much cash will be available when a kid begins college. Parents should be careful, however, in investing in this type of bond.

Some financial experts believe that baccalaureate bonds are risky because they're tied to inflation and interest rates, and experts therefore recommend that they be only one part of an entire financial portfolio. Other experts suggest that selection should be limited to bonds with an AAA or AA rating. Baccalaureate bonds can be purchased only through a broker.

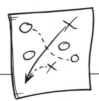

Action Plan

Bonds are rated on an alpha scale from AAA to EEE, where AAA is the highest rating that a bond can receive. It is an indication that the organization (government agency, corporation, or other issuer) that has issued the bonds is financially stable and will in all likelihood meet its bond debt obligations. The lowest rating (EEE) indicates doubt about the financial integrity of the issuer and its ability to meet its bond debt obligations. As a general rule, the lower the bond rating, the higher the interest that's paid on the bonds.

Tax-Exempt Trust Accounts

A *trust* is a legal instrument that holds and manages your real property as well as your tangible and intangible property. When you put assets into a trust, you're transferring them from your ownership to the ownership of the entity known as the trust. Sorry for the abbreviated legal explanation, but if you're a parent, it's important for you to know that certain types of trusts allow you to transfer a portion of your assets into a trust fund for your kid or kids. Why would you want to do this? Because it may allow you to declare a lower asset base when you file for financial aid, and any income earned by income-producing assets in the trust avoids taxes until the money is withdrawn.

Charitable Remainder Trusts

A *charitable remainder trust* is useful for families with a lot of money. This planning vehicle allows parents to combine a charitable gift with a financing plan for their college-bound child. Parents can present a gift to a charitable institution with the provision that a certain amount of the gift be set aside for the kid's tuition account.

There are, however, tax consequences to a charitable trust investment. The interest earned is subject to federal, state, and local taxes. Further information on this type of trust may be obtained from a certified financial planner, banker, or accountant.

Clifford Trusts

Clifford Trusts are legal arrangements transferring some type of property from one person to another. The properties are managed by a trustee for the benefit of the beneficiary. Anyone can be named the beneficiary of the trust, and there may be several beneficiaries. The trust can be funded for a kid after his or her fourteenth birthday.

Crummey Trusts

In *Crummey Trusts,* parents name the student as the beneficiary. Under the terms of the agreement, parents may make annual tax-free gifts of up to $20,000 if they are married, and $10,000 if they are single. Income can remain in this type of trust for an indefinite period of time. Parents should seek the advice of financial experts for more information on this type of trust arrangement.

Custodial Accounts

A *custodial account* is one way that parents can transfer some of their financial assets to their children. The Tax Reform Act of 1986, however, introduced the so-called "kiddie tax," which made custodial accounts less attractive financially than was previously the case.

For example, if a kid is under the age of 14, the first $650 of income is tax-free and the second $650 is taxed at the kid's rate, usually 15 percent. Anything over that amount is taxed at the parents' rate until the kid reaches age 14, when income is again taxed at the kid's rate. However, it's important to remember that students must contribute 35 percent of their assets, and parents are required to contribute only 5.6 percent of theirs.

College Sure CDs

College Sure certificates of deposit (CDs) are the only savings plan that depends on the increase in college costs. Other savings plans are tied to the *prime rate,* which is the rate at which the Federal Reserve System loans money to banks.

Introduced in 1987 to help parents meet new increases in education costs, College Sure CDs allow a variable rate of return based on the inflation of college costs. Each July, interest rates reset at 1.5 percent below the rate of annual inflation in college costs for the index.

Some of the advantages of College Sure CDs include

➤ If tuition suddenly skyrockets, this CD could protect the long-range saver from the decreasing purchasing power of inflation.

➤ The minimum deposit is only $1,000 per CD.

➤ They're insured by the Federal Deposit Insurance Corporation (FDIC) up to $100,000.

Some of the disadvantages of College Sure CDs include

➤ Interest earned is taxable.

➤ College Sure CDs are less profitable when tuition inflation rates are low.

➤ CDs lack the significant long-term growth potential of stocks and mutual funds.

Money Market Mutual Funds

Because college fees approach so terribly soon, don't even think about investing money in any kind of unstable investment. Maybe you couldn't start a good savings plan 18 years ago. Perhaps you've already spent everything you'd saved because you didn't think your children wanted to go to college. Now your kids are telling you they want to go. *Money market mutual funds* allow you to set up a relatively short-term investment and make a reasonable return on your money before you'll need it for college.

Most money market mutual funds slot money into government and corporate bonds. You can collect a fair amount of interest from these shortest of short-term bonds. Although they're not insured by the FDIC, these funds provide low-risk investments with fairly high returns. They typically plug your investment money into low-risk government securities, commercial certificates from well-established corporations, and bank certificates.

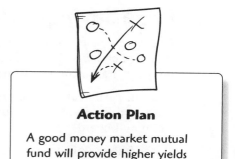

Action Plan

A good money market mutual fund will provide higher yields than bank savings accounts and most CDs.

Education IRAs

The *Education IRA* is another way to save for college. The federal government allows parents to contribute up to $500 per year to the education fund of each child under 18. The contributions are not tax-deductible, but earnings do accumulate tax-deferred. And better yet, as long as the monies are used to pay for education-related expenses (tuition, room and board, textbooks, and fees), they are not taxed at the time of withdrawal.

Education IRAs are an option for single taxpayers earning less than $95,000 per year Adjusted Gross Income (AGI) or married taxpayers filing jointly earning less than $150,000 per year of AGI. Before the named beneficiary turns 30, however, the IRA fund must be spent or transferred to another minor family member.

529 IRA Plans

The relatively new education IRA that we covered in the preceding section offers a puny $500 annual contribution. Most mutual-fund companies won't even open an account for $500. Even if they would, saving such a tiny sum each year wouldn't make a real dent in the cost of a college education anyway.

But a little-known 1997 piece of tax legislation has come to the rescue. Under Section 529 of the tax code, state college plans now enjoy tax-deferred growth and estate tax advantages, which are referred to as 529 Plans. As a result, more states are starting to offer college savings plans. This new breed of college plan is a major improvement over both the Uniform Gifts to Minors Act and the prepaid tuition plans that had been established by a number of states. These state savings plans are a great way for grandparents to help their grandchildren, and lower estate taxes at the same time. If you want to learn more about the 529 Plan, check out the Web site at www. savingforcollege.com/.

College Savings Plans

College savings plans offer parents a way to save money for college expenses and get great tax benefits. These plans are more flexible than prepaid tuition plans, since they do not dictate which institution your kid must attend.

You can participate in college savings plans with colleges inside or outside of your state, and the funds can be used for all kinds of college expenses, not just tuition and room and board.

Other features of the plans include tax-deferred earnings until your kid enters college. Withdrawals are taxed at the student's low tax bracket, not at the higher bracket of the contributor, who is usually the parent.

If you're worried about the rising cost of tuition, this type of college savings plan might be for you. In general, prepaid tuition plans allow families to prepay for college expenses at discounted rates. However, the plans vary from state to state, so be sure to investigate all of the details for this type of plan in your state. Some plans can be used at both public and private universities within your state, while others are more limiting. Check with your state's financial aid office, listed in Appendix C.

Some of the features of prepaid tuition plans are

➤ There are several types of payment options, such as one-time, lump sum payments or payment schedules that allow you to spread the payments over time.

➤ If the parents are the contributors, then they maintain control of the account.

➤ Income level is not a limiting factor, and you can contribute over $100,000 per year.

➤ If the intended beneficiary does not attend college, the funds can be transferred to another family member or refunded to you, minus a penalty fee.

For parents or students trying to meet the higher cost of education, tax-saving opportunities have been limited. However, with the renewed national interest in education, things are beginning to change. Congress is becoming increasingly focused on education as a top national priority and on tax incentives to ease the cost burden of education.

The Least You Need to Know

➤ If you're interested in saving money for college that's either tax-deferred or tax-exempt, you should know about the multitude of savings programs that are available to you for that purpose.

➤ Educational IRAs are a great way to save tax-deferred dollars for college.

➤ Opening up a trust account on behalf of your kid offers you a legal way to reduce your asset base and earn tax-deferred income on assets in the trust.

➤ The recently introduced 529 Plan for state college tax savings is an improved plan which gives you tax-deferred growth and new estate tax advantages.

Financial Aid Consulting Services

The new arrival on the college scene is the *college financial aid consultant,* an expert who leads families through the financial aid process. The good ones know how to work with you to develop strategies that meet your family's objectives, and they can assist you in filling out forms to attract the maximum financial aid. They can also work with you to appeal a rejected claim, negotiate a better aid offer, or help you compare financial aid offers to determine which one is the best for you.

How Much Do They Cost?

Good college financial aid consultants cost money but can save you more than their cost if you hire a good one. Over a four-year period, expert planners can save you thousands of dollars. Their payment terms range from hourly charges as high as $125 or more, to package prices of $500 and up for a year's service. Their fees depend on the level of service you need.

For example, suppose you only want your FAFSA completed. Are your financial affairs simple or complex? If your money matters are uncomplicated, and you hired a tax preparer to complete a short form 1040A or 1040EZ tax return, you probably paid about $50. Expect to pay approximately the same amount for your rudimentary FAFSA. If, however, your fiscal situation is complex enough to require a 1040 long form, you probably paid a tax preparer $300 or more to fill it out. Expect to pay a financial aid consultant a fee in the same neighborhood for a comparable task.

Should you seriously look for a good college financial consultant? Yes, if you're a middle-income family and need to learn about alternative loans, state residency requirements, institutional policies on award packaging, financial aid appeals processes, or future financial aid award structuring. In this situation, it may be well worth investing as much as $300 to $500 per year with a college financial aid consultant.

Help

If you have the time to learn about the complete financial aid process, then you probably don't need to hire a financial aid consultant.

How Much Is Too Much?

When are charges from a college financial aid planner higher than normal? Avoid planners who are charging over $1,000 per year. The more you pay for services does not mean the more you'll get in financial aid.

Who Are the Experts?

Experts have special knowledge derived from training or experience. Many, perhaps most, financial aid experts have worked as financial aid counselors on a college campus. Sometimes, they later were hired by banks or loan agencies and delivered education loans to college students and their families. Many have professional degrees and have worked first at foundations or private financial aid family services. Experts have been in the field and know the process from the inside out:

Warning

Anyone can hang out a financial aid shingle. No certification, degree, or license requirement exists for an individual to open a financial aid service and charge a fee for consulting. Like many other consultants, financial aid professionals come in two basic groups: experts and incompetents.

➤ They know which regulations are changing and how your family will be affected by the changes.

➤ They have a client base across the United States that consistently feeds them with information from the financial aid trenches.

➤ They're on call throughout the financial aid process to keep you informed about where you are in the process.

➤ They know which appeal letters work with which colleges, states, and federal agencies.

➤ They know which out-of-state public universities award only loans and jobs, and no gift aid.

➤ They will certify on the FAFSA that they assisted in preparing the FAFSA as required by federal regulation.

➤ They will be able to develop a four-year financial plan for you that accommodates the multitude of documents, regulations, and college inquiries; and the plan will be both legal and ethical.

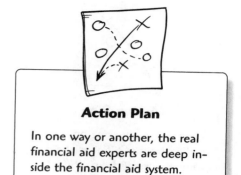

Action Plan

In one way or another, the real financial aid experts are deep inside the financial aid system.

Who Are the Incompetents?

Incompetents may have exhaustive knowledge of taxes or other financial planning strategies, but they lack detailed, up-to-date knowledge of local and state educational grants, specific scholarships, or effective ways to deal with the financial aid structure at various institutions. Incompetents usually have a superficial knowledge, if any, of the financial aid system, recommend unethical strategies, guarantee results, and overcharge. Stay clear of incompetents.

If a financial aid consultant suggests any of the following, you'd be wise to find someone else:

➤ Promises to slip into a college's side door to intercede with the financial aid officer on your behalf. The expert knows that the college's financial aid officer has high legal exposure if student confidentiality is breached. Influence peddling doesn't happen among reputable professionals. Watch out for the consultant who pretends to have connections and can make an award "a sure thing" for your kid.

➤ Suggests that your assets be hidden. An asset that's hidden on these forms may reappear when the college asks for additional information. It's also possible that the vehicle suggested to hide assets from the financial aid office will keep that money out of a family's hands for quite some time. If assets are frozen, a family might not be able to meet its expected contribution, which could mean that the student can't go to college after all.

➤ Wants to be paid up-front for four years. If you quit school before graduation, don't expect a refund. The expert charges either by the hour or by the year.

Incompetents know that their reference base is thin, so they use smoke and mirrors to look reputable. They'll claim that they belong to the local Better Business Bureau, to a state professional financial aid association, or even to the National Association of Student Financial Aid Administrators. They may, in fact, be members. Anyone can become a member of these organizations by paying membership dues.

The incompetent focuses on paying college costs for a single year, rarely on a comprehensive plan.

Incompetents have been known to direct parents to keep two sets of forms, one for the IRS and the other for the completion of the FAFSA. This duplicity may be discovered if a college asks for a signed waiver to obtain your tax records from the IRS. Another trick is the so-called Grannie Loan. Incompetents frequently tell families to lower their expected family contribution by claiming that family assets belong to others.

Action Plan

When you're checking on the qualifications of a financial aid planner, referrals from satisfied clients work best. Also call your high school guidance counselor and the college's financial aid officer. The expert will be recommended; the incompetent will not.

All in all, it's not a good idea to hire anyone who's intent on helping a family beat the system. The financial aid planner will collect a fee and not have any liability, but the family will be taking an enormous risk.

Warning

If your family is racing to send you off to college, researching financial aid may seem like a time-hogging task. You feel as though you don't have two minutes to rub together, and bingo! you spot an ad that jumps out at you: "Money for College – Results Guaranteed!" Such seductive ads are often run by firms that claim to tailor a computerized scholarship search to your individual needs for a fee. Watch out!

What to Expect from a Planning Meeting

To assist you in setting up a financial aid plan, experts will ask you to come their office (which may be their residence), because that's where the professional resources are located. Of course, incompetents may also invite you to an office.

Before you go to that meeting, make sure you've asked for and investigated the consultant's references. Referrals from satisfied clients work best. Call your high school guidance counselor for recommendations.

An expert should be prepared to discuss with you such topics as

➤ **Family structure**   Are you married, separated, thinking about separation, divorced, single, or widowed?

➤ **Home equity**   The family's equity in its primary home is important to anticipate possible effects on other forms of assets and documents required by a college.

➤ **Retirement accounts**   The history of retirement accounts is important, since these funds must be reported on some college applications.

➤ **Employment history**   The parents' job record is important because some colleges require business and farm supplemental income documents.

The incompetent financial aid person probably won't know about these issues and is not likely to bring them up or answer your questions satisfactorily. Conversely, a competent consultant should be able to answer all of your questions to your satisfaction. He or she will offer you insights that could help improve your chances of getting a better financial aid offer.

Computer Search Services

Computer-based research companies that do the legwork for you at a modest price can be a quick fix if you're in a time-crunch for finding private scholarships. But only a few scholarship search firms provide serious returns. We identify some of the best of the breed in the "Scholarships, Grants, and Fellowships" section of Appendix B, "Directory of General Financial Aid Resources." The unhappy truth is that some computerized search firms have proven to be borderline fraud cases, and they taint the entire industry with a bad odor. Some were such rip-offs that in recent years the Federal Trade Commission, state attorneys-general, and other government scam squads shut them down.

Computer-based scholarship search firms, however, continue to take advantage of time- and tuition-short students and their families. Some persuasive services claim that for a one-time fee ranging from $300 to $1,000 they'll set up your financial aid research for the next four years. Many of these firms last only a few months before disappearing. Moreover, anyone familiar with college life knows that few students know how long they'll be in school. You're wiser to use the college financial aid office's free resources.

Action Plan

A good scholarship search firm allows you to pay as you go, one hour, one week, one month, or one year at a time.

Free Scholarship Search Services

Some reputable search firms offer their search for free over the Internet. They can do so because the service is advertising-driven. What that means is that they sell your name and contact information to mailing list houses to use for direct mail promotions and telemarketing solicitations. Because schools don't monitor the quality of online financial aid searches, the results of your search may disappoint you. If privacy is a concern, ask if the service keeps your information confidential. A good scholarship search firm can be for fee or for free, but it does not sell your name without your permission.

Help

Your high school guidance office, college financial aid office, and library offer materials to conduct searches for financial aid at no cost.

Database Quality

The quality of the scholarship database is all-important. You need accurate, current information that matches your criteria.

Scholarship criteria change from year to year. Researchers who know their business are knowledgeable enough to update their information only after the sponsor's board of directors has met to determine the ground rules for the following year's awards. Normally, the boards meet between March and August. To merely verify this info on an arbitrary date is useless; for instance, verifying in January results in simply getting last year's data. Experienced researchers know when the boards meet because it's their business to know—they ask and note the dates in their working files.

Some scholarship search firms advertise that they update every quarter. This claim is marketing hype. Scholarship rules don't change with the seasons—they change once a year. A good scholarship search firm maintains its own research staff and updates its database annually, using savvy research methods.

Questions to Ask Search Services

Find out whether you'll be told about scholarships for which you're ineligible. A good scholarship search firm doesn't try to stick you with inapplicable scholarships, for example, ones that are specific to geographic regions or colleges you're not considering, or scholarships for groups of people to which you don't belong. Here are two important questions to ask:

➤ **What percentage of the service's database consists of portable awards?**—You want financial aid you can take to any college or to any group of colleges that participate in a specific scholarship award, such as the National Merit Scholarship Program.

➤ **How large is the database and how much has it grown in the past two years?**—A typical size is a couple of hundred thousand scholarship sources. Incompetents claim that their databases balloon by the hundreds per day or week; genuine services admit that although they constantly add new sources, outdated information keeps total tallies low.

A good scholarship search firm doesn't oversell the size of its database from year to year. A smaller database with high-quality scholarships can prove far more valuable than a large one with the kitchen sink thrown in. One search firm, for instance, will not include any scholarship in its database that awards less than $1,000 per student. Another search firm, however, incorporates scholarships as small as $50 book awards.

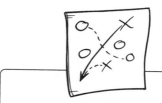

Action Plan

Don't mistakenly assume that any computer search, no matter how credible the firm or reliable the data, can do all the heavy lifting for maximizing your college money. Look at printed publications that list sources of financial aid.

The Least You Need to Know

➤ The best way to find a competent financial aid consultant is to seek out one who is recommended to you by friends or your high school or college counselors.

➤ Find out if the consultant is competent by asking lots of appropriate questions when you meet.

➤ Raise a red flag if you run across a consultant who wants a large "up-front" advance before agreeing to start working on your kid's application.

➤ Beware of unethical advice, which can get you, not the consultant, into hot water later on.

➤ If you decide to pay for computer search services, first review the information on them in this chapter so you'll know what questions to ask.

Part 4

From Applications to Offers

Most, if not all, of us hate filling out forms. Filling out financial aid forms is complicated, and even unsettling for some. You're required to disclose all kinds of personal information that will be reviewed by some unknown processor. Do you have a choice about it? Not when you apply for FAFSA (federal) funds, which is the first step in getting any type of financial aid.

The chapters in this section show you how to fill out the forms correctly so you can avoid having them rejected: Make no mistake about it: If you don't complete the forms properly, your application for financial aid will be rejected. In these chapters you'll also learn what a financial aid offer looks like, how to compare offers, how to negotiate for more funds, and what to do if your application for aid is rejected.

Chapter 18

What's Inside a Financial Aid Package?

In This Chapter

➤ Finding out what's in a financial aid package and how to dissect its parts

➤ Learning how to avoid an automatic rejection by submitting a properly completed form in the first place

➤ If your college requires you to write an essay, seeing what a winning essay looks like

➤ Mastering the process of evaluating and comparing aid packages

---

Financial aid is supposed to go to students who need it the most. In reality, most of the money goes to those who best understand how to find and apply for it. Unfortunately, the process has become more complicated over the years. At first glance, it seems simple enough. You fill out a financial aid application (FAFSA, covered in Chapter 19, "Decoding the Forms") and e-mail it to a central processing office, where the computers figure out how much your family can afford to pay for college.

If your family's contribution is short of the mark, the government and the college are supposed to help pay the difference. That's how the "simple" system is supposed to work. In fact, applying for college aid is one of the most complex and difficult financial processes you'll ever experience. In this chapter, we disperse much of the mystique in the financial aid system. Read what's here and you'll have a good chance of getting at least your fair share of the pie.

What You Should Know

You should *always* apply for federal and state financial aid. Most colleges and universities cannot consider applicants for their own scholarship and loan programs until the applicants have been denied aid from federal and state sources. The amount of a family's expected contribution will be affected by the cost of the college and the school's financial aid policies, so it's possible to receive more aid by attending an expensive school.

Always ask questions such as the following about the school's financial aid policies:

➤ Is it the school's policy to fully meet the financial needs of all aid recipients? Or does the school meet only a portion of need? Is aid provided after the first year?

➤ What is the average indebtedness of recent graduates? The answer will give you clues about the school's awarding policy.

➤ Is the school meeting the full need of all its financial aid applicants with loans, work-study programs, grants, and gifts?

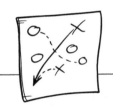

Action Plan

Apply for aid as early as possible. Deadlines vary, but your application for Federal Student Aid can be sent anytime after January 1. An early application will help you get the best financial aid package possible.

Most colleges and universities offer their students money from institutional funds. Some awards are based on financial need, and others on merit. Schools may offer special scholarships or grants to students with particular talents in, for example, music, drama, or journalism. Find out about the criteria the college uses to make these awards and the average amount awarded.

When students submit aid applications, many colleges and universities will provide estimates of what their financial aid will be. Always ask for an estimate; having one means you won't have to guess at how much money you'll need from your own resources to finance your college education.

Your Expected Contribution

The school to which you're applying will prepare a financial aid package to help you meet your financial need. *Financial need* is the difference between your cost of attendance at school, including living expenses, and what you'll be expected to pay. Your aid package cannot exceed your financial need, but some forms of self-help assistance may be used to meet your expected family contribution (EFC).

The school will notify you of your aid package by sending you an award letter. You must maintain eligibility for the aid programs in order to receive the awards. If you're selected for the verification process, you may be required to submit certain documentation, such as a copy of your family's IRS tax forms, prior to receiving any aid.

Shop Before You Buy

Once a college acknowledges a family's or student's "need," it's more than likely that its financial aid office will prepare a plan for meeting the cost of college. It may include a combination of grants, loans, scholarships, work-study, and payment programs. This "financial aid package" is designed in accordance with federal and college regulations.

The financial aid package may come in one of two forms: a firm offer or a tentative plan subject to change on the basis of additional information from the family, or one subject to changes in the college's financial aid program funding levels.

Shopping for a financial aid package and a college to attend should go hand in hand. Beginning early in your junior year of high school, start exploring which schools you would like to attend, and sign up for and take the standardized tests (the SAT, for example) required by most colleges for admission.

Preview as many college catalogues as possible. Remember that these catalogues are useful sources of information. Look at the courses offered, speak to counselors about the programs various schools offer in the areas you're interested in, check out the overall environment of the campus, and, if at all possible, talk to graduates or to students currently attending those colleges.

Look closely at tuition and other related costs, but do not rule out a school because the price seems too high. More-expensive schools often offer larger financial aid opportunities. The bottom line is not the total amount of aid, but the amount you will have to pay, or repay in the form of loans.

Action Plan

Who's receiving financial aid? Public institutions (26 percent), nonprofit institutions (35 percent), and profit institutions (39 percent).

Take Care of the Paperwork

College catalogues will tell you how to apply for admission and financial aid. Each school will likely have a different application process, so follow the directions carefully when filling out the many forms.

Most colleges will want to know about the student's and the family's financial background. This family financial statement will include questions about the family's annual income, debts, mortgage, financial holdings, and investments. Be prepared to answer very specific and personal questions. If you have a problem or question, contact the college's admissions or financial aid office.

When applying for financial aid, your kid may be expected to file as a dependent of yours. If he or she has been employed and filed federal tax returns for two years, and had income of at least $4,000 a year, your son or daughter may be able to file as an independent student. If so, you cannot claim your student as a dependent on your tax return. By filing as an independent, however, your kid may become eligible for far more funds, in terms of grants and scholarships, than those you save by claiming him or her as a dependent.

Applicants who are 24 or older or meet special circumstances may be expected to file as independents. It's important to note that students who try to apply as independents but who do not in fact meet the requirements are in violation of federal laws and may be subject to a fine. The forms that you fill out, at this point, represent the beginning of the process of determining whether your kid is eligible for financial aid. Get an early start.

Forms should be completed and submitted to the college as early as January of your kid's senior year in high school. Most schools reply in about one month, giving an analysis of your financial position and of what the school interprets as your "need." The initial reply may also include an offer of financial aid. The filing of these initial forms might not constitute an application for grants, scholarships, loans, or other forms of financial aid. Read the instructions carefully to see if there are further steps you must take.

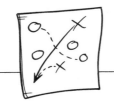

Action Plan

Your financial aid package is likely to include funds from the U.S. Department of Education, which provides 70 percent of all student financial assistance.

What If They Require an Essay?

Some colleges require that the student submit an essay when applying for financial aid. Each college has different requirements, which will be spelled out in the application that they send you.

Writing the college application essay can be one of the most daunting parts of applying for financial aid. The most important part of it is the subject matter. You should expect to devote about one to two weeks to simply brainstorming ideas. When you brainstorm with your friends, you may come up with a subject that's a winner. Here's an example of a winning essay:

Hiking to Understanding

Surrounded by thousands of stars, complete silence, and spectacular mountains, I stood atop New Hampshire's Presidential Range awestruck by nature's beauty. Immediately, I realized that I must dedicate my life to understanding the causes of the universe's beauty. In addition, the hike taught me several valuable lessons that will allow me to increase my understanding through scientific research.

Although the first few miles of the hike up Mt. Madison did not offer fantastic views, the vistas became spectacular once I climbed above the tree line. Immediately, I sensed that understanding the natural world parallels climbing a mountain. To reach my goal of total comprehension of natural phenomena, I realized that I must begin with knowledge that may be uninteresting by itself. However, this knowledge will form the foundation of an accurate view of the universe. Much like every step while hiking leads the hiker nearer the mountain peak, all knowledge leads the scientist nearer total understanding.

Above the tree line, the barrenness and silence of the hike taught me that individuals must have their own direction. All hikers know that they must carry complete maps to reach their destinations; they do not allow others to hold their maps for them. Similarly, surrounded only by mountaintops, sky, and silence, I recognized the need to remain individually focused on my life's goal of understanding the physical universe.

At the summit, the view of the surrounding mountain range is spectacular. The panorama offers a view of hills and smaller mountains. Some people during their lives climb many small hills. However, to have the most accurate view of the world, I must be dedicated to climbing the biggest mountains I can find. Too often people simply hike across a flat valley without ascending because they content themselves with the scenery. The mountain showed me that I cannot content myself with the scenery.

When night fell upon the summit, I stared at the slowly appearing stars until they completely filled the night sky. Despite the windy conditions and below-freezing temperatures, I could not tear myself away from the awe-inspiring beauty of the cosmos. Similarly, despite the frustration and difficulties inherent in scientific study, I cannot retreat from my goal of universal understanding.

When observing Saturn's rising, the Milky Way Cloud, and the Presidio meteor shower, I simultaneously felt a great sense of insignificance and purpose. Obviously, earthly concerns are insignificant to the rest of the universe. However, I experienced the overriding need to understand the origins and causes of these phenomena. The hike also strengthened my resolve to climb the mountain of

Help

Refer to the subjects in "Scholarships, Grants, and Fellowships" found in Appendix B, "Directory of General Financial Aid Resources," for more information on how to write an essay.

knowledge while still taking time to gaze at the wondrous scenery. Only then can the beauty of the universe and the study of science be purposefully united. Attaining this union is my lifelong goal.

What makes this a good essay? In the opening paragraph, the student who wrote the essay vividly captures the way in which the experience with nature drives his or her desire to learn more through scientific research. In the next two paragraphs, the student dynamically shows how the hike helped to focus his or her life goals of "understanding the physical universe." The rest of the essay reinforces the student's focused direction. If you were considering this student for admittance into your college based on the words in the essay, you could conclude that this person has a clear and definite sense of what he or she wants to achieve in life, and will know how to get there.

When Do You Get the Package?

Congratulations! You've taken the first step in the financial aid process, assuming you've completed and submitted a FAFSA form.

It will take three to four weeks for the Feds to process your form before you'll receive a Student Aid Report (SAR) by mail. Keep these things in mind regarding the SAR:

➤ Your SAR will summarize the data that you reported on your application. Check the information carefully to make sure that it's accurate.

➤ Make sure that you keep a copy of the report and note the *Data Release Number (DRN)* in the upper-right corner of the first page. You'll need it if you decide to apply for additional aid.

➤ If the information is complete, an Expected Family Contribution (EFC) will be printed next to the DRN. The EFC is based on the income and expense information that you provide on the FAFSA, and your school will use it to award your financial aid.

Help

If you're wondering, "Why do they ask that question?" see "FAFSA Online" and "FAFSA Form," both in Appendix B. The FAFSA site at www.ed.gov/ prog_info/SFA/FAFSA/index.html answers questions and discusses how personal information should be reported.

The Award Letter

When your college has all the information it needs, it puts together an aid package that will probably include a combination of grants, loans, and work-study employment. Your award letter notifies you of what your aid package contains and gives you an idea of your probable cost of attendance. The letter also tells you how your need was determined, what your need turned out to be, and the composition of your financial aid package. If you're satisfied with the aid package, you sign the documents that come with the letter and return them to the school.

Even if you haven't decided which school to attend, you should keep your options open: If you're offered several aid packages, after you've evaluated them, move quickly to accept the best ones. Schools set response deadlines, and if you don't respond to your aid letter in time, you could miss out on the funds that have been offered to you.

Before you accept any award, read everything in the aid package carefully and compare what's being offered with other offers you've received.

Consider the following as you evaluate the offer:

➤ Don't be fooled by big numbers. Pay special attention to how much of the offer is made up of grants versus loans.

➤ Note which schools are tossing in special awards for academic or athletic merit.

➤ If scholarships are offered, are they renewable or are they one-shot deals that go away at the end of the year?

➤ Break out your calculator and compare the loan interest rates offered by different lending institutions. Check out whether the loan payment requirements are especially onerous.

➤ If you're offered a work-study program, will you be able to juggle your study and school schedule with work so that your grades won't be affected?

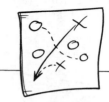

Action Plan

Accepting an aid package does not obligate you to attend the school. This isn't to say that you should keep 10 colleges on a string—make your choices as quickly as possible so that the schools you don't choose can distribute the money to other students.

Important: You may accept part of the award and reserve the right to appeal any objectionable parts.

Eligibility

Eligibility for all federal grants, subsidized loans, and work-study programs is based on a need analysis. When you send your FAFSA to the Feds for processing, they will determine your family's Expected Family Contribution (EFC) and mail you a Student Aid Report (SAR) containing the results of their determination.

The Offer

The college financial aid need (level of eligibility) in this model is under $6,500 and may include self-help funds (from loans and/or work) and some gift money in the form of a grant or scholarship. The formula for calculating your need is as follows:

Example

Total estimated cost of one year of college:	$12,000
Minus Expected Family Contribution (EFC):	$7,000
Amount of demonstrated financial need:	**$5,000**

You don't have to wait for your Student Aid Report form or the even more elusive response from your chosen college. You can easily estimate your EFC ahead of time on the Web at finaid.org.

After you know how much colleges will expect you to shell out, you can start scrimping—or not scrimping. Simply enter your financial data next to the mathematical symbols in each box. Using the symbols, calculate figures until you reach the final boxes, which estimate the student's and parents' contributions (divided by the number of family members in college).

If you believe you have special circumstances that should be taken into account, such as a significant change in income from one year to the next, you should contact the financial aid administrator at the school(s) you're applying to. If the circumstances warrant it, the aid administrator has the authority to change your dependency status or to adjust the data used to calculate your EFC. Please note that the aid administrator's decision is final and cannot be appealed to the U.S. Department of Education.

Warning

Don't turn down an award just because there's something in it you don't like. You have the right to appeal any aspect of it that you object to.

The Least You Need to Know

➤ The financial aid package that you receive after you've filed the FAFSA discloses the amount of aid you qualify for.

➤ College catalogues explain any special requirements they might have for financial aid requests (such as essays).

➤ The dependent versus independent tax status of college-bound students will affect the amount of aid they're eligible to receive.

➤ Read and carefully compare all aid offers before you decide which ones to accept.

➤ You can accept part of an award and appeal any parts you find unacceptable.

Chapter 19

Decoding the Forms

In This Chapter

➤ Finding out where you can get help completing the FAFSA form

➤ Learning how to complete many of the forms online to save time

➤ Knowing how to avoid making the most common mistakes when completing a FAFSA

➤ Get line-by-line guidance on filling out the FAFSA

There are a number of ways to apply for federal financial aid—but it all starts with the *Free Application for Federal Student Aid (FAFSA)*. The federal forms are required for anyone applying for federal funds for college and are used by many institutions, but some schools require additional forms, so check with your school to determine exactly which forms they'll want from you.

You can file electronically through your school, or you can use the Department of Education's FAFSA Express software. It runs on computers that use the Windows operating system and have a modem. Computers with the program set up and running can be found at many high schools, public libraries, and Educational Opportunity Centers. You can download a copy yourself from the Department of Education's Web site at www.fafsa.ed.gov/. Or you can order the software on diskette by calling 1-800-801-0576. If you want to forego technology altogether, you can get a form that comes on old-fashioned paper by writing to:

Federal Student Aid Information Center
P.O. Box 84
Washington, D.C. 20044

Help

For more information about the FAFSA form, used to apply for federal aid and public funds such as Pell Grants and Stafford or Perkins Loans, call 1-800-4 FEDAID (33-3243).

Warning

The Student Aid Report (SAR) is where the rubber meets the road in the race for financial aid. That's when blundering students discover they goofed in filling out their FAFSA. When they receive their SAR, they woefully discover that they were awarded little or, worse yet, no financial aid!

Completing the FAFSA on the Web

The FAFSA is available online. While FAFSA on the Web offers an alternative to the paper application, students will need to sign and submit an original signature to fully complete the application process. If the student has a printer available, the software will print a copy of the applicant data and the signature page.

After receiving the student's FAFSA, the U.S. Department of Education (DOE) allows 14 days for the student's signature page to arrive. If the student does not send in a valid signature page within 14 days, the DOE will print a Student Aid Report (SAR) and request that the student and parent sign it and return it to the FAFSA processor. Once all appropriate signatures are sent to the FAFSA processor, the DOE can calculate your Expected Family Contribution (EFC).

FAFSA Express

Another way to send your FAFSA electronically is by downloading FAFSA Express software to your computer. You'll need a PC equipped with Windows and a modem to complete this electronic form and to send your completed FAFSA to the Department of Education. The FAFSA Express site is www.fafsa.ed.gov/.

FAFSA in PDF

If your computer can't support an electronic FAFSA or if you'd rather obtain a printed version of the form and send it to the DOE by mail, you may want to download and print the application form in Portable Document Format (PDF). Adobe Acrobat Reader software is required to print the PDF version of the FAFSA.

Download it for free from Adobe Systems at www.adobe.com/products/acrobat/readermain.html. You can also download and print instructions to assist you in completing the FAFSA.

Sending FAFSA to College

If you want your application information sent to schools that you might attend, you have to enter the Federal School Codes for those schools on the FAFSA. If you don't know your schools' codes, contact the schools directly or visit their Web sites to obtain this information. Or, you can use the FAFSA search function on the Web to locate school codes.

You don't need to put something in every search box. Provide only the information that you know is accurate. For example, if you enter "Tech" without quotes in the School Name search box and then click the search button, the results page will list schools with the word "Technical" in their name as well as technology and polytechnic schools. Spell out words like "Saint" and "Mount" in the School Names box instead of using common abbreviations like "St." and "Mt.," and omit quotes. State names retain their common abbreviated form but do not have periods, as in AZ for Arizona.

Line-by-Line Instructions for Completing the FAFSA

In this section, we walk you through the steps for properly filling out the FAFSA. Any error that you make on this form could sink your chances of getting financial aid. You'll find a copy of the FAFSA form in Appendix B. Make a copy of it so you can refer to it as you go through this section.

Help

Apply electronically, or get a paper FAFSA from your high school, college, or local public library. To receive a paper copy by mail, call the Federal Student Aid Information Center at 1-800-433-3243. If you're unable to dial the toll-free number from your area, an alternate number is 319-337-5665. Call 1-800-801-0576 if you have technical questions about submitting an electronic FAFSA.

Insight

You'll be asked to create a **PIN number** when you begin to fill out the FAFSA online. Your PIN number is the identifier that lets you access personal information in various U.S. Department of Education systems. You must have a PIN to file an online renewal FAFSA or to make online corrections to your FAFSA.

Step One: Personal Information

Lines 1–3	Use your proper full name.
Lines 4–7	Use a permanent address because that is where all of your financial-aid-related mail will be sent to you.
Line 8	You must have and enter a Social Security Number to be eligible for financial aid.
Line 9	Make sure you enter your correct birth date. An incorrect birth date can cause your application to be rejected.
Line 10	The telephone number you enter on this line is the one they will use if they need to talk to you.
Line 11	Enter Yes or No if you have a drivers license.
Lines 12–13	Enter your driver's license number and the state that issued the license.
Lines 14–15	If you are a U.S. citizen, enter "yes" and go on to the next line. There are special instructions in the application package for non-U.S. citizens.
Lines 16–17	Enter your marital status and the month and year of that status.
Line 18-22	Indicate whether you will be a "full time," "¾ time," or less than "half time" student for the semesters or quarters indicated. Note that you are instructed to mark "full time" if you are not sure.
Lines 23–24	Enter the highest level of education your father and mother achieved.
Lines 25 –27	Enter the state code where you are a legal resident and the date you became a legal resident of your state.
Line 28	You are asked to enter "1" in the box provided if you have been convicted of any illegal drug offense, and are instructed to call a special number for additional instructions. Note that this does not necessarily make you ineligible for aid.
Lines 29–30	If you are a male student, you are asked if you have enrolled in the Selective Service, which is generally a requirement to receive financial aid.
Line 31	You're asked to enter a numeric code for your course of study. The codes are in the application package. For example, 01 is the code if your course of study is in agriculture.
Line 32	Enter your grade level. You are instructed to refer to a table to select a number that corresponds to your grade level.
Lines 33–36	These questions should be relatively easy for you to answer, but they are very important. They will be used to determine the type of financial aid you are eligible to receive.

Step Two: Tax Status Information

Lines 37–48   Note the questions you do not need to answer if you are not married.

Lines 49–53   You are asked to disclose your current net worth, which will influence the amount of financial aid you are eligible to receive. The financial aid instructions that come with the form tell you how to determine your net worth. Make sure you keep copies of any documents you used to determine your net worth in case your application is audited.

Step Three: More Basic Questions

Lines 54–59   Most students will answer "no" to the next six questions. Note that if you answer "yes" to any one of the questions, you can skip Step Four. You must complete Step Four if you answered "no" to any question.

Step Four: Household Information

Lines 60–85   These questions pertain to the tax status of your parents and will be used to help determine the amount of financial aid that you qualify for. Note that you are asked to disclose the Social Security Numbers of both of your parents. The Department of Education has the legal right to validate the information on your parents' tax returns. Therefore, keep copies of all tax returns and W2 statements that you used to answer Step Four questions in the event that you're audited.

Step Five: More Household Information

Lines 86–87   These questions pertain to the number of people in your household. Complete this step only if you answered "yes" to any question in Step Three.

Step Six: Request for Schools to Receive Your Financial Aid Information

Lines 88–99 You can list the names and addresses of up to six colleges and universities to which you want the results of your FAFSA sent. You must include the unique school code next to the name of each school. You can get the school code either by calling the appropriate college or by looking it up on the Web (at Finaid.com).

Step Seven: Releases and Signatures

Lines 100–104 Make sure you and your parents sign and date the form before you send it in, or the form will automatically be rejected and nothing will happen to your request.

Mistakes You Don't Want to Make

Many of the questions on the FAFSA seem too easy. Just because the form asks for information you can recite in your sleep doesn't mean you should take the form lightly when you fill it out. You'll soon discover there are myriad lines requesting numbers, and they may require some digging. Applicants often make mistakes out of pure carelessness, which can cost them a rejected application. As you and your folks complete the application, double-check every entry you make.

Even when well-meaning parents fill out the FAFSA, they sometimes make simple mistakes, such as entering their own Social Security Number on the line where the form requests their kid's. The same parents, with stunning consistency, often go on to enter their own birth date instead of their kid's. It can be dangerous: When the application reviewer looks at the age listed on the form, he or she will probably classify the applicant as an adult independent student.

If you're a student filling out the FAFSA, some of the questions you'll be asked are:

➤ **The marital status of your parents**. Legal separation isn't required for this question. If your parents are living apart for the purpose of eventually becoming divorced, answer the question

Warning

Make sure you complete all of the appropriate parts of Steps Six and Seven. If you enter the wrong codes, list the wrong schools, forget to sign the forms (yours and your parents' signatures required), your application will probably be rejected. Also, don't send in the form for processing before January 1.

"separated." Complete the rest of the form using the information about the parent you live with or who provided the most financial support during the last 12 months.

➤ **The number of people in your family who will be attending an eligible college program at least half time while you're attending college.** The more family members you can claim are in college, the more financial aid you're eligible to receive. If your parents are attending college, make sure you include them, even if their employer is paying for their tuition. Who pays for the tuition expenses is not relevant to this question.

➤ **Tax figures that were reported on your parents' income tax return.** Most parents use the long form, also known as the 1040 form. But if your parents make less then $50,000, they'll be eligible for more aid if they file the short form (either the 1040A or 1040EZ form). If they use the short form and net less than $50,000, they don't need to complete Section G on the FAFSA, which requires them to list assets.

➤ **Disclosure of any assets that are owned under the student's name.** You can generally qualify for more financial aid if you have minimal assets. For example, if your parents opened a savings account on your behalf when you were young and started to make generous deposits into the account to help fund your education, it could reduce the amount of aid you'll receive. Students are penalized 35 cents on the dollar for their assets. Parents are better off keeping the money in their own account.

Checklist for Filing the FAFSA

❏ Find out and note the federal deadline for submitting your FAFSA.

❏ Find out and note your college's deadline for financial aid applications.

❏ Obtain the FAFSA form at your high school or college's financial aid office or online.

❏ You can contact your financial aid office to request additional materials that may be required by the U.S. Department of Education.

❏ If you're already in college and applying for financial aid for the first time, request that your financial aid transcripts be sent to the college you're attending. You must do the same thing if you transfer to another college.

❏ Complete your taxes or an estimation of your taxes as soon as possible.

Help

Students and parents can receive assistance in completing the FAFSA on the Web by calling 1-800-801-0576.

❏ If you're a dependent, make sure you have copies of your parents' tax returns so that you can record their tax information on your FAFSA.

❏ Submit your FAFSA online or through the mail prior to the deadline.

❏ Complete and submit any additional materials required by your college's financial aid office by their deadline date.

This chapter offered tips on how to fill out the FAFSA form and pointed out common mistakes to avoid. The bottom line is that the form is relatively easy to complete if you take your time and carefully check it over before you send it to the Feds. It can get complicated if you make a dumb mistake like entering a wrong Social Security Number or birth date. Going through the correction process is a pain in the neck and will cost you valuable time, so check and double-check the form before you send it in.

The Least You Need to Know

➤ If you're applying for any form of federal financial aid for college, you must submit a FAFSA.

➤ If you prepare your FAFSA online, you'll improve the turnaround process and benefit from some of the automated editor features that have been built into the online systems.

➤ Do it right the first time. Make sure your FAFSA is error-free before you send it to the Department of Education.

Chapter 20

What Does an Offer Look Like?

In This Chapter

➤ Learning how financial aid offers work

➤ Finding out what to look for to determine the best deal for you

➤ Considering the advantages and disadvantages of accepting a deal that includes work-study

➤ Finding the errors in your Student Aid Report that could have caused your rejection

➤ Getting financial aid in your own state even if you get rejected by the Feds

Aid from the Student Financial Assistance Programs will be paid to you through the school. Your aid awards will almost always be paid to you by the time of your college's semester or quarter enrollment period.

A college will first use the aid to pay any tuition, fees, and room and board charges owed to the school. The remainder will be paid to you for your other living expenses. Aid funds may not be credited for books, supplies, and other school expenses unless you have given the college written authorization.

When you receive an award letter, all you need to do is indicate that you are accepting for the mid-year term. If you wait until the fall to apply for the spring or mid-year, you'll probably get only federal loan money and perhaps a Pell Grant. You may not get free money from your state, your college, or private scholarships. Remember: You cannot apply for financial aid until after January 1. Award letters are usually received four to six weeks from the date your application is received by the processor.

Figuring Out Your Best Deal

Celebrate when your award letters begin to arrive, and then be critical. Analyze each award letter you receive, and figure out what it's offering. Is it a good deal for you? Don't take the words in any award letter you receive personally because they don't tend to be very personal. Award letters are kicked out by computers programmed with specific criteria, and most college financial aid counselors don't have the time to review each letter before it's mailed. Also see Chapter 18, "What's Inside a Financial Aid Package?" for more on award letters.

Because the letters are computer-generated, you should go over yours with a fine-toothed comb.

➤ **Look for your best deal** among the various awards, and keep an eye out for reasons to appeal for even more aid.

➤ **To keep your options open, immediately accept each award** by signing and returning each college's acceptance form, which will be attached to its award letter. Even if you later turn down a particular school and its award, you want to be sure that the school doesn't give your aid to someone else while you're making up your mind.

➤ **Compare competing offers,** and when you finally decide on which school and aid offer to accept, notify the financial aid offices of the rejected schools as quickly as possible. Your thoughtfulness allows them to offer the vacated admission seat to another student.

Warning

Never burn your bridge with any college by not responding to their reward offerings. It could eliminate your chances of applying for financial aid with them in the future.

What if the offer you finally select contains a job or a college work-study position, and you don't want to be employed during your first year, when you're uncertain how much time you'll need for studies? Can you turn down work opportunities and accept only the gift aid? Will you make a big mistake if you do?

Consider these factors:

➤ Employers hiring new graduates consistently favor applicants who gained work or internship experience during their college years.

➤ Conventional wisdom says that a job will not interfere with your college education experience as long as you don't toil beyond 14 hours a week.

➤ Working improves your time management skills, which will prove to be a blessing throughout your entire life.

➤ If you're a marginal student who needs every free hour to study, perhaps you shouldn't work during your undergraduate years. But whether you're a marginal or a good student, if you do decide to turn down the work portion of the award, the financial aid counselor may bounce the money-gap ball back into your court, leaving you on your own to solve the shortage of funds.

What Does an Award Letter Look Like?

The following letter is an example of a typical college's offer of a scholarship or gift aid. Note that the scholarship becomes part of a financial aid offer that will come either with the letter or follow at a later date. (See our example of the financial aid award offer following the letter.) The award becomes firm once you sign and return the obligatory paperwork.

Dear John Doe Student:

Congratulations on your acceptance to ABC College. We are delighted to inform you that you have been awarded a merit scholarship in recognition of your high school academic achievements. You will receive a $4,000 academic scholarship for the current academic year beginning September 15, 20XX.

This scholarship will automatically renew for an additional three years provided that you are a full-time student and maintain a 3.0 cumulative grade-point average. You are therefore eligible to receive a total award of $16,000 over the next four years. Since you have applied for financial assistance, we have attached a copy of your Financial Aid Award Offer to this letter.

If you have any questions, please feel free to contact our Financial Aid Office at your convenience. We look forward to meeting you at the college reception for new students in September.

Yours Truly,

Jane Doe, Ph.D.
President of ABC College
Financial Aid Award Offer

Financial Aid Award Offer	
Estimated Expenses	
Resident Tuition & Fees	$3,600
Room & Board	$5,400
Books & Supplies	$700
Estimated Personal Expenses	$2,100
Transportation	$850
Medical	$1,200
Total Estimated Expenses	$13,850
Financial Aid	
Scholarships	$4,000
Pell Grant	$1,500
College Grant	$1,000
Parent PLUS Loan	$850
Subsidized Stafford Loan	$6,500
Total Financial Aid	**$13,850**

Many Americans believe that financing their children's education is beyond their ability and that the increasing cost of going to college will make higher education unaffordable for all but the wealthy. For most families, financing a college education is a major undertaking. However, as we hope you learn from this chapter, the award of financial aid can help your kid get into college.

What If Your Application Is Rejected?

When you receive your Student Aid Report (SAR), it will be accompanied by a letter explaining what you need to do to receive aid. However, the letter may say: "Based on the information you provided, it appears that you are not eligible to receive a Federal Pell Grant at this time," or some other qualifying statement. Unfortunately, many students interpret this to mean that they are not eligible for any financial aid, which may not be the case. It is not what the statement means.

The correct interpretation of the SAR statement used in the example is that you cannot receive aid out of the Federal Pell Grant money bucket. You may be eligible to receive aid from the state, the college you plan to attend, the federal government (in the form of a subsidized loan), or some other source. You just won't get money from the Pell program. Before you start looking for other sources, review every line on your SAR for errors that may have caused the rejection, such as a wrong birth date or Social Security Number.

Check Your SAR

If your aid application is rejected, the first thing to do is go through the following steps to see if you made any errors on your SAR that may have been responsible for the rejection:

1. Start with your Social Security Number. If it's wrong on your SAR, you'll be missing in action in a college's financial aid office because that's how they keep track of you. If the office can't find you on their computer, you don't exist.

2. Make sure that all colleges you potentially want to attend are listed on your SAR. If a school is missing, call the Federal Student Aid Information Center (319-337-5665) to report the omission. The center will ask for your SAR's PIN number, so have it ready. If a school doesn't get your SAR, you won't be able to get any money from that school.

3. Check to see how you answered this question on the SAR: "Do you have a bachelor's degree?" Many students think that a high school diploma is a bachelor's degree. If you already have a bachelor's degree, you automatically become ineligible for Federal Pell Grants, Federal Supplemental Educational Opportunity Grants, and most state grants. That's a mistake you don't want to make!

> **Warning**
>
> Whether you communicate in writing or by phone with federal, state, or private individuals about the status of your financial aid application, always have your PIN number available. This is the one number that they use to tie everything together on your behalf. If you don't have it, they won't know how to function.

Don't Lose Aid Because You Won't Respond

Colleges are required by federal laws to verify by random sample the eligibility of 30 percent of the students filing for aid. You may receive a standard verification form that requires you to verify such things as the number of family members listed as household residents on your FAFSA, to declare any untaxed income, and to submit copies of income tax returns and W-2 statements.

Many families have a problem with this process because they believe they are being audited in the same way that the IRS audits taxes. This is not so. A verification is not an audit. It's an effort by the college to verify the integrity of the financial aid process. If you did make an error when you completed your FAFSA, you could be eligible for more aid or less. You can't ignore a verification request; it's the law. If you do fail to respond to the verification request, you are no longer eligible for any kind of financial aid.

College financial aid offices can't award federal money to students who have previously attended a postsecondary institution until they receive a *Financial Aid Transcript (FAT)* from the previous college(s). The FAT is required even if you never received financial aid in the past. Unfortunately, many students think they took care of this issue when they requested that academic transcripts be sent in. An academic transcript reports grades, whereas a financial aid transcript reports money or shows that you didn't get any money if that was the case. Your aid will be held up until your FAT(s) is received. Accepting or regretting college offers is not as casual as accepting or regretting social invitations.

Don't Get Rejected Because You Didn't Renew

Pick up financial aid packets from your college's financial aid office to continue or initiate awards for next year. Many colleges do in fact initiate aid renewals automatically, but they are not responsible if your renewal slips through the cracks.

The federal government sends out renewal FAFSA forms to remind you that it's time to start the process all over again. Renewal FAFSA forms are available on the Web. Just because you didn't get federal money or a state scholarship one year does not mean you'll be ineligible forever. Eligibility can boomerang as a result of changes in income, parents' marital status, revisions in assets and savings, fresh money in a college's resources, and changes in the federal budget.

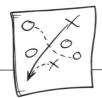

Action Plan

In many respects, state financial aid agencies play a more significant role in the financial aid award process than the federal government does. That's because the Feds collect most of the aid money through the country's tax system and then distribute the funds to the states for dispersal.

Ask Your State for Help

Don't forget to apply to your state for financial aid, even if your request for federal financial aid was denied. Some states are more generous than the federal government in determining whether you qualify. Federal awards are based on your adjusted gross income, which includes some notice of your assets. In contrast, some states award aid based solely on taxable income, without regard to your assets.

In some states you can own an estate, a condominium in Aspen, and several Ferrari sports cars, and still qualify for thousands of state aid dollars, as long as your taxable income falls within state limits. Many states award a full ride, including room and board, to in-state students who participate in the federal free lunch program. State rules vary significantly from state to state.

Don't overlook inquiring about possible aid awards at your state's student financial aid agency. If the application forms for student aid aren't available at your high school or college Financial Aid Office, contact your state's Department of Education. States vary in the information they need to decide whether you're eligible for aid. Some will use the data from the FAFSA; others will require a supplemental aid form that is processed by the state's Department of Education.

Look to your state (and its financial aid office, listed in Appendix C, "Alphabetical State Financial Aid Listings") to play a substantial role in supporting your education. Tuition at state schools is always much less costly when you're a state resident. The difference between being an in-state student and an out-of-state student can be as much as $10,000 or more per year.

Establishing State Residency

Although establishing residency in a state used to be fairly simple, rules have tightened over the years. Many states now require that parents pay state taxes and have a primary residence in the state. If you have your eye on another state's public university, find out what it takes to become a resident. It may be worth your while to drop out of college for a year, work in that state, and pay state taxes to establish residency. Make sure you know exactly what you must do to meet all the residency rules of the state.

Residency requirements not only vary from state to state, but often from school to school within a state. Don't count on starting school during the year that you're establishing your residency. Community colleges, which are usually operated by a county, add another requirement for residency. Not only do you have to live in the state, you also have to live in the school's county to be eligible for their residency tuition.

When you contact a state's financial aid agency, don't expect the agency to know details about state residency requirements, which may change from year to year. Most will only know about their state's financial aid programs, but they should be able to tell you whom to contact to verify residency requirements. The most common answer will be the college's financial aid office.

Different institutions in a state require more or fewer years to establish residency. Always verify residency requirements with the college you hope to attend.

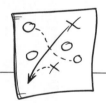

Action Plan

If you snag aid from one state but attend school in another, you'll have to contact your state financial aid agency to learn the ropes. Addresses of all state aid offices are listed by state in Appendix C.

The Least You Need to Know

➤ Know how to compare the various offers you'll get to determine which offer is right for you.

➤ Understand how offers will be presented to you so that you'll know in advance what to expect.

➤ Always verify the accuracy of the information on your SAR. An error can prevent you from getting financial aid.

➤ Just because you got turned down for one type of aid doesn't mean you're ineligible for another type.

➤ Don't overlook applying for financial aid in your home state. States can be more generous than the Feds.

Chapter 21

Negotiating a Better Offer

In This Chapter

➤ Gaining a clear understanding of what you need to do to negotiate a better offer

➤ Knowing how to research information that will strengthen your negotiating position

➤ Learning how to write an appeal letter that will improve your negotiating position

---

It's the spring of your high school senior year, and you're looking forward to entering college next fall. You know you're about to embark on some of the best years of your life, but the next couple of months are pure torture as you await answers from the colleges you applied to for financial aid. You live from one mailbox visit to the next, ready for good news or, perish the thought, dreading bad news.

Suddenly, the envelopes start to arrive. At first glance, you're happy to see that they're all thick acceptance letters rather than thin rejection notes. Everything is going great until you get a reduced offer from your favorite college. Good grief, their financial aid award is $4,000 short of the amount you need to make it through the year. What went wrong, when all of the other colleges are meeting your financial needs? What are your options?

Before you think about hanging yourself, don't give up. The $4,000 shortfall in our example doesn't spell doom for your chances of attending your preferred college. If you organize a good negotiations strategy, you may be able to get them to come up with the additional $4,000 you need. We show you how to do it in this chapter.

Check Your Appeal Options

Most colleges have an appeals process. If you're not sure about the process at the college you're interested in, call their financial aid officer and ask about it. If the college doesn't offer an appeals process, then don't waste your time trying to appeal. They won't listen. If they do have one, make sure you understand exactly what you need to do to submit an appeal. You're going to get only one shot at it.

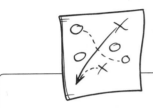

Action Plan

If parents are paying most of a student's college expenses, then they're the ones who should conduct the negotiations.

One of the surest ways to win an appeal is to provide a good and sincere reason for needing the additional aid. Base all of your negotiation on facts, because subjective issues will not be considered.

Call attention to information on your application that the aid counselor may have overlooked. Always remember that the need amount you requested was based on the facts in your application. If the facts haven't changed since then and you feel shortchanged, then you can logically conclude that their interpretation of the facts is different from yours. Try to get them to tell you why they arrived at a lower number. Is there something they may have overlooked?

How to Negotiate for More Aid

Parents more often than their kids conduct financial aid negotiations because they usually have more negotiating skills. Even though thousands of dollars may be at stake, in this chapter we address most of our suggestions to students, who probably need practice in the dynamics of negotiating.

Colleges usually state their appeals policies early on in their award letters. When you're in doubt about their negotiation policy, anonymously call the financial aid office and ask if award appeals are accepted. The colleges that imply "take our offer or leave it" tend to be elite, top-tier schools. They can take a rigid stance because they can afford to. Esteemed institutions like Harvard enjoy a surplus of academically qualified applicants whose parents are able to pay cash without a quibble.

Fortunately for most students, there are relatively few colleges that refuse to negotiate award offers. The great majority of colleges in the United States are pressured to enroll students at discounted tuitions in order to accommodate students' financial needs whenever possible. If you provide good reasons for needing more aid or you make a sincere plea for guidance, they'll negotiate their financial aid award offers.

Remember: Base your negotiation on facts by presenting new information or calling attention to factors that the financial aid counselor may have overlooked. It's the surest way to win an appeal.

If new facts can't be found, make an emotional appeal to the college's financial aid counselor. Admit that you have a financial problem, and ask the counselor to help you find more aid. Try to make your appeal face-to-face. If that's not possible, write your appeal in a letter and follow up with a telephone call.

Negotiating Tactics

Initiating an award appeal that pays off is easier when you can bring up new or overlooked information.

As a negotiating strategy, consider omitting a minor special circumstance to keep the door open for an appeal. Save your major special circumstances for later.

Warning

Determining whether or not a sudden change in your financial situation is a major or minor circumstance can be a subjective call. What *you* may consider to be a minor financial circumstance may conversely be considered a major one as far as the government financial aid agencies are concerned. If you're not sure about how a change in your financial situation will affect your aid application, seek out the advice of your high school counselor.

What would be considered a minor special circumstance? Childcare expenses or health insurance for students no longer covered by parental health plans are two examples. A special circumstance you've forgotten to mention in your original aid request need not be earth-shattering in importance, just logical enough to give you a graceful entry into the appeals process.

Get Ready to Bargain

Colleges with large endowments have a better chance of meeting students' financial needs. They have more flexibility than those that are less endowed because, quite simply, they have more free money to work with. This is a well-kept secret within the collegiate financial aid industry and is one you should know about.

A college's financial aid process doesn't always result in the best deal for every student. Often the opening bid is less than you need and less than the college can deliver. It's not uncommon for colleges to submit to you their "low ball" offer first, even though they know you're eligible for more funds. The rationale is that the offer can always be raised if that's what it takes to get you enrolled. When you bite and accept the initial offer without trying for more, the college is richer and you are poorer.

Before you launch an appeal, it pays to determine the school's norms in aid awards. A computer probably ground out your award letter with programming based on specific parameters. If you give financial aid counselors new information that makes the parameters unreasonable, they routinely modify awards.

Get the Facts

Anyone who has tried to get more of anything knows that background information is needed to unravel the basic dynamics of negotiating a better deal. Look at the underlying factors and family complexities that impact the aid process and that can influence your request for more aid. Your family-based special circumstance will not be taken into consideration in your aid appeal if you fail to include documentation. Here are some ideas that will help you get started:

➤ **Printed information**—The college's catalogue or letters to you are the first stops on your research trail. Make sure you understand exactly what they can and cannot offer in the form of financial aid to their students. If you try to ask for something they don't offer, you're wasting your time.

Action Plan

Learn all you can about the college financial aid system. Use that knowledge to prepare a plan on how you will pay for college. If you don't know something, ask questions.

➤ **Personal inquiries**—Ask an admissions counselor at the college's admissions office what percentage of demonstrated need the college has historically granted. Is your offer above or below their average offer? Admissions personnel should have this information because these numbers have to be reported to the federal government.

➤ **College Web sites**—Each college's Web site may also contain additional information not in their catalogue about how it awards financial aid.

➤ **Network your friends**—Reaching out for information from your friends and their friends who attend or have graduated from the college may provide the data you need to pull the financial aid system's levers.

➤ **Discover trends**—Is their enrollment down? If it is, a college may be vulnerable. They need students. When a college is receiving a smaller-than-usual number of student applications, they may be frantic to add students, which will improve your odds of negotiating a better offer.

➤ **Loss of job**—You or your spouse lost your job after you applied for financial aid. If this occurs, you have a strong case for an appeal.

➤ **Diversion of income**—One of your parents is suddenly confined to a nursing home, and your family has to pay the extra expenses that are not covered by Medicare. That's the same money you planned to use for college.

➤ **Know the rules**—If something has changed in your family that can influence your eligibility for more aid, contact your financial aid counselor immediately.

➤ **Develop a winning strategy**—Always negotiate for a better financial aid offer in a professional manner.

Insight

All colleges and universities are required by state and federal laws to disclose an incredible amount of information about the disbursement of financial aid funds to their respective students. This is "public domain" information. If you run into an official who tries to tell you that the information is confidential, remind him or her of this fact. If the official still refuses to give you the information that you desire, report his or her action to someone one level of authority above that person.

Compare Tuition Costs

Check the college's fees against those of other comparable colleges. For example, if their tuition is 20 percent higher than it is at other institutions in the state, then they may have room to offer you a lower tuition rate. Colleges with high tuition rates have more room to negotiate discounted tuitions. With the exception of the top colleges that are not looking for students, colleges that charge high tuitions generally have more room to negotiate than colleges that charge lower tuition rates.

Incorporate research into your appeal, noting that state colleges charge about a quarter of what it costs to go to private colleges. Ask whether there is possibly enough margin in the tuition structure to offer you more consideration. By researching tuition at somewhat similar colleges, you can refine your comparison even more by citing the tuition at "comparable private schools."

Making Your Appeal

Does your research reveal that a large proportion of the college's student population is receiving financial aid? If so, the college's financial aid professionals are sensitive to the institution's high costs and the students' needs. This college is probably more student-oriented than others with lower student-aid support. They should be receptive to aid appeals. Pull out all the stops with a factual and heartfelt appeal.

Competitive Offers

Although most colleges don't like to admit it, they are like any other business operating in a competitive world.

Let's assume that you have a better offer. When you're negotiating with a financial aid officer, politely tell him or her about the other offer and ask whether it can be matched. This negotiating strategy assumes, of course, that your kid would rather go to their institution than to the one who made the better offer.

Let the financial aid officer know up front that your son or daughter is set on attending this college, not the one that made the better aid offer. This will make it clear that you're not playing the officer's college against another one.

Warning

If a college doesn't increase its award offering, don't make the mistake of irately threatening to send your child elsewhere. Another college may be one of your options, and you may have to call it to their attention, but do it in a professional manner. If your tone is threatening, you won't be given any options at all!

When dealing with financial aid officers, be sensitive to how you leverage one financial aid offer against another to increase the lower offer. Always use tact and polite language, or you'll be told to take the other offer and run. If you're sincere and fair with them, they may come back and match, or even beat, a competing offer.

Do They Need Students?

All colleges desperately want to start off their school year at full enrollment. Anything less amounts to lost revenue that they can never recover. Find out from the admissions office what the enrollment figures have been over the past year. Then ask what their full enrollment figure is. If they're below the full enrollment figure, you might suggest to the aid officer that an enrolled student paying at a reduced rate is a lot better than having no student at all.

Add Diversity

Whether you offer new facts or make a personal plea, when your research shows that your intended alma mater is blessed with endowment money, think diversity.

Emphasize your geographical desirability as an enrichment to other students on campus. For example, an East Coast campus may want to attract students from the West Coast who can share their experiences with the school's predominately East Coast student population. Liberally use the word "diversity" in your appeal. Say you can contribute to the cultural richness of the student body, but that you need help with the level of your financial aid.

If you're planning on attending an out-of-state college, then you may have some additional room to negotiate. Most colleges actively recruit out-of-state students to add diversity. Some colleges even go so far as to embrace students from particular sections of the country. Check with the admissions office, and see if you can find out what areas turn them on. Emphasize how you can contribute to the cultural richness of the student body.

Insight

Colleges are pressured by the Feds, states, their alumni, faculty members, and even their students to increase minority student representation on campus. In the United States, a fourth of college students comes from minority groups. We cover this subject in more detail in Chapter 13, "Minority and Other Special Programs."

Changes in Your Family

The amount of financial aid that you're offered is based on a standard formula that is applied to all families and is based on the FAFSA forms they've submitted. However, your family may have some nonstandard issues that aren't covered in the standard formula. If so, bring up the issues when you start negotiating for a better deal. You must be able to prove that circumstances have occurred within your family that justify increasing the amount of financial aid you need.

➤ Is a new sibling coming on the scene? A central element in calculating your eligibility for aid is the number of household members. Count all your family's children who will receive more than half their support from your parents between July 1, 2001, and June 30, 2002. Your appeal is based on your mother being pregnant and expecting to give birth in the spring of 2001, which adds another mouth to feed during your school year.

➤ The college financial aid counselor has no way of knowing if one of your parents is planning to retire during your school year. If one is, explain the retirement benefits, which usually are lower than employment earnings. Ask the counselor to calculate a new aid base.

➤ If you and your parents are financially overextended, have a bad credit history, or for other reasons can't borrow more college money, share that fact with your financial aid counselor. The counselor may be sympathetic and award you more aid funds.

➤ Do other members of your family have uncommon costs that take away from your family's ability to pay the assessed expected family contribution? Perhaps a brother or sister is required to attend a private school because of learning disabilities, for example. The FAFSA form has no place to record such information.

Loss of Income

Social Security benefits for children are reduced at age 18 or on the last day of high school attendance, whichever date comes last. Usually this occurs after the FAFSA documents are filed, which means that the college's financial aid counselor has no way of knowing that your SS benefits are lower and your family will have fewer dollars for college.

Another income cut that your financial aid officer won't know about unless you announce it in an appeal occurs when parents split up. Most noncustodial divorced or separated parents are not obligated to contribute child support after the children's 18th birthday. If your parents get divorced or separated after you've submitted your financial aid form, all income and asset information must be corrected. Tell your financial aid counselor how much child support and home maintenance support your custodial parent expects to receive from the other.

Action Plan

Don't be afraid to confide in financial aid officers. Their official mission in life is to help you get the aid you deserve. Ask them what steps you and/or your family need to take to increase your eligibility for financial aid. They'll give you an honest answer.

In any event, your expected family contribution is likely to be lower under the new arrangement. The divorce or separation must have legally taken place. It can't be an action that may happen in the future. If the parent who was a wage earner during the base year of income is no longer able to contribute, your income drops and aid rises.

If your aid package requires you to complete an internship, co-op education assignment, or other program that requires an automobile for transportation, ask for additional aid funding to cover the related expenses. If you're enrolled in college for credit and must complete a study-abroad program to fulfill curriculum requirements, you may be able to get more money for transportation and living expenses abroad.

Prove Everything on Your Appeals Claim

Prove everything you are claiming by supplying documents such as retirement letters, canceled checks, medical bills, divorce papers, employment termination notices, and Social Security notifications. Many parents are caught in the "sandwich" generation, providing for their children and for their own aged parents. Costs of providing parent care in a home or a nursing facility can be overwhelming. Use such expenses in an appeal, because the higher the expense total, the greater your demonstrated need will be.

Example of an Appeal Letter

Many avenues for appeal are open once you begin to think through the college's issues and your family's fiscal fitness. Learn to write a good appeal letter. Even when you plan a face-to-face encounter in the financial aid office, take with you a letter stating the facts and give it to the financial aid officer at the beginning of the conversation so he or she will have an official letter that documents your position.

Here is a sample letter written by a mother on behalf of her son:

To: Office of Student Financial Aid
Subject: Letter of Appeal, Loss of Income
Re: John Doe (Student) SSN 000-000-000

This is to inform you of my loss of income for the current year. I understand that students' financial aid is based on their demonstrated need, which involves the parents' and students' income and assets for the calendar base year.

My income has been reduced significantly. I have enclosed a copy of a letter from the International Medical Group that confirms that my service agreement with them will not be renewed. On my current income tax return, I listed the income from this contract at $21,000. My income, however, will consist only of my full-time job, which pays me a salary of $58,000. This is a tremendous decrease from the original $79,000.

I hope you can consider this new and disheartening information in a reevaluation of my son's financial need. John and I would greatly appreciate it.

Thank you for what you have already done for John; our family would treasure any additional assistance toward John's education as he pays his own way at Adelphi University.

Sincerely yours,
(Mother of Student)

Negotiating is an important skill to learn because a college financial aid counselor has the authority to use professional judgment on a case-by-case basis. Third-party scholarships prove the point. The average award package is made up of 60 percent self-help funds from loans and/or jobs and 40 percent gift funds. When you receive an outside (third party) scholarship, some colleges want to take back their gift aid in like proportion, leaving you with the same amount of debt. Good negotiation may modify that disappointment by persuading the college to reduce each type of assistance in the award letter by 50 percent of the outside award.

Action Plan

A special circumstance you forgot to mention in your original financial aid request need not be earth-shattering as long as it is true and can help you negotiate more aid.

For example, suppose you win an outside scholarship of $2,000, and your award letter specifies a $3,500 loan and a $2,000 grant. You want your loan reduced by $1,000 and your grant reduced by $1,000. You don't want your grant reduced by $2,000, leaving you with $3,500 to pay off. If you don't fully understand the financial aid formulas and don't know what's going on, you're going to pay thousands of dollars more than you really have to. In any industry—and education is an industry—business managers try to get you to pay as much as possible, while you try to pay as little as possible.

After you've gathered all of your facts and made your appeal, ask whether it isn't better to have a student paying at a reduced rate than to have an empty seat in the classroom or an empty bed in the dorm. You need not mention an anemic enrollment, because school managers are well aware of the problem.

The Least You Need to Know

➤ Before you negotiate for more aid, first get all the facts about the colleges you're interested in.

➤ To negotiate a better financial aid option for yourself, support your position with adequate documentation.

➤ Consider every possible basis for making an appeal for more aid.

Part 5

Okay, You're Accepted and You Have Aid: Now What?

These chapters are full of advice for students who are about to begin a very challenging and exciting period of their lives. We give you ideas on how to earn while you learn and how to find work that can be a learning experience as well as a way to pay for some of your college expenses. We also give you tips and strategies on how to cut your living costs, and we tell you about the many innovative tuition plans that can trim your college bills.

Knock all bottles down, win a Scholarship

Chapter 22

Opportunities Are Everywhere

In This Chapter

➤ Learning how to make your own breaks by searching for money in the right places

➤ Discovering ways to grow your own opportunities by promoting yourself

➤ If you have to work, getting a job where you can learn and get a head start in your chosen field

This chapter focuses on individual actions you can take and choices you can make to ensure you'll continue to get financial aid. Perhaps none of our suggestions are startling news, but consider them timely reminders to act now to increase your chances for success in the future. Always remember that a good education and money go hand in hand. Unless you're one of the select few who wins an all-expenses-paid four-year tour, you will need to pay for your own education.

Continue to Get Good Grades

Granted, other criteria can win you college funds, but a stellar grade-point average can make you eligible for many financial aid programs. If you're not the type to blank out under pressure, test your mettle for money in academic competitions. Many merit-based scholarships consider test scores.

Look for Contest Money

You'd never guess that acting in school plays, painting still-life oils, or other hobbies you might have could be a cash cow in your future. The interests you develop during your high school years can indicate potential that may lead to scholarship dollars. Millions of contest dollars go out sponsors' doors each year to students who have honed their hobbies, activities, and talents to a competitive level. For example:

➤ **Communicative Arts scholarships**—Sponsored by the Educational Theater Association/International Thespian Society, these scholarships require a 2.7 or better GPA to enter the competition. However, your academic record doesn't count in the judging; your high school activities do. Selection criteria include, for example, an acting award you received for your performance in a high school play, and how well you do in an interview with the judges. Each year about 10 scholarships worth $1,000 each are awarded.

➤ **Graphic arts scholarships**—The National Scholarship Trust Fund offers this award program to high school and college undergraduate students who wish to pursue a career in graphic communications. Finalists are selected based on SAT/PSAT scores, transcripts, recommendation letters, and their demonstrated ability to apply graphic arts. Over 160 awards ranging between $500 and $4,000 go to winners annually.

➤ **Guideposts Youth Writing Contest**—*Guideposts* magazine sponsors this nonfiction contest, which pays better than what many professional writers earn for similar work. High school juniors and seniors are invited to write about their most memorable and inspiring true experience. The judges assess the originality of the writing; the sincerity of the author; and the values of kindness, spirituality, fairness, and morality expressed in the essay. Over 30 students annually win between $1,000 and $4,000.

Action Plan

Like it or not, getting good grades is the single best way to qualify for all kinds of financial aid programs that simply are not available to students who have poor grades.

Community Service Payoffs

While you are doing good works through volunteering in community service activities, you can simultaneously build career skills and leadership experience. Not only that, many community service organizations return the favor with scholarships toward your education.

For example:

➤ **Soroptimist Foundation's Regional Youth Citizenship Awards**—Scholarships are given on the basis of service, dependability, leadership, and sense of purpose. Academic criteria (grades, test scores) aren't considered. The foundation gives over 50 scholarships annually worth several hundred dollars each, plus one $2,000 scholarship to study abroad.

➤ **The Tylenol Scholarship Fund**—These scholarships recognize students who provide leadership in community and school activities. What counts? School awards, academic record, activities, and honors are considered. Each year, 500 scholarships worth $1,000 each and 10 awards of $10,000 each are passed to up-standing students.

➤ **The U.S. Senate Youth Program**—Sponsored by the William Randolph Hearst Foundation, this program acknowledges students who have been elected to leadership offices in their high school student governments. It distributes over 100 scholarships annually.

➤ **The Toyota Community Scholars Program**—Each year 100 students who show dedication to community service as well as academic leadership receive these awards. The program was launched in 1997 with a bang of big bucks: The four-year awards range from $10,000 to $20,000. To be considered, you must have initiated, or been actively involved in, a service program that addresses a school or community need.

Get an Inside Job

A part-time, student assistant job in the college's financial aid office can expose you to knowledge about how awards are determined and how students win them. Just by working in this office, you can pick up valuable information you may otherwise miss. Your close contact with the office's inner workings can unveil the perfect financial aid for you.

Working in the alumni office offers you opportunities to find out which alumni are helping financially strapped students complete their education. As an added benefit, if you can get to know the alums who do the talent scouting for their companies, they may offer you summertime work, or even a job after you graduate.

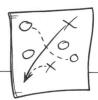

Action Plan

Have you ever heard the expression "It's who you know, not what you know"? This trite but true statement reflects reality. If you can land a job in an influential office on campus, you'll have access to important decision makers who can offer you all kinds of assistance, both during and after your college years.

Find a Sponsor

Are you a pleasant, sincere, hard-working, and deserving person? If so, you may be able to find a sponsor who will pay part or all of your way through college. If you think such generosity doesn't happen, it does: Multimillionaire Eugene Lang is well known for backing not just a single student but entire groups of students with his "I Have a Dream Project." Lang began with sixth-grade students at a Harlem school in New York City, promising that he'd pay for their college education if they graduated from high school. His program has since expanded into 20 cities.

If you want to find your own sponsor, you can't be shy about asking teachers, friends, professionals, and community leaders to recommend potential sponsors. Ask whether they'll introduce you to people who might undertake a sponsorship. An Arizona State University student turned his sponsor search into an art by passing out self-marketing packets containing his transcript, personal profile, and recommendation letters to potential sponsors. As a result of his effort, he received several private scholarships. If you're lucky enough to find a sponsor, be sure to keep in touch with him or her, and always say "thank you."

Market Yourself

Are you as good as you say you are? Well, of course you are. There are many organizations that are willing to sponsor a deserving student if the idea is properly presented to them. You might ask the question, Why would they be willing to do that? Most if not all organizations are keenly interested in maintaining an excellent public relations image. It's good for business. Offering a deserving student a scholarship is a great way to build their public profile through media coverage. They'll get free press releases, radio and local television exposure, plus lots of other free publicity that money can't buy.

You can't be shy when you start looking for a sponsor.

1. Start off by asking your friends and teachers for names of business and community leaders that you might talk to.

2. Call every major business that is, say, within a 25-mile radius of where you live and ask to speak to their public relations officer. Most public corporations have one. Smaller organizations may not have a public relations department, but they will usually have someone in their marketing department covering that function.

3. Many sponsor prospects will ask you to send a letter to formalize your request. Prepare a dynamite one-page letter that states what you're looking for (college sponsors, for example) and why you need the money (to pay for college tuition, for example), and gives a brief summary of your qualifications. Before you send out the letter, show it to as many friends and associates as you can to get their

opinions and ideas for improvement. Ask your high school English teacher to proofread it. See if your local newspaper will help you find sponsors or maybe even publish the letter in one of its daily editions.

Employment Program Opportunities

One way to reduce college costs is by working. Several studies indicate that most students who work between 10 and 20 hours a week actually do better academically. It is not unrealistic for a student to expect to earn between $2,000 and $4,000 during the school year. Summer employment can easily add $2,000 or more to your college funds. If you multiply that sum by the four years you'll spend in college, you can make a substantial contribution to your school expenses. That's money you will not have to borrow and your parents will not have to find.

When you think of working while you're going to college, look at it not only as an opportunity to earn a portion of your college expenses, but also as an integral part of your long-term career plan. Your college employment can be career-related or even lead to a job after graduation.

Federal, state, institutional, and private work programs are available to college students both on and off campus. Investigate all sources covered in this section. Some work arrangements offer free room and board in exchange for household help. Ask your school counselor whether this type of arrangement is available. Try to find part-time employment that is career-related; it will add to your job credentials when you graduate. You'll gain valuable experience and earn money at the same time.

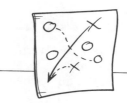

Action Plan

Your school's financial aid director, career counselor, and placement officer can all help you find the right job. Seek assistance and advice from the counselors in these offices and use the resources they can provide.

Work Experience Programs

Some colleges and universities award credits based on work experience, thereby reducing the number of courses and credits you're normally required to take to graduate. Check with your college's admissions office for further information on what you need to do to qualify. If you qualify, not only will you save on college fees, but also, by graduating early, you'll start earning money faster than you had originally planned.

Federal Work–Study Program

One of the most popular work programs is the *Federal Work-Study Program (FWS)*, which provides employment on and off campus for students in postsecondary institutions. Although the subject has been discussed throughout the book, it is worthy of additional coverage because, quite frankly, it's a great program.

Work-study is a need-based program that's administered through colleges' financial aid offices. The federal government pays 50 percent of the student's wage for private sector jobs and 70 percent if the student is employed on campus. Jobs are available to undergraduate, vocational, and graduate students. The dollar-earning amount allocated to students may vary from year to year based on funding levels. It is also limited by the students' financial needs, based on the amount of their allocations as determined by their financial aid directors.

Federal Work-Study funds are awarded along with other financial aid. To be considered for this program, students must be U.S. citizens or permanent residents and must be enrolled or accepted for enrollment at an eligible institution. They must also maintain satisfactory academic progress to stay in the program.

Student Educational Employment Program (SEEP)

The federal government's *Student Educational Employment Program (SEEP)* employs students through its internship and fellowship programs. Opportunities are available at both the high school and college levels.

High school students should seek the advice of their guidance counselors about employment opportunities under the Junior Fellowship Program (described later in this chapter).

College students may obtain information about SEEP federal internship opportunities from their school's financial aid office or employment office.

Institutional Employment Programs

Many schools have placement offices that help students find employment. Almost all schools have personnel offices that hire students to work on campus. These *institutional employment programs* are not need-based. Check with your college's personnel director for more information.

Most colleges and universities offer tuition reduction or waiver programs to their employees. Under this plan, school employees and their dependents receive either full tuition remission or partial reductions in tuition costs. These programs are not need-based and provide an excellent opportunity to attend college at practically no cost.

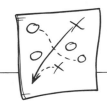

Action Plan

When you make your rounds of the various offices on campus looking for a part-time job, always ask the person you are talking to if he or she knows of any job opportunities in other campus offices. Make sure you get the name of the person you should talk to.

Private Sector Employment Programs

In *private sector employment programs,* local businesses hire students. Check with your school's placement office for a list of off-campus employment opportunities. Try to find a job in your major field of interest. You may be able to turn part-time student work into a full-time job after graduation.

Resident Adviser (RA) Program

A *resident adviser program* provides financial assistance to students in the form of reduced tuition or board costs in exchange for working in residence halls. The RA may live in the dorm and be responsible for students on his or her floor. Interested students should contact the dean of students on their campus for further information and eligibility requirements.

State Work–Study Programs

Many states provide employment to residents under *state-sponsored work-study programs.* These employment programs are administered by state organizations and follow most of the federal eligibility requirements. Check with your school's financial aid office or state Department of Education (see Appendix C) for further details.

Employer Tuition Plans

Employer tuition plans are the great unclaimed area of financial aid, with billions of dollars available to millions of employees. Unfortunately, many companies won't hire you for a good position until you have your college degree. But if you're willing to attend college part-time and start in a low-paying position, you'll find many companies that will pay for your higher education. Although directories of employers who have such programs are commercially available, they tend to be expensive; however, you can find these sources in the public library or through your school library or guidance counselor.

Companies that pay employees' education bills want to make sure they'll get their money's worth, so tuition plans generally come with a hitch or two. The most important hitch: You have to make the grade—that means a B or better. This is the way it works:

➤ In reimbursement plans, you put up the tuition money and you get the money back only when you've successfully completed the course—in some programs, "successfully" means a grade of B.

➤ In other programs the company pays upfront, but if you drop out or flunk, you have to reimburse your employer.

➤ You may have to prove that the courses you're taking are somehow related to your work. Still, an understanding boss can help you to frame your educational needs in such a way that they fit in nicely with company objectives.

Insight

According to the U.S. Department of Education, 40 percent of co-op students continue working for their co-op employer after graduation. Another 40 percent find work in fields directly related to their co-op assignments. Add up those percentages, and it's pretty easy to see that co-oping leads to jobs.

Help

For further information about cooperative programs, call or write: National Commission for Cooperative Education, 360 Huntington Avenue 384 CP, Boston, MA 02115-5096; or call 617-373-3770.

Cooperative Education

Each year over 250,000 college students work at "co-op" jobs. Over 1,000 colleges and universities participate in cooperative education.

In *co-op education,* you combine your time in the classroom with practical experience on the job. It's something for everyone: You the student get a job, and the employer gets a highly motivated workforce. Co-op programs not only put money in your pocket but also provide you with job contacts for the future. You get an opportunity to work in your chosen profession to make sure you're on the right career track. There's another significant advantage to consider. The firm for which you're working will often offer you a job after you graduate.

How Does the Co-Op Program Work?

Cooperative education programs allow students to alternate between working full-time and studying full-time. If you're in the program, it generally takes five years to complete a four-year bachelor's degree. Although the federal government remains the largest employer, many businesses participate in cooperative education programs. These programs are not based on financial need and are available to undergraduate and graduate students, and students seeking professional degrees. The most important and attractive feature of employment programs is matching the students' future career plans with relevant employment.

Who's in the Program?

Roughly 1,000 colleges have cooperative programs of some kind or another; in some schools virtually all the students are in cooperative education programs. Some 50,000 employers hire on the co-op plan, including the largest provider of co-op jobs, the federal government, which hires nearly 12,000 students each year.

The Program Takes Time

Co-oping takes time. Whether you alternate semesters of work and study or work part-time while attending school, the programs usually require five years. Still, 200,000 students each year seem to feel the time is worth spending.

Get Help from Associates

If you've decided on a career to pursue, you may be eligible for aid from the professional association that specializes in your career field. If you want to get financial aid in your chosen career field and want to get a head start, you should consider attending a college that has a cooperative education program. But if your school doesn't provide such programs, then you might be able to get help from the appropriate professional association.

There is an industry group for almost every trade and profession, from dental hygienists to hotel managers to wine experts. Most of this money gravitates toward schools that have well-regarded programs in the field, engineering at MIT, for example.

For suggestions on the strongest schools in your career area, you should consult guides such as *Ruggs Recommendations on the Colleges*. Still, many professional groups offer "portable" scholarships that are not tied to a particular school.

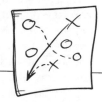

Action Plan

There are literally thousands of professional and trade associations worldwide, and we could not include all of them in Appendix B. Associations are easy to find in reference books such as *Gales Encyclopedia of Associations*. The book is available at the research desks of most libraries and provides descriptions, addresses, and telephone numbers of national and international associations. Once you have the addresses, write and request their scholarship information. Include a stamped, self-addressed envelope to ensure a prompt response.

Junior Fellowship Program

The *Junior Fellowship Program* resembles cooperative education but has some important differences. For one, your boss is the federal government. For another, you join the program in high school, but you don't begin working until you're in college, when you work during term breaks. You apply to the program through your high school guidance counselor. If your high school guidance counselor doesn't have information on the Junior Fellowship Program, contact: Director, Office of Personnel Management, 1900 E Street NW, Washington, D.C. 20415. Unlike cooperative education, which is offered only through certain schools, junior fellows can attend any college of their choice.

To qualify for a Junior Fellowship, you must have very good grades and prove financial need. Although the program is limited to 5,000 participants at a time, it historically has had vacancies. What a great opportunity!

Other Sources of Aid

Many organizations provide scholarships, though the amounts are usually small. If you've already received all you're going to get from the major sources of financial aid—federal government, state government, and college programs—you may be able to get additional money from sources you haven't considered previously.

Help

You can get some college aid information from local unions. To get the fullest picture, write for the comprehensive AFL-CIO guide, which is free to members: AFL-CIO Guide to Union Sponsored Scholarships, Awards, and Student Financial Aid; Department of Publications, AFL-CIO; 815 16th Street NW; Washington, D.C. 20006; or call 202-637-5000.

Your Local Government

Your city, county, or even your school district may have scholarship money or other special programs for you to consider. Although many of these programs amount to only a few hundred dollars, some do offer significant funds, like in the thousands. Finding them involves investigative work on your part, since relatively few of them make their way into the big scholarship databases. But you can find them: Your high school or college financial aid officer should have some information about local government programs. Your local Chamber of Commerce may have leads as well. Watch for scholarships in the news section of your local newspaper or in a national newspaper such as *USA Today*.

Unions

Many unions offer college grants for the education of their members' children. Information about some of these programs can be found in the scholarship roster or listing that you can get by contacting the union's business office. However, for more specific information, contact the union's main office. Union programs are offered by both the national organization and the local chapters.

Community Organizations

Don't forget to check into scholarship programs available from community organizations.

An example is the American Legion, which offers a multitude of awards, including a $2,000 scholarship at the national level for children of veterans called the American Legion Auxiliary National President's Scholarship. They also sponsor a National High School Oratorical Contest with a grand prize of $16,000, and many $1,000 scholarships. The Legion is most valuable to students who are the children of veterans, but any student can apply.

Help

For the most up-to-date listing of the American Legion's programs and contests, you should send $3 dollars to get a copy of *Need a Lift?* Write to: The American Legion National Emblem Sales, P.O. Box 1050, Indianapolis, IN 46206; or call 317-630-1200.

Religious Organizations

Churches and religious organizations also grant money to college-bound students. Groups like the Aid Association for Lutherans host contests and offer scholarships and loans. Find these groups through your church's business office. You can find the addresses and telephone numbers of most religious organizations listed in *Gales Encyclopedia of Associations*.

You may run into a few restrictions, including a requirement of religious study or attendance at a church-sponsored school.

The Least You Need to Know

➤ Maintaining good grades is a prerequisite to getting ahead.

➤ Contest money is everywhere if you know where to find it—and it's fun to go after!

➤ Employer tuition plans are plentiful, and a great way to mix learning with earning.

➤ Community service programs and part-time jobs can give you an early start on your career, along with making you some extra money.

Chapter 23

Cost-Cutting Strategies

In This Chapter

➤ Discovering how to cram four years of college into three, and save a bundle

➤ Finding out how you can get a head start by taking college classes while you're still in high school

➤ Knowing why you should consider two-year colleges first before you leap into a four-year institution

➤ Uncovering innovative tuition plans you never knew existed

➤ Learning how to cut unnecessary expenditures

If you're looking for ways to reduce the costs of going to college, then this chapter was written for you. We identify a variety of approaches that you can apply to substantially reduce college expenses. Some of these strategies require a financial or academic about-face, whereas others call for minor changes in lifestyle.

The Three-Year Program

Most students finish college in four or five years, but a lot of students are now graduating in three years. How? In a *three-year program,* you carry 20 hours per semester and attend college in the summer to pick up the extra credits you need.

Even though you'll have extra bills for summer tuition, your total tab will fall well below what you'd pay over four years. You'll also enter the job market ahead of your class, which gives you an extra year of income and seniority over your classmates. That might even be enough to get that sports car you've always wanted!

Action Plan

Although colleges don't like to talk about it, most of them can offer you a three-year degree program if you'll just ask. Their three-year programs are not widely publicized because colleges would rather collect tuition and fees from you for four years. You owe it to yourself to ask the admissions office what you would need to do to graduate in three years, even if you plan to graduate in four. You'll at least know what your options are if you need to reduce costs.

Think of how much money you could save if you graduated in three years instead of the normal four. For example, if you're spending $12,000 a year for college, you could potentially save $12,000 by cutting a year out of the program. How do you do that? A typical full-time student must earn 15 credits per semester, or 120 total semester credits, to graduate in four years. To complete 120 credits in three years, you would need to earn 20 credits per semester (120 ÷ 6 semesters). That's a heavy load, and not all students would be able to accommodate it. However, if you're willing to go to summer school, you can earn the additional 10 credits you need without changing your 15-credit workload.

Insight

The International Baccalaureate (IB) Program offers college preparatory courses at some high schools in the United States and abroad. If you are interested in participating in the program, visit their Web site at: www.iastate. edu/~adm_info/cbe_ib.html.

Take College Classes in High School

Another way to decrease college costs, if your high school allows it, is to attend a nearby college and take up to 12 semester hours of college-level courses before you graduate from high school. You may have to meet certain selection criteria, and your options may be few because your hours of attendance would be limited, but you'd have a head start on college.

Advanced Programs

The College Board has agreements with more than half of the nation's colleges to honor its *Advanced Program (AP)* exams, which give credit to students who take AP classes and pass the exams. More than 150,000 students take AP exams annually, and two-thirds of them pass. Needless to say, if you pass an AP exam, you save on tuition by not having to take that course. More than 10,000 students were eligible last year to place-out of all freshman year courses.

The College Board offers over 20 tests covering English, calculus, American history, European history, biology, chemistry, physics, computer science, art, music, and many languages.

Go to a Community College First

Two-year community colleges are among the best buys in higher education. Their courses cost about half of those at four-year institutions, and the first two years of general education courses are roughly the same, no matter where you attend college. When money's a problem, beginning your studies at a community college is your best solution.

If you can manage to afford doubling up on your community college classes and going to summer school, you could be out in a little over a year. When you join a four-year institution as a junior, you'll be a half-year ahead of the game and will have saved a bundle on tuition.

Most community colleges coordinate their curricula with four-year institutions, so check that your four-year college or university will accept the credits you earn at a two-year institution before you sign up for specific classes. Contact an admissions counselor at the four-year institution you plan to attend and ask which community college courses will transfer for full credit. Get the counselor to sign the agreed-upon list of transferable courses for your records. Don't accept an oral agreement that certain courses will transfer for credit; you could find out when the time comes that the college won't give you the credits and the college official you've talked to has no recollection of the conversation.

Help

You can take the AP tests through your school for a fee of $50 per test. Some high schools will subsidize the costs of the tests for students. Contact the College Board, 45 Columbus Avenue, New York, New York 10023 for more information.

Warning

If you take courses at a community or junior college, make sure in advance that the four-year college(s) of your choice will allow you to transfer every credit you earn. The college admissions office can provide you with this information.

Co-Op Your Way Through

Wouldn't you like to gain some hands-on experience so that upon graduation you won't be considered a rookie when you enter the job market? *Cooperative education programs* allow you to gain "real world" experience as you complete your education. You study some, work some throughout your college years, and earn money as you go. Over a thousand colleges operate cooperative education programs in which students typically take about five years to complete an undergraduate degree.

One of the problems that new college graduates face when they search for a job is their lack of work-related experience. The first question a potential employer is likely to ask is, "Do you have any experience that will qualify you for this job?" Wouldn't it be great to answer with a resounding "Yes"? You could do that if you become a co-op student, alternating semesters of study with work for a company in your chosen field. And, you get paid for it!

The potential downside is that you will probably take longer to graduate because of your work schedule, but at least you'll have some money to help pay for college. Many students earn enough money through cooperative programs to pay for all of their college expenses. When you graduate, you may even have an opportunity to go to work full-time for the company that you've been working for. You'll get to know each other; and after you graduate, if there's a job in your field, you could be in.

Action Plan

Magazines such as *Money* and *US News & World Report* annually publish reports on bargain schools where tuitions are modestly priced and the educational standards are high.

Help

If you need more information about cooperative education programs, you can order *A College Guide to Cooperative Education*—free, from the National Commission for College Education, 360 Huntington Ave, Boston, MA 02115. You can also check out work-study programs at: www.collegefundingonline.com.

Earn While You Learn

Yet another moneysaving option is to work, either part-time or full-time, while taking a partial or a full load of classes. Granted, working part-time and attending college full-time can take all your energy and time, but more students than ever have to double up on work and school to pay for everything. And literally thousands of students, many of them parents, do it the other way around: They hold full-time jobs and attend school part-time. The University of Phoenix is exclusively a night program school and has over 50,000 students enrolled.

Challenge Classes

Many colleges will release you from having to take required course work if you can prove you know the material well enough not to need the course. It's known as taking *challenge classes*. Ask at your college admissions office about obtaining credits for passing tests without taking courses or about receiving credits by providing relevant proof of life experience. For example, let's say you have worked with computers either in a job or in the military, you could escape a required $600 computer competency course, or you could take the school's computer competency exam. If you pass (test-out), that's one less course you'll have to take.

Innovative Tuition Plans

Most colleges and universities increase their tuition fees annually, and because they are the benevolent souls they are, they're always looking for ways to take the sting out of paying tuition. Most offer programs that allow you to pay on monthly plans rather than having to pay in one or two annual lump sums. There are as many programs as there are colleges, and programs at different schools that sound similar may have significant differences between them.

Help

If you want a free booklet explaining testing-out procedures, order *Information for Candidates* from College-Level Examination Programs, The College Board, Box 886, New York, New York 10101.

Colleges are also getting smarter about giving students and their families more ways to pay for college. Many schools now allow tuition to be paid through regular electronic fund transfers from bank accounts or through credit cards.

Installment Plans

More colleges now allow students to pay tuition on an *installment plan*. Installments plans can run monthly, two payments per semester, or they can be stretched out over several years. Check with your school for more details.

Banks and private companies are also working with colleges to create installment-plan tuition programs. Many colleges manage their own installment plans, while others have private companies run them. Contact your state's guaranty agency (listed in Appendix B) for more information on college installment plans.

Prepayment Discounts

Schools like having money in the bank, and the sooner they get it, the better. They can earn interest on it and invest it, which is why they're willing to make attractive offers to you in return for getting money quickly.

Many colleges offer *prepayment discounts* on tuition for students who pay their entire tuition in a single up-front payment. It can save you in excess of 10 percent. Contact your state's guaranty agency (see Appendix B) for more information about advanced tuition plans.

Help

There's no substitute for getting the full description of all of your school's programs from the school itself. However, if you need a broad survey of programs available at different schools, you can order a chart-filled paperback from College Check Mate, Octameron Associates, P.O. Box 2748, Alexandria, VA 22301.

Leadership Programs

Some schools offer tuition breaks for students who are willing to take leadership roles in student organizations, such as student government. Participation in student referral programs and a variety of other programs may also produce discounts. Check to see whether the college you want to attend offers any of the programs in the following sections.

Legacy Programs

Some schools reduce tuition for children of alumni in programs referred to as *legacy programs*. Many schools now offer discounts for referring other family members to their "sacred halls." They may also give a tuition discount for convincing a friend to attend.

Test the Waters Programs

Some colleges are letting prospective students *test the waters* during their first semester by attending at a discount to see whether they like the place.

Tuition-Matching Programs

Some private schools now offer *tuition-matching programs* in which they match tuition with public schools to stay competitive. Many states offer scholarship programs to equalize tuition rates between public and private schools.

Moral Obligation Scholarships

Moral obligation scholarships are gifts from the school to you that are granted with a "moral obligation" to pay back the money after graduation. These programs pack a potent tax benefit. Since the payback is technically construed to be a gift to the school, the student gets a tax deduction. Colleges are constantly thinking up new, headline-grabbing alternatives. Keep an eye on the media for gift programs that pop up unexpectedly.

You can expect moral obligation scholarships to be scrutinized by the IRS. In fact, any program that promises to help people save money for college at low tax rates will attract the attention of the IRS. So it's important to check with the school to see whether the IRS has ruled that the school's "too-good-to-be-true" program really is too good to be true.

Warning

It's a fact of life! Many of the great college tuition plans end up running afoul of the IRS sooner or later. One previously popular method of saving for college—shifting assets to children in order to take advantage of lower taxation rates for parents—has been all but eliminated by changes in the tax laws. The IRS is already taking a hard look at long-term tuition prepayment plans.

Wait Before You Buy Anything

College students tend to use shopping sprees to escape from study sessions. Somehow, they get their parents to spring for new wardrobes and dorm supplies, forgetting that materialistic trappings rarely improve higher learning. As a rule of thumb, don't buy anything until you know you really need it.

Before you buy any clothes, first see what your classmates are wearing. A surprising amount of money is wasted on new clothes that never leave a student's closet. The best wardrobe investments you'll make during college will be the cap and gown you'll wear during the graduation ceremony and the suits you'll need for job interviews.

Watch for student discounts on everything you buy. Put every practical need like clothes, bookshelves, and computer equipment on a wish list. Share it with relatives near major holidays.

If you're as preoccupied as most students, you may think that take-out food costs the same as grocery store food. Those $5 fast food meals twice a day add up to $300 per month!

If you buy food items, buy in bulk whenever it makes sense. Bulk items are typically 25 percent cheaper per weight of measure than their smaller counterpart packages. Use an electric frying pan to fix your own meals. Save your money and get a small re-frigerator that will fit under your desk; then you can buy soft drinks and healthy snacks in quantity from a supermarket, and store them in the frig.

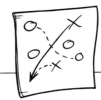

Action Plan

Watch for student discounts. When you walk into any store to buy whatever, automatically ask, "Do you offer student discounts?" Many stores do but don't advertise it. Some that don't may offer you a one-time discount. You can also ask when items you're interested in buying will be going on sale.

Schedule your travel well in advance of known travel dates. That's when you'll find the discounted tickets, not two days before Thanksgiving.

Buy Used Books

Try not to choke when you discover what it costs to buy a single textbook these days. Some of the ways you can cut textbook costs are:

➤ Always buy used books if you can, which can save you as much as 50 to 75 per-cent of the new book price. Look for bookstores on or off campus that sell used books. If the store wants you to buy the "new" book because it has just been "revised," ask your instructor whether the revisions are significant enough to warrant buying new as opposed to used.

➤ Check with your friends who are taking the same classes you'll be taking next semester. They might be interested in selling or trading their books when they've finished their courses.

➤ College bookstores often have exclusives on assigned textbooks, so try to buy their used ones. They can cost half of what you'd pay for a comparable new textbook.

➤ Don't automatically believe the book list you're told to get for your classes. Talk to your instructor before the first day of class and find out which books you should have first, and take it from there. You may not really need all the books on the instructor's list. If you do, you may have plenty of extra time to shop for a good used one.

➤ If a course requires an especially pricey book and you don't expect to ever read it again after the final, see whether you can check it out of the library.

➤ Sell or trade any textbooks you don't plan to use again.

Travel Smart

Some college towns are so well designed that you won't need a car most of the time. A friend's car, a bus, a subway, or a taxi can come in handy occasionally (and there's always walking), but the expense of purchasing, maintaining, parking, fueling, and paying insurance on your own car can eat up sparse dollars. Consider saving your money for your dream car after you graduate. Schedule your trips home when a friend is driving to your area, so you can share expenses.

Other Cost-Cutting Moneymaking Strategies

Allow your mind to wander as you think about all of the possible ways you can save money or even make money when you go to college. We cover some ideas for you to think about in this section.

Live at Home

Some families save money by having their kid live at home. This option saves dorm or apartment rental costs and looks very attractive on the surface. Yet there are a number of hidden costs to staying at home, the least of which is losing out on a major part of the college social experience by not being at the center of things. Another is commuting costs, which can cut away at the money that living at home saves.

Another reason why staying at home is more expensive than it looks is food. Students who live at home won't be able to eat all meals at home because of the odd hours they keep. They'll spend more money in campus-area eateries, while students in dorms buy a relatively inexpensive meal plan or keep small refrigerators stocked. Meal plans may be available for nondormers and are worth looking into.

Barter for Deals

Some colleges will make a deal with parents to exchange a wide range of gifts for tuition. Almost any type of property can be swapped under such a program. Even if the college can't use what you have to offer, they might resell it; this occurs often when corporations make odd gifts to schools, such as yachts, for tax purposes. Ask about a barter program at the college.

Find Your Own Deal

Instead of relying on your college for a moderate- to low-paying work-study job, why not strike out on your own? If you have an entrepreneurial flair, you might find that a little investment of time and effort can provide you with a comfortable living while you're in school and after. Michael Dell began selling computers while he was in college—now his company sells millions of dollars worth of computers each year under the Dell Computer logo.

Become a Part-Time Salesperson

You might find plenty of sales opportunities in your student group. Students know students. Find an item that you need and that they need. Buy it in bulk and offer it to others who share your need. This same strategy is responsible for the proliferation of student-run services that offer discounts on everything from computer diskettes to lecture notes.

Help

For students interested in the entrepreneurial route, one book could serve as a wellspring of ideas: *How to Pay Your Way Through College (The Smart Way)*, by John J. Lyons ($7.95, Banbury Books). This lively book presents more than 50 money-making opportunities for college students, ranging from resumé-writing to selling cut-rate diskettes and CDs.

Learn to think like an entrepreneur, and you'll come up with all kinds of creative ways to finance your college education.

The clearinghouse for information on entrepreneurship in college is the Association of College Entrepreneurs, a group founded by college students in 1983, which now numbers more than 4,500 members. It's based in Wichita, Kansas, but has local chapters nationwide. And your own campus business department might have people who can give you pointers: More than 600 schools across the nation have entrepreneurship courses.

In conclusion, I sincerely hope that my book lived up to your expectations. It should be clear to you by now that there are literally thousands of financial aid opportunities out there for you and your kids to explore. And, with the current political environment favoring enhanced educational programs, you can look forward to increased funding for all financial aid programs.

The trick is to know how to find and apply for financial aid. If you check out the comprehensive appendixes in this book, they'll help you seek out and find the opportunities that are right for you. There are also hundreds of Web sites that cover every aspect of the financial aid process. All of the major ones are listed in Appendix B. I wish you the best of luck in your search for the financial aid your family deserves.

The Least You Need to Know

➤ There are all kinds of ways of graduating from college in three instead of four years.

➤ Working part-time while you're in school offers you an opportunity to gain "real world" working experience and earn some money at the same time.

➤ The myriad innovative tuition plans are well worth looking into.

➤ If you watch how you spend your money, you can save a bundle.

Glossary of Financial Aid Terms

AA   An associate of arts degree. Can be earned at most two-year colleges.

AAMC   American Association of Medical Colleges.

AAS   An Associate of Applied Science degree. Can be earned at some two-year colleges.

academic year   A measure of academic work to be accomplished by a student. A school defines its own academic year, but federal statute and regulations set minimum standards to determine federal financial aid awards.

accounting period   The time period for which financial records are maintained and at the end of which financial statements are prepared.

accrual basis   Type of accounting under which income is recorded when earned.

accrued interest   Interest on a loan that is not paid during the period of the loan but accumulates and is paid in installments at a later time.

achievement tests   Tests required by some colleges to measure student achievement in specific areas of study, such as English, Math, or Science.

ACT test   Published by American College Testing to measure a student's ability in math, verbal comprehension, and problem solving. Usually taken by students during their junior or senior year of high school.

adjusted gross income (AGI)   Taxable income after all allowable tax deductions are made.

advanced placement (AP) test   Test used to earn credit for college subjects studied in high school and scored on a scale from 1 to 5 (the best possible score).

aid package   A combination of financial aid (scholarships, grants, loans, and/or work-study) determined by the financial aid office of a college or university. See also *award letter*.

ALP   Alternative Loan Program that is used to supplement the funds students need to attend college.

amortization   The process of gradually repaying a loan over an extended period of time through periodic installments of principal and interest.

annual percentage rate (APR)   The total annual cost of a loan, including all fees and interest.

APR   See *annual percentage rate.*

asset protection   A sum subtracted from a family's total assets when determining the expected family contribution to college costs.

assets   The amount a family has in savings and investments. This includes savings and checking accounts; a business; a farm or other real estate; and stocks, bonds, and trust funds.

ASVAB (Armed Services Vocational Aptitude Battery)   A test designed to measure aptitude in 10 different career-related skills.

award   A specific amount of financial assistance to pay for education costs, offered to a student through one or more financial aid programs.

award adjustment or revision   An action by a financial aid office resulting in an increase, decrease, program-source substitution, or cancellation of a student's financial aid award.

award letter   An official document issued by a financial aid office listing all the financial aid awarded to the student. Also see *aid package.*

award year   An award year begins on July 1 of one year and extends to June 30 of the next year.

BA and BS   Bachelor of Arts and Bachelor of Science, respectively.

base year   For need-analysis purposes, the base year is the calendar year preceding the award year.

borrower   Anyone who obtains money from a lender. The borrower signs a promissory note, which serves as the formal promise to repay the loan.

business office   The school office responsible for an institution's financial accounting, including Title IV aid program activity. The office disburses financial aid award payments to students.

campus-based programs   Financial aid programs administered by the university. The federal government provides the university with a fixed annual allocation.

cancellation of a loan   Nullifying the borrower's obligation to repay all or a designated portion of the principal and interest on a student loan upon the condition that the borrower has met specific requirements. It may also be referred to as *discharge.*

CASHE (College Aid Sources for Higher Education)   Free financial aid service offered by Sallie Mae.

certificate   Award granted for the successful completion of a sub-baccalaureate program of studies.

citizen eligibility requirements   To be eligible for federal student aid, the borrower must be either a U.S. citizen; U.S. national (including natives of American Samoa or Swain's Island); or U.S. permanent resident (who has an I-151, I-551, or I-551C [Alien Registration Card]).

claim   An application made to a guarantor for payment of an insured student loan because of loss of payment due to borrower's death, total and permanent disability, bankruptcy, default, or school closure.

COA (cost of attendance)   The total cost of attending a postsecondary institution for one academic year.

coborrower   Person who signs a promissory note in addition to the borrower and is responsible for the obligation if the borrower does not pay.

consolidation loan   Combines several loans into one loan. This sometimes results in a lower interest rate, for example when a consumer loan is used to pay off high-interest credit card balances.

collateral   Something of value pledged as security for a loan. Banks do not require collateral for all loans.

college   A postsecondary school that offers general or liberal arts education, usually leading to an associate's, bachelor's, master's, doctor's, or first professional degree. Junior colleges and community colleges are included under this terminology.

College Board   A nonprofit membership organization of colleges, secondary schools, and education associations that administers the SATs and runs the College Scholarship Service.

College Scholarship Service   Arm of the College Board and one of the agencies that process financial aid information and applications.

commercial bank   An institution whose primary function is making loans to businesses.

cosigner   A second creditworthy party who signs a promissory note with a borrower who does not have collateral or a good credit history.

default   Failure to repay a loan in accordance with the terms of the promissory note. Default can also occur if a student fails to submit a request for deferment or discharge (cancellation) in a timely manner.

deferment of a loan   A period of postponement during which the repayment of loan principal is suspended because the borrower meets one or more deferment requirements established by law.

deferred interest   Interest payments that are delayed while a borrower is not gainfully employed.

delinquency   You are delinquent if your payment is not received by the due date. Delinquencies greater than 30 days are reported to national credit bureaus.

dependency status   The degree to which the student is expected to have access to parental financial resources. An independent student is one who is 24 years old.

dependent student   A student who, under federal criteria, is considered to be financially dependent on his or her parents or guardians. Most full-time students are considered dependent until they are 24 years old.

Direct Loan   See *Federal Direct Loan Program.*

disbursement   The release of loan funds to a school for delivery to the borrower. Disbursements are usually made in equal multiple installments copayable to the borrower and the school.

discharge   The release of a borrower from the obligation to repay his or her loan.

disclosure statement   A statement of the total cost and amount of a loan, including the interest rate and any additional finance charges.

doctor's degree   An earned degree carrying the title of Doctor. The Doctor of Philosophy degree (Ph.D.) is the highest academic degree and requires mastery within a field of knowledge and demonstrated ability to perform scholarly research. Other doctorates are awarded for fulfilling specialized requirements in professional fields, such as education (Ed.D.), musical arts (D.M.A.), business administration (D.B.A.), and engineering (D.Eng. or D.E.S.).

DRN   Data release number. A number appearing on the Student Aid Report (SAR) in the upper right corner of the first page (next to the printed EFC). It is needed to identify the appropriate FAFSA data for release to schools beyond the six (maximum) listed by the student in the original FAFSA submission.

due diligence   The requirement by the federal government that a lender, holder, or servicer exercise reasonable care and diligence in the making, servicing, and collection of insured federal student loans in order to retain the insurance (against default claims) of the loans.

early action   A college admissions program that consists of earlier deadlines and notification dates than for the regular admissions process, but that does not require a binding commitment from the student to enroll if admission is offered.

early decision   A college admissions program that consists of earlier deadlines and notification dates than for the regular admissions process, and that requires a student's binding commitment to enroll if admission is offered.

education IRA   A tax-deferred savings and investment account for educational expenses. Parents are allowed to put away $500 a year for each child or grandchild under the age of 18. Contributions aren't tax-deductible, but withdrawals are tax-free. The money must be used by the time the student turns 30.

Educational Testing Service   The company that produces and administers the SAT and other educational achievement tests. Also known as ETS.

EFC   Expected family contribution. The amount a family is expected to contribute to a student's education, based on family earnings, net assets, savings, size of family, and number of siblings in college.

eligible institution   A public or private nonprofit institution of higher education, a postsecondary vocational school, or a proprietary institution of higher education that meets all the criteria to participate in Title IV student financial aid programs.

eligible program   A course of study that requires a certain minimum number of hours of instruction and period of time and that leads to a degree or certificate.

endowment   Funds owned by an institution and invested to produce income to support the operation of the institution.

enrollment status   An indication of whether you are a full-time or part-time student. Generally you must be enrolled at least half-time (and in some cases full-time) to qualify for financial aid.

entitlement counseling   Students with federal educational loans are required to receive counseling before they receive their first loan disbursement. The borrower's rights and responsibilities and the loan terms and conditions are reviewed with the student.

exit counseling   Students with federal educational loans are required to receive counseling before they graduate or withdraw (leave school), during which the borrower's rights and responsibilities and loan terms and conditions are reviewed with the student.

expected family contribution   See *EFC.*

extended repayment plan   A recent addition to repayment options for the federal loan programs that extends the repayment terms on federally sponsored loans.

FAA   See *financial aid administrator.*

FAFSA (Free Application for Federal Student Aid)   The form that must be completed by students and parents when applying for Federal Title IV student aid.

FAT (financial aid transcript)   A record of all federal aid received by students at each school attended.

Federal Direct Consolidated Loan   A loan arranged through the U.S. Department of Education's Direct Loan Servicing Center. The loan is designed to combine Title IV education loans (including non–Direct Loans) into a single loan with one monthly repayment.

Federal Direct Education Loan (FFEL) Program   Group of federal education loans that include Federal Stafford Loans (both subsidized and unsubsidized), Federal PLUS (parent) Loans, and Federal Consolidation Loans. All of these are long-term loans insured by state or private nonprofit guaranty agencies that are reimbursed by the federal government for all or part of the insurance claims paid to lenders.

Federal Direct Loan Program   Program of four types of education loans to student and parent borrowers: Federal Direct Stafford/Ford Loan, Federal Direct Unsubsidized Stafford/Ford Loan, Federal Direct PLUS Loan, and Federal Direct Consolidation Loan.

Federal Direct Stafford Loan   Federally financed low-interest loan that is government-subsidized only when based on student financial need.

Federal Family Education Loan Program (FFELP)   Stafford and PLUS loans, which are financed by private lenders and guaranteed by the federal government.

Federal Methodology Formula   Used to determine an expected family contribution (EFC) for Pell Grants, campus-based programs, FFEL programs, and Direct Loan programs.

Federal Pell Grant Payment and Disbursement Schedules   Charts published annually by the U.S. Secretary of Education. They determine the dollar value of student Federal Pell Grant awards on the basis of schools' costs of attendance (COA) and students' Expected Family Contributions (EFC).

Federal Pell Grant Program   A need-based grant program for undergraduate students who have not completed a first baccalaureate degree.

Federal Perkins Loan (FPL) Program   Campus-based loan program providing low-interest student loans to undergraduate and graduate students with financial need.

Federal PLUS Loan   Loans for parents borrowing for the education of their dependent children.

Federal Processor   The organization that processes the information submitted on the Free Application for Federal Student Aid (FAFSA) and uses it to compute eligibility for federal student aid.

Federal Register   Government publication published each weekday that prints regulations, regulatory amendments, notices, and proposed regulatory changes for all federal executive agencies.

Federal Student Aid Information Center (FSAIC)   The office associated with the Department of Education that assists students and families in applying for financial aid from the federal government.

Federal Student Financial Aid Handbook   The Department of Education publication that explains procedures that schools should follow in administering federal student financial aid (SFA) programs.

Federal Supplemental Educational Opportunity Grant (FSEOG) Program A campus-based and need-based aid program that provides grant assistance to students in undergraduate programs who have not earned a bachelor's degree or first professional degree.

Federal Work-Study Program A program providing part-time jobs for undergraduate and graduate students with financial need.

fellowship A form of aid given primarily to graduate students to help support their education.

financial aid Financial assistance in the form of scholarships, grants, work-study, and loans for education.

financial aid administrator (FAA) A college or university employee involved in administering financial aid. Also known as financial aid advisor, officer, or counselor.

financial aid award The total amount of financial aid (federal and nonfederal) in scholarships, grants, loans, and/or work-study that a student has been awarded. Also called a financial aid package.

financial aid officer See *financial aid administrator.*

financial aid package See *financial aid award.*

financial aid transcript A record of all federal aid received by students at each school attended.

financial need Difference between the cost of attendance at a college and the Expected Family Contribution (EFC). Also known as financial aid eligibility.

financial responsibility An institution's demonstrated ability to responsibly participate in federal Title IV student aid programs.

forbearance on a loan A *temporary* cessation or reduction of payment amounts allowed by an FFEL lender (or the U.S. Department of Education for Direct Loans) for subsidized or unsubsidized Federal Stafford, Federal PLUS, Federal Perkins, or Federal Direct Loans.

General Educational Development (GED) Test A test administered by the American Council on Education as the basis for awarding high school equivalency certification.

gift aid Financial aid, generally in the form of a grant or scholarship, that a student is not required to repay or earn through employment.

grace period The time period beginning the day after a loan recipient ceases to be enrolled at least half-time, and ending the day before the loan repayment period starts.

Graduate Record Examination (GRE) Multiple-choice examination administered by the Educational Testing Service (ETS) and taken by applicants who plan to attend certain graduate schools.

graduate student A student in a postsecondary institution who is enrolled in a master's or higher-level degree program.

graduated repayment A repayment schedule in which the monthly payments are smaller at the start of the repayment period and become larger later on.

grants Financial aid awards that do not have to be repaid. Grants are available through the federal government, state agencies, and colleges.

gross income Income before taxes, deductions, and allowances have been subtracted.

guaranty agency A state agency or private nonprofit institution that insures student loans for lenders and helps administer the federal loan programs.

holder The institution that owns a loan.

home equity line of credit A variation of the home equity loan that allows a homeowner to draw money (write checks) against his or her home's equity on an ongoing basis.

HOPE Scholarship Provides a family with a tax credit of up to $1,500 maximum per year for two years for each dependent student.

independent student A student who is either married, 24 years of age or older, enrolled in a graduate or professional education program, has legal dependents other than a spouse, is an orphan or ward of the court, or is a veteran of the U.S. Armed Forces.

individual retirement account (IRA) Individual tax-deferred savings and investment account meant to accumulate funds for retirement.

information review form A document associated with the Student Aid Report (SAR) on which the borrower can correct any incorrect information on the SAR.

institutional loan A loan specific to a college, university, or other postsecondary educational institution.

institutional methodology A specific formula used by a college or university to determine financial need for allocation of the school's own financial aid funds.

institutional student information record A report about a student sent by the Department of Education to the student's chosen schools after the student's application for federal aid has been received via the FAFSA.

insurance An agreement between the guaranty agency and the lender in which the guaranty agency agrees to reimburse the lender for its losses on claims.

insurance fee   A fee charged by guaranty agencies that is deducted from loan proceeds and used to insure against defaulted loans.

interest subsidy   Interest the federal government pays on certain loans during authorized deferment or grace periods or while borrowers are in school.

interest-only payment   Payment that covers only accrued interest owed on a loan but that does not prohibit borrowers from making additional or larger payments at any time.

international student   A student who is not a citizen or resident of the United States and intends to attend, or is attending, a college, university, or other postsecondary educational institution in the United States.

internship   A type of part-time job in which a student receives supervised learning and work experience during the academic year or the summer months.

Leveraging Educational Assistance Partnership (LEAP) Program   A program that provides grant aid for education costs to postsecondary students with substantial financial need through matching formula grants to the states.

Lifetime Learning Tax Credit   A tax credit of up to $1,000 per family per tax year for postsecondary education courses. Claimant must file a tax credit and owe taxes for that tax year.

loan counseling   Students with federal educational loans are required to receive counseling before they receive their first loan disbursement.

loan disclosure statement   A statement sent to a loan borrower by the lender before or at the time a loan is disbursed and before the start of the repayment period.

master promissory note   The note a student signs when taking out a Stafford Loan (subsidized or unsubsidized).

National Service Trust   A U.S. national community service program. If you participate in this program before attending college, its funds may be used to pay your educational expenses.

National Student Loan Clearinghouse   A central repository for the collection of postsecondary enrollment status and related information.

need-based analysis   The formula used to determine a student's need for financial assistance for college expenses. It determines the family's ability to contribute to the student's cost of attendance.

net income   Income after taxes, deductions, and allowances have been subtracted.

National Merit Scholastic Qualifying Test (NMSQT)   A test given during the junior year of high school in the form of the Preliminary Scholastic Assessment Test (PSAT). Sometimes abbreviated as PSAT/NMSQT. See also *PSAT.*

Office of Student Financial Assistance (OSFA)   The office of the U.S. Department of Education that is responsible for administering federal student financial aid programs and for developing aid policies and procedures.

origination   The process whereby the lender, or a servicing agent on behalf of the lender, handles the initial application processing and disbursement of loan proceeds.

origination fee   An up-front charge deducted from a loan to pay part of the loan's administrative costs.

over award   The amount of loan proceeds that exceed the borrower's educational need.

Parent Loans for Undergraduate Students (PLUS)   Federally insured loans for parents of dependent students. The amount of the loan is generally limited to the actual cost of attendance minus any financial aid already received.

parents' contribution   As determined by the Federal Methodology, the expected contribution by parents to the yearly cost of their children's education.

part-time enrollment   The number of students enrolled in higher education courses with a total credit load less than 75 percent of the normal full-time load.

payment period   A school-defined length of time for which financial aid funds are paid to a student.

payment reimbursement method   A method certain schools must use to request federal financial aid funds from the Department of Education.

pay-off balance   The amount you would pay if you were to pay off your loan today. It includes the outstanding principal plus any unpaid accrued interest.

Pell Grants   Grants generally awarded to undergraduates based on need and family income qualifications. Maximum award for the 1999–2000 award year was $3,000.

period of enrollment   The time period during which aid is granted. It coincides with the school's academic terms such as the academic year, semester, and so on.

Perkins Loan Program   Federally insured low-interest loans repayable over an extended period. Funded by the federal government and awarded by the school.

personal income   Current income received by persons from all sources.

PLUS Loan   See *Parent Loans for Undergraduate Students*.

postsecondary   A term meaning "after high school." It refers to all programs for high school graduates, including programs at two- and four-year colleges and at vocational and technical schools.

prepaid tuition plan   A college savings plan guaranteed to increase in value at the same rate as college tuition.

prime rate Fluctuating interest rate that banks charge for short-term loans to corporations or individuals whose credit standing is excellent.

principal The amount borrowed, which may increase as a result of interest capitalization. Also, the amount on which interest is calculated. Also known as principal balance.

private school A school or institution that is controlled by an individual, agency, or board rather than by the government, and is usually not supported primarily by public funds or operated by publicly elected or appointed officials.

professional judgment The financial aid administrator's ability to make changes to a student's financial aid package based on extenuating circumstances.

Profile The customized financial aid application form required at certain colleges to determine eligibility for institutional aid.

promissory note The contract between a borrower and a lender that includes all the terms and conditions under which the borrower promises to repay the loan.

proprietary school Postsecondary school that is private and legally permitted to make a profit. Most offer technical and vocational courses.

PSAT (Preliminary Scholastic Assessment Test) The test that helps prepare high school students for the SAT—and, if taken during the junior year, is one of the qualifying criteria for the National Merit Scholarship Program. Usually taken during the sophomore year or early in the junior year. Sometimes abbreviated as PSAT/NMSQT. See *National Merit Scholastic Qualifying Test.*

racial/ethnic group Classification indicating general racial or ethnic heritage based on self-identification, as in data collected by the Bureau of the Census, or on observer identification, as in data collected by the Office for Civil Rights. These categories are in accordance with the Office of Management and Budget standard classification scheme.

renewal FAFSA Version of the FAFSA that students may use if they applied for federal financial aid the previous award year.

repayment policy An institutionally established policy that determines the amount of education-related expenses (noninstitutional costs) reasonably incurred during a student's actual period of attendance.

repayment schedule A specific timetable detailing the amount of principal and interest in borrower's installment payments and the number of payments required to pay off the loan.

repayment period The time during which a borrower actively pays back an education loan.

Reserve Officers Training Corps (ROTC) Programs that combine military education with baccalaureate degree study, often with financial support and required commitment to future service in the Armed Services. Scholarship recipients participate in summer training while in college and meet a service commitment after college.

resources   As defined in federal regulations for campus-based programs, other student aid that must be taken into account to prevent an over award in the campus-based programs.

SAP   See *satisfactory academic progress.*

SAR   See *Student Aid Report.*

SASE   Self-addressed stamped envelope.

SAT I   The Scholastic Aptitude Test, which is used to measure a student's ability in math, verbal comprehension, and problem solving. SATs are administered during the junior and senior years in high school.

SAT II Subject Test   A test offered in many areas of study, including English, mathematics, many sciences, history, and foreign languages. Some colleges require students to take one or more SAT II tests when they apply for admission.

satisfactory academic progress (SAP)   To be eligible to receive federal student aid, a student must maintain, based on the school's written standard, satisfactory academic progress toward a degree or certificate.

scholarships   Funds used to pay for higher education that do not have to be repaid. Scholarships may be awarded based on any number of criteria, such as academics, achievements, hobbies, talents, affiliations with various groups, or career aspirations.

Scholastic Aptitude Test   See *SAT I.*

secondary market   Institutions that buy student loans from the institutions that originated or owned them.

Selective Service   Registration for the military draft. If required by law, you must register, or arrange to register, with the Selective Service to receive federal student aid.

self-help aid   Financial aid in the form of student loans or student employment.

servicer   An organization that administers and collects loan payments.

Simplified Needs Test   Basis on which only the first part of the FAFSA form is required. Asset information is not required if the parents of a dependent student have income of less than $50,000 and the relevant family members were non–tax filers or were eligible to use a 1040A or a 1040EZ to file their taxes.

Stafford Loans   Subsidized (need-based) and unsubsidized (non-need-based) loans guaranteed by the federal government and available to students to fund their education.

Statement of Educational Purpose   A legal document in which the student agrees to use his or her financial aid for educational expenses only.

Student Aid Report (SAR)   A report sent to a student by the federal government summarizing financial and other information reported on the FAFSA. The student's financial aid need or eligibility is indicated by the Expected Family Contribution (EFC), which is printed on the document.

Student Financial Aid (SFA) Programs   The programs administered by the Office of Student Financial Assistance Programs within the U.S. Department of Education. These include Federal Pell Grants, Federal Supplemental Educational Opportunity Grants, Federal Work-Study, Federal Perkins Loans, Federal Direct Stafford/Ford Loans, Federal Direct PLUS Loans, Federal Stafford Loans, Federal PLUS Loans, and State Student Incentive Grants.

Subsidized Stafford Loans   These are awarded to students based on financial need. Interest is subsidized by the Department of Education while borrowers are enrolled in school at least half-time, and during grace and deferment periods.

Supplemental Educational Opportunity Grant Program (SEOG)   Federal grant funds made available through some schools to a limited number of undergraduate students with financial need.

tax credit   The amount subtracted from your federal income taxes dollar-for-dollar for the cost of education. Taxes must be owed for the given tax year, and a tax return must be filed to receive any tax credit.

teaching assistantship (TA)   A form of financial aid that is given to graduate students and that usually provides them with a waiver of all or part of tuition, plus a small stipend for living expenses.

transcript   A list of all the courses a student has taken in high school or college and the grades received.

tuition and fees   Payment or charges for instruction or compensation for services, privileges, or the use of equipment, books, or other goods.

undergraduate student   A degree-seeking student at a college or university who has not earned a first bachelor's degree.

Uniform Gifts to Minors Act (UGMA)   Legislation that introduced a tax-effective manner of transferring property to minors without the complications of trusts or guardianship restrictions.

university   An institution of higher education that consists of a liberal arts college, a diverse graduate program, and usually two or more professional schools or faculties, and is empowered to confer degrees in various fields of study.

U.S. Department of Education (DOE)   The government agency that administers several federal student financial aid programs, including the Federal Pell Grant, the Federal Work-Study Program, the Federal Perkins Loan, the FFELP, and the FDLP. Also known as the ED.

U.S. Department of Health and Human Services (DHHS, HHS)   Government agency that administers several federal health education loan programs, including the HEAL, HPSL, and NSL loan programs.

variable interest   Interest rates for the Federal Stafford Loans (subsidized and unsubsidized) are set by the government each year and therefore vary from year to year.

verification   A procedure by which a school checks the information a student reported on the FAFSA, usually by requesting a copy of the student's signed federal tax returns.

vocational education   Organized educational programs, services, and activities that are directly related to the preparation of individuals for paid or unpaid employment, or for additional preparation for a career.

work-study   A generic term for programs designed to provide part-time employment as a source of funds to pay for postsecondary education, and for a federal program that is administered through postsecondary institutions.

Directory of General Financial Aid Resources

In many respects, Appendix B is one of the more exciting parts of our book. How in the world can an appendix be exciting? Well, for starters, it offers a comprehensive index of where you can go to find any additional information you may need on financial aid. You'll also discover financial aid sources that you may not have considered previously. For even more information and listings, see Appendix C, "Alphabetical State Financial Aid Listings," where you can find addresses and other useful resources listed by state.

The table of contents shown here will help you locate the topic you're looking for:

Appendix B Contents

Associations Related to Financial Aid

There are literally hundreds of associations that are directly or indirectly associated with the financial aid process. Here's a partial listing of the major associations that you may want to contact. For state-by-state alphabetical listings of financial aid resources, see Appendix C.

American Association of University Women (ASUW)   The Educational Foundation of the association is dedicated to improving women's access to the education system. Contact them at 319-337-1716 for more information.

Council of Better Business Bureaus   The council is dedicated to ensuring fair and legitimate practices within the financial aid process. Contact them at 703-276-0100 for more information.

Higher Education Washington, Inc.   This is an information resources company serving the student financial aid administrator community. Resources include publications and conferences. Visit their Web site if you need more information: **www.hewi.net.**

Institute of International Education   The Institute helps students gain access to international colleges and universities. Contact them at 212-883-8200 for more information.

> **Highly Recommended**
>
> **Americorp National and Community Service Program** Americorp is an excellent source for scholarships, work–study, and community service programs. Contact them at 1–800–942–2677 for more information.

National Association for College Admissions Counseling (NACAC)   NACAC is an education association of secondary school counselors, college admissions officers and counselors, and related individuals who work with students as they make the transition from high school to postsecondary education. Members of NACAC join together because they recognize that, for students and their families, a real choice demands information and communication. The school admissions counselors are often the primary sources of information about the transition process and are uniquely aware of the concerns held by the people they serve. Contact them at 703-836-2222 or visit their Web site if you need more information: **www.nacac.comindex.html.**

National Association of Student Financial Aid Administrators   These are the people who decide how much you get. They've assembled a nice collection of basic information for parents and students, including an online version of the popular brochure "Cash for College." Visit their Web site if you need more information: **www.nasfaa.org.**

National Society of Fund Raising Executives (NSFRE)   NSFRE is a major professional organization that lists educational opportunities and other services. Visit their Web site for more information: **www.nsfre.org.**

Northwest Education Loan Association   Information on student loans, financial aid, and college planning for students and families in the Pacific Northwest is available through this association: **www.nela.net.**

Pennsylvania Higher Education Assistance Agency (PHEAA)   This is a full-service student financial aid organization and a national leader in providing affordable and efficient access to higher education. Visit their Web site for more information: **www.pheaa.org.**

Western Interstate Commission for Higher Education (WICHE)   WICHE offers exchange programs among member colleges in the western states. Eligible students get a reduction in tuition. Contact them at 303-541-0210 for more information.

Adult Financial Aid Programs

As more and more adults attend college on a part-time basis, there's renewed interest in the development of financial aid programs for the adult population. The following are several programs to consider.

Distance Learning Programs   If you're thinking about school, Peterson's excellent Web site offers information about distance learning programs, as well as a discussion area for graduate students. Visit their Web site for more information: **www. petersons.comgraduate/indexfa.html**.

The University Alliance   The Alliance offers news resources for nontraditional education and options for adult re-entry into the higher education system. Get the inside scoop on financial aid, distance education, graduate school, employment, internships, and educational trends. Visit their Web site for more information: **www.back2college.com**.

The Virtual College   This guidebook by Pam Aixon shows how to use distance learning in your career plan. If you are interested in ordering the book, visit **www. amazon.com** or your local bookstore, or call Peterson's at 1-800-338-3282.

Athletic Scholarships

Athletic scholarship programs are very competitive, but if you know where and how to look for them, you can dramatically improve your odds of getting one.

All American Athletes On-Line   This online college athletic recruiting resource allows high school athletes to post their profiles on the Web for review by college coaches. Your Web profile is available in their searchable database for up to four years! A hard copy of your profile is mailed directly to coaches at five universities of your choice. Instant e-mail notification of new profiles goes out to thousands of coaches and recruiters who use the database to find high school talent. You have real-time access to your profile so you can make changes and updates to maximize your chances of getting an athletic scholarship. All American Athlete's Web site gets over 50,000 visits a month from coaches and student athletes. Visit the site for more information: **www.allamericanathletes.com**.

College and University Volleyball Scholarships   This Web site specializes in helping students get volleyball scholarships. Visit the site for more information: **www.volleyball.org/college/index.html**.

CSA College Recruiting   CSA offers information updated daily on the nation's top high-school athletes. Visit their Web site for more information: **www.csasports.com**.

Florida Bluechip Report   At this Web site covering the state of Florida, recruiters can browse through over 275 Florida high school prospects for college football.

Features include a variety of ways to mine and sort the data, as well as ways of checking updated news for each profile. For more information or to file your profile, visit **www.floridabluechips.com**.

Kurelic Recruiting   Well-respected analyst Bill Kurelic gives Midwest football recruiting reports and analyses in the Kurelic Recruiting Report. Visit his Web site for more information: **www.floridabluechips.com**.

National Recruiting News   Gator Country's Automated National Recruiting News covers football and basketball scholarship recruiting. Visit their Web site for more information: **www.gatorcountry.org/recruitnews.html**.

PrepStar College Recruiting   PrepStar offers information updated daily on the nation's top football and basketball prospects. Since 1982, PrepStar has helped thousands of qualified and deserving student-athletes in all sports obtain athletic scholarships and financial aid for college. Their online recruiting center is used by thousands of college coaches nationwide as a vital tool for recruiting efforts. Visit their Web site for more information: **www.prepstar.com**.

Rivals 100   Famed analyst Bobby Burton covers the college football recruiting scene and ranks the top 100 prep players in the country. Visit his site for more information: **rivals100.rivals.com**.

Budgeting

If you go to college without first setting up a budget, you'll have little or no idea where your money is being spent, and you'll miss opportunities to save money on key items in your budget.

BACK Calculators   A Web site which offers an entire set of specialized calculators to complete every aspect of the budget process. Visit the site for more information. **www.statesavingsbank.com/calculators.html**.

Budget Calculator   Build a budget and stick to it! Using wired scholar's budget calculator, you can quickly get an overview of where your money goes. You may be able to cut expenses or increase your income to avoid having to borrow. Check out their Web site at **www.embark.wiredscholar.compaying/lt_financial_planning/ltfp_monthbud.jsp**.

Budgeting for College Spending   Money from home and from savings will help you set up and maintain a budget. If you need help budgeting your money, check out this excellent Web site: **www.emich.edu/public/coe/nice/budgetws.html**.

College Cost Estimator   This Web site will not only help you estimate what it will cost to go to college, it offers a financial aid checklist which you can review to be sure you haven't left out any college costs. Visit the site at **www.state.nj.us/treasury/osa/studenttools/index.html**.

Career Guidance

Many freshmen enter college with no idea of what subject they want to major in. Somewhere in their sophomore year, they'll decide on a major, only to find out that many of the courses they've already taken can't be credited toward their selected major. To take the additional required courses, many of these students have to spend another semester in college—and that's an expensive proposition that might have been avoided if they'd sought career advice from organizations such as the following:

Career and Guidance Foundation   This Web site lists over 8,100 college catalogs online! Visit the site for more information: **www.cgf.org/home.asp.**

The Coalition of Colleges and Universities   This group has assembled advice for students and their parents on preparing for college, choosing the right school, and finding ways to pay for it. Their Web site includes recommendations on which middle school and high school courses to take and offers many good Internet links. Visit the site for more information: **www.collegeispossible.org.**

Major Databases   Major databases provide information for specific majors or career interests, such as art, computer science, journalism, and nursing. FinAid's Web site describes scholarships and other forms of aid available. Visit their Web site for more information: **www.finaid.org/otheraid/majors.phtml.**

Mapping Your Future   At this site, you'll find information to help you plan your career, select a school, and pay for your education. This site is sponsored by guaranty agencies, who participate in the Federal Family Education Loan Program (FFELP) and are committed to providing information about higher education and career opportunities. Visit their site for more information: **mapping-your-future.org.**

College Admissions Requirements

Before you apply to a college, make sure you understand its admissions requirements. If you can't meet the admissions requirements, don't waste your time applying unless you have talked to someone in the admissions office who has told you that you might have a chance of being admitted.

Common Applications   The recommended application form for admission to undergraduate programs at many independent colleges and universities is known as the *Common Application*. It was developed to simplify the college application process. Students complete the form and send copies to any of the participating colleges to which they wish to apply. Paper and disk copies of the Common Application are available at most high schools. The form can also be downloaded or completed online at: **www.commonapp.org.**

Fish Net   Fish Net is a service that allows you to order admissions information for almost any college or university through its Web site! Visit the site for more information: **www.mycollegeguide.org/index.html.**

College Financial Aid Directory

Virtually every college in the country offers financial aid of some sort, and the types of aid programs offered vary. If you want to get the inside story on what's available at the colleges that you're interested in, contact their financial aid offices.

College Quest   Choosing the right school is difficult. Even narrowing your choices to a few likely candidates can be an exercise in frustration. With thousands of schools in the United States, how will you ever find the right one for you? College Quest's Web site provides you with selection criteria that are important to you and that help you narrow your list. Visit their site for more information: **www.collegequest. complugin.nd/CollegeQuest/pgGateway.**

Community Colleges

Community colleges offer students an opportunity to complete the first two years of college for significantly less than what it would cost at a four-year institution.

The Community College Web   This site contains a searchable index to the Web sites for community colleges in the United States, Canada, and elsewhere in the world. The interface allows you to search alphabetically or geographically, or by location, Web address, or keywords in the college name. Visit the site for more information: **www.mcli.dist.maricopa.edu/cc/index.html.**

Two-Year College Directory   If you're interested in attending a two-year college, this online directory will provide you with the names, addresses, and telephone numbers of junior colleges throughout the country. Visit their Web site for more information: **cset.sp.utoledo.edu/twoyrcol.html.**

Consulting Services

If you're a busy parent without the time to check out all of your financial aid options, then you may want to consider hiring a financial aid consultant to do it for you. Here's how to find a good one:

Ask the Expert   Sixty financial aid administrators and financial aid professionals have graciously volunteered to answer questions submitted via this forum. Visit their Web site for more information: **www.finaid.org/questions.**

Key Education Resources   This group offers a range of education planning and financing products that can help you meet your education goals. Whether your kid is going to graduate school, starting college, or entering a private school, this group has several programs to offer. Visit their Web site for more information: **www.key. comtemplates/t-ps2.jhtml?nodeID=H-1.3.**

Directory of Colleges and Universities

If you don't know the addresses or Web sites of the colleges that you're interested in attending, or if you need more-detailed information to narrow your list, you can assess your options by using the following Web sites:

College Admissions This Web site details what colleges look for and how they make admissions decisions. Visit the site for more information: **www.collegeboard. comfeatures/parentgd/html/admssn.html.**

College Resources This college and career resource from *U.S. News & World Report* includes a searchable directory of colleges, a yearly ranking of colleges, information on financial aid, and more. It features a special section on over 1,200 community colleges. Visit their Web site for more information: www.usnews. comusnews/edu.

FAFSA Form

Filling out a FAFSA application is the first step in applying for student aid. Line-by-line instructions for completing the form (see the sample form on the following pages) are in Chapter 19, "Decoding the Forms."

FAFSA Online

You have the option of completing the FAFSA online. This section tells you how to get answers to the most commonly asked questions about the FAFSA form and gives instructions for completing it.

Completing the FAFSA If you're wondering, "Why do they ask that?" or if you find yourself saying, "My family situation is different; now what do I do?" check out this Web site. It explores the purpose of FAFSA questions and discusses how information should be reported in some unusual cases. Visit the site for more information: **www.ed.gov/prog_info/SFA/FAFSA/ index.html.**

FAFSA on the Web Completing the FAFSA on the Web is the fastest way to apply for student financial aid! Students who applied for aid last year can also complete a renewal FAFSA application online at **www.fafsa.ed.gov.**

Free Application for Federal Student Aid

OMB 1845-0001

July 1, 2000 — June 30, 2001 school year

Step One: For questions 1-36, leave blank any questions that do not apply to you (the student).

1-3. Your full name (as it appears on your Social Security card)

1. LAST NAME   2. FIRST NAME   3. M.I.

4-7. Your permanent mailing address

4. NUMBER AND STREET (INCLUDE APARTMENT NUMBER)

5. CITY (AND COUNTRY, IF NOT U.S.)   6. STATE   7. ZIP CODE

8. Your Social Security Number

9. Your date of birth — MONTH / DAY / YEAR   1 9

10. Your permanent telephone number — AREA CODE

11. Do you have a driver's license?   **Yes** ○ 1   **No** ○ 2

12-13. Driver's license number and state

12. LICENSE NUMBER   13. STATE

14. Are you a U.S. citizen? Pick one. **See Page 2.**

a. Yes, I am a U.S. citizen. .... ○ 1

b. No, but I am an eligible noncitizen. **Fill in question 15.** ○ 2   **15.** ALIEN REGISTRATION NUMBER   A

c. No, I am not a citizen or eligible noncitizen. .... ○ 3

16. Marital status as of today

I am single, divorced, or widowed. ○ 1

I am married. ○ 2

I am separated. ○ 3

17. Month and year you were married, separated, divorced, or widowed   MONTH / YEAR

For each question (18 - 22), please mark whether you will be <u>full time</u>, <u>3/4 time</u>, <u>half time</u>, less than half time, or not attending. Mark "Full time" if you are not sure. See page 2.

18. Summer 2000   Full time ○ 1   3/4 time ○ 2   Half time ○ 3   Less than half time ○ 4   Not attending ○ 5

19. Fall semester or quarter 2000   Full time ○ 1   3/4 time ○ 2   Half time ○ 3   Less than half time ○ 4   Not attending ○ 5

20. Winter quarter 2000-2001   Full time ○ 1   3/4 time ○ 2   Half time ○ 3   Less than half time ○ 4   Not attending ○ 5

21. Spring semester or quarter 2001   Full time ○ 1   3/4 time ○ 2   Half time ○ 3   Less than half time ○ 4   Not attending ○ 5

22. Summer 2001   Full time ○ 1   3/4 time ○ 2   Half time ○ 3   Less than half time ○ 4   Not attending ○ 5

23. Highest school your father completed   Middle school/Jr. High ○ 1   High school ○ 2   College or beyond ○ 3   Other/unknown ○ 4

24. Highest school your mother completed   Middle school/Jr. High ○ 1   High school ○ 2   College or beyond ○ 3   Other/unknown ○ 4

25. What is your state of legal residence?   STATE

26. Did you become a legal resident of this state before January 1, 1995?   **Yes** ○ 1   **No** ○ 2

27. If the answer to question 26 is "**No**," give month and year you became a legal resident.   MONTH / YEAR

28. If you have **never** been convicted of any illegal drug offense, enter "1" in the box and go to question 29. A drug-related conviction does not necessarily make you ineligible for aid; call 1-800-433-3243 or go to http://www.fafsa.ed.gov/q28 to find out how to fill out this question.

29. Most male students must register with Selective Service to get federal aid. Are you male?   **Yes** ○ 1   **No** ○ 2

30. If you are male (age 18-25) and not registered, do you want Selective Service to register you?   **Yes** ○ 1   **No** ○ 2

31. What degree or certificate will you be working towards during 2000-2001? **See page 2** and enter the correct number in the box.

32. What will be your grade level when you begin the 2000-2001 school year? **See page 2** and enter the correct number in the box.

33. Will you have a high school diploma or GED before you enroll?   **Yes** ○ 1   **No** ○ 2

34. Will you have your first bachelor's degree before July 1, 2000?   **Yes** ○ 1   **No** ○ 2

35. In addition to grants, are you interested in student loans (which you must pay back)?   **Yes** ○ 1   **No** ○ 2

36. In addition to grants, are you interested in "work-study" (which you earn through work)?   **Yes** ○ 1   **No** ○ 2

— Page 3 —

289

Step Two: For 37-51, if you (the student) are now married (even if you were not married in 1999), report both your and your spouse's income and assets. Ignore references to "spouse" if you are currently single, separated, divorced, or widowed.

37. For 1999, have you filed your IRS income tax return or another tax return listed in **question 38**?

    a. I have already filed. ○ 1   **b.** I will file, but I have not yet filed. ○ 2   **c.** I'm not going to file. **(Skip to question 44.)** ○ 3

38. What income tax return did you file or will you file for 1999?

    a. IRS 1040 .... ○ 1   **c.** A foreign tax return. **See Page 2.** .... ○ 3

    b. IRS 1040A, 1040EZ, 1040Telefile ...... ○ 2   **d.** A tax return for Puerto Rico, Guam, American Samoa, the Virgin Islands, the Marshall Islands, the Federated States of Micronesia, or Palau. **See Page 2.** ...... ○ 4

39. If you have filed or will file a 1040, were you <u>eligible to file a 1040A or 1040EZ</u>? See page 2.   Yes ○ 1 No/don't know ○ 2

For questions 40-53, if the answer is zero or the question does not apply to you, enter 0.

40. What was your (and spouse's) adjusted gross income for 1999? Adjusted gross income is on IRS Form 1040–line 33; 1040A–line 18; 1040EZ–line 4; or Telefile–line I. $ ▢▢▢ , ▢▢▢

41. Enter the total amount of your (and spouse's) income tax for 1999. Income tax amount is on IRS Form 1040–line 49 plus 51; 1040A–line 32; 1040EZ–line 10; or Telefile–line K. $ ▢▢▢ , ▢▢▢

42. Enter your (and spouse's) exemptions. Exemptions are on IRS Form 1040–line 6d, or on Form 1040A–line 6d. For Form 1040EZ or Telefile, **see page 2.**   ▢▢

43. Enter your Earned Income Credit from IRS Form 1040–line 59a; 1040A–line 37a; 1040EZ–line 8a; or Telefile–line L. $ ▢▢▢ , ▢▢▢

44-45. How much did you (and spouse) earn from working in 1999? Answer this question whether or not you filed a tax return. This information may be on your W-2 forms, or on IRS Form 1040–lines 7, 12, and 18; 1040A–line 7; or 1040EZ–line 1. Telefilers should use their W-2's.   **You (44)** $ ▢▢▢ , ▢▢▢   **Your Spouse (45)** $ ▢▢▢ , ▢▢▢

46. Go to page 8 of this form; complete the column on the left of **Worksheet A**; enter student total here. $ ▢▢▢ , ▢▢▢

47. Go to page 8 of this form; complete the column on the left of **Worksheet B**; enter student total here. $ ▢▢▢ , ▢▢▢

48. Total current balance of cash, savings, and checking accounts $ ▢▢▢ , ▢▢▢

For 49-51, if net worth is one million or more, enter $999,999. If net worth is negative, enter 0.

49. Current <u>net worth</u> of <u>investments</u> (<u>investment value</u> minus <u>investment debt</u>) See page 2. $ ▢▢▢ , ▢▢▢

50. Current <u>net worth</u> of business (<u>business value</u> minus <u>business debt</u>) **See page 2.** $ ▢▢▢ , ▢▢▢

51. Current <u>net worth</u> of investment farm (Don't include a farm that you live on and operate.) $ ▢▢▢ , ▢▢▢

52-53. If you receive veterans education benefits, for **how many months** from July 1, 2000 through June 30, 2001 will you receive these benefits, and **what amount** will you receive per month? Do not include your spouse's veterans education benefits.   **Months (52)** ▢▢   **Amount (53)** $ ▢▢▢

Step Three: Answer all six questions in this step.

54. Were you born before January 1, 1977? .... Yes ○ 1 No ○ 2

55. Will you be working on a degree beyond a bachelor's degree in school year 2000-2001? .... Yes ○ 1 No ○ 2

56. As of today, are you married? (Answer yes if you are separated, but not divorced.) .... Yes ○ 1 No ○ 2

57. Answer **"Yes"** if: (1) You have children who receive more than half of their support from you; **or**
    (2) You have dependents (other than your children or spouse) who live with you and receive more than half of their support from you, now and through June 30, 2001.... Yes ○ 1 No ○ 2

58. Are you an orphan or ward of the court or were you a ward of the court until age 18? .... Yes ○ 1 No ○ 2

59. Are you a <u>veteran</u> of the U.S. Armed Forces? See page 2. .... Yes ○ 1 No ○ 2

If you (the student) answer "No" to every question in Step Three, go to Step Four.

If you answer "Yes" to any question in Step Three, skip Step Four and go to Step Five.

(If you are a graduate health profession student, you may be required to complete Step Four even if you answered "Yes" to any question in Step Three.)   **Page 4**

Step Four: Complete this step if you (the student) answered "No" to all questions in Step Three. Please tell us about your parents. **See page 7 for who is considered a parent.**

60. Parents' marital status as of today? (Pick one.)　　Married ○ 1　　Single ○ 2　　Divorced/Separated ○ 3　　Widowed ○ 4

61-62. Your father's Social Security Number and last name

61. FATHER'S/STEPFATHER'S SSN

62. FATHER'S/STEPFATHER'S LAST NAME

63-64. Your mother's Social Security Number and last name

63. MOTHER'S/STEPMOTHER'S SSN

64. MOTHER'S/STEPMOTHER'S LAST NAME

65. How many people are in your <u>parents' household</u>? **See page 7.**

66. How many in question 65 (**exclude your parents**) will be <u>college students</u> between July 1, 2000, and June 30, 2001? **See page 7.**

67. What is your parents' state of legal residence?

STATE

68. Did your parents become legal residents of the state in question 67 before January 1, 1995?

Yes ○ 1　　No ○ 2

69. If the answer to question 68 is "No," give the month and year legal residency began for the parent who has lived in the state the longest.

MONTH　　YEAR

70. What is the age of your older parent?

71. For 1999, have your parents filed their IRS income tax return or another tax return listed in **question 72**?

a. My parents have already filed. ○ 1

b. My parents will file, but they have not yet filed. ○ 2

c. My parents are not going to file. (Skip to question 78.) ○ 3

72. What income tax return did your parents file or will they file for 1999?

a. IRS 1040 .... ○ 1

b. IRS 1040A, 1040EZ, 1040Telefile ..... ○ 2

c. A foreign tax return. **See Page 2.** .... ○ 3

d. A tax return for Puerto Rico, Guam, American Samoa, the Virgin Islands, the Marshall Islands, the Federated States of Micronesia, or Palau. **See Page 2.** ...... ○ 4

73. If your parents have filed or will file a 1040, were they <u>eligible to file a 1040A or 1040EZ</u>? **See page 2.**　　Yes ○ 1　　No/ don't know ○ 2

For 74 - 85, if the answer is zero or the question does not apply, enter 0.

74. What was your parents' adjusted gross income for 1999? Adjusted gross income is on IRS Form 1040–line 33; 1040A–line 18; 1040EZ–line 4; or Telefile–line I.　　$ ____ , ____

75. Enter the total amount of your parents' income tax for 1999. Income tax amount is on IRS Form 1040–line 49 plus 51; 1040A–line 32; 1040EZ–line 10; or Telefile–line K.　　$ ____ , ____

76. Enter your parents' exemptions. Exemptions are on IRS Form 1040–line 6d or on Form 1040A–line 6d. For Form 1040EZ or Telefile, **see page 2.**　　____

77. Enter your parents' Earned Income Credit from IRS Form 1040–line 59a; 1040A–line 37a; 1040EZ–line 8a; or Telefile–line L.　　$ ____ , ____

78-79. How much did your parents earn from working in 1999? Answer this question whether or not your parents filed a tax return. This information may be on their W-2 forms, or on IRS Form 1040–lines 7, 12, and 18; 1040A–line 7; or 1040EZ–line 1. Telefilers should use their W-2's.

Father/ Stepfather (78) $ ____ , ____

Mother/ Stepmother (79) $ ____ , ____

80. Go to page 8 of this form; complete the column on the right of **Worksheet A**; enter parent total here.　　$ ____ , ____

81. Go to page 8 of this form; complete the column on the right of **Worksheet B**; enter parent total here.　　$ ____ , ____

82. Total current balance of cash, savings, and checking accounts　　$ ____ , ____

For 83–85, if net worth is one million or more, enter $999,999. If net worth is negative, enter 0.

83. Current <u>net worth</u> of <u>investments</u> (<u>investment value</u> minus <u>investment debt</u>) See page 2.　　$ ____ , ____

84. Current <u>net worth</u> of business (<u>business value</u> minus <u>business debt</u>) See page 2.　　$ ____ , ____

85. Current <u>net worth</u> of investment farm (Don't include a farm that your parents live on and operate.)　　$ ____ , ____

Now go to Step Six.　　　　**Page 5**

Step Five: Complete this step only if you (the student) answered "Yes" to any question in Step Three.

86. How many people are in your (and your spouse's) <u>household</u>? **See page 7.**

87. How many in question 86 will be <u>college students</u> between July 1, 2000, and June 30, 2001? **Do not include your parents. See page 7.**

Step Six: Please tell us which schools should receive your information.

For each school (up to six), please provide the federal school code and your housing plans **(enter "1" for on campus, "2" for off campus, and "3" for with parents)**. Look for the federal school codes on the Internet at **http://www.ed.gov/studentaid**, at your college financial aid office, at your public library, or by asking your high school guidance counselor. If you cannot get the federal school code, write in the complete name, address, city, and state of the college.

Federal school code *OR* Name of college	College street address and city	State	Housing Plans
FIRST SCHOOL CODE 88.			89.
SECOND SCHOOL CODE 90.			91.
THIRD SCHOOL CODE 92.			93.
FOURTH SCHOOL CODE 94.			95.
FIFTH SCHOOL CODE 96.			97.
SIXTH SCHOOL CODE 98.			99.

Step Seven: Please read, sign, and date.

By signing this application, you agree, if asked, to provide information that will verify the accuracy of your completed form. This information may include a copy of your U.S. or state income tax form. Also, you certify that you (1) will use federal and/or state student financial aid only to pay the cost of attending an institution of higher education, (2) are not in default on a federal student loan or have made satisfactory arrangements to repay it, (3) do not owe money back on a federal student grant or have made satisfactory arrangements to repay it, (4) will notify your school if you default on a federal student loan, and (5) understand that **the Secretary of Education has the authority to verify income reported on this application with the Internal Revenue Service.** If you purposely give false or misleading information, you may be fined $10,000, sent to prison, or both.

100. Date this form was completed.

MONTH / DAY / 2000 ○ or 2001 ○

101. **Student** signature (Sign in box)

Parent signature (one parent whose information is provided in Step Four.) (Sign in box)

If this form was filled out by someone other than you, your spouse, or your parent(s), that person must complete this part.

Preparer's Name and Firm _____

Address _____

102. Social Security # ___ – ___ – ___
OR
103. Employer ID # ___ – ___

104. Signature and Date _____

SCHOOL USE ONLY
D/O ○
FAA SIGNATURE
Federal School Code

MDE USE ONLY
Special Handle ___ – ___

Page 6

292

Federal Financial Aid

The U.S. Department of Education disburses financial aid money to the states and is fairly lenient about how it allows the different states to distribute the money. Make sure you contact the Department of Education in the state(s) where you plan to attend college to find out how their programs work. They are all different. See Appendix C for state-by-state listings of state Departments of Education.

Department of Education's Student Guide   This online guide provides information about financial aid from the U.S. Department of Education. Visit their Web site for more information: **www.ed.gov/prog_info/SFA/StudentGuide.**

Federal Student Aid Information Center   The government has a toll-free number to provide you with information about federally subsidized loans, grants, and scholarships. Operators are on hand to answer questions about your FAFSA or a particular school's loan interest rates. Call them at 1-800-433-3243, write them at P.O. Box 84, Washington, D.C. 20044-0084, or visit their Web sites if you need more information: **www.ed.gov/offices/OPE/Students/index.html, www.ed.gov/money.html.**

Information on Financial Aid   This Web site is one of the most comprehensive resources for objective and unbiased information about student financial aid. Visit the site for more information: **www.finaid.org.**

Federal Financial Aid Regional Offices and Related Sites

The country is divided up into 10 financial aid regional offices, which are listed in this section. Related sites follow. (You can find any state's Department of Education listing and listings for other state offices compiled by state in Appendix C.)

Region I (Connecticut, Maine, Massachusetts, New Hampshire, Rhode Island, Vermont)
U.S. Department of Education
Student Financial Assistance Programs
J.W. McCormack Post Office and Courthouse, Room 502
Boston, MA 02109
617-223-9338

Region II (New Jersey, New York, Puerto Rico, Virgin Islands, Panama Canal Zone)
U.S. Department of Education
Student Financial Assistance Programs
75 Park Place, Room 1206
New York, NY 10007
212-264-4022

Region III (Delaware, District of Columbia, Maryland, Pennsylvania, Virginia, West Virginia)
U.S. Department of Education
Student Financial Assistance Programs
3535 Market Street, Room 16200
Philadelphia, PA 19104
215-596-0247

Region IV (Alabama, Florida, Georgia, Kentucky, Mississippi, North Carolina, South Carolina, Tennessee)
U.S. Department of Education
Office of Student Financial Assistance
101 Marietta Tower, Suite 2203
Atlanta, GA 30323
1-800-433-3243

Region V (Illinois, Indiana, Michigan, Minnesota, Ohio, Wisconsin)
U.S. Department of Education
Office of Student Financial Assistance
111 North Canal Street, Room 830
Chicago, IL 60605
1-800-433-3243

Regions VI and VII (Arkansas, Iowa, Kansas, Louisiana, Missouri, Nebraska, New Mexico, Oklahoma, Texas)
U.S. Department of Education
Student Financial Assistance Programs
1200 Main Tower, Room 2150
Dallas, TX 75202
214-767-3811

Region VIII (Colorado, Montana, North Dakota, South Dakota, Utah, Wyoming)
U.S. Department of Education
Office of Student Financial Assistance Programs
1391 North Speer Boulevard, Suite 8
Denver, CO 80204-2512
303-844-3676

Region IX (Arizona, California, Hawaii, Nevada, American Samoa, Guam, Federated States of Micronesia, Marshall Islands, Republic of Palau, Wake Island)
U.S. Department of Education
Office of Student Financial Assistance
50 United Nations Plaza
San Francisco, CA 94102
415-437-8293

Region X (Alaska, Idaho, Oregon, Washington)
U.S. Department of Education
Office of Student Financial Assistance Programs
1000 Second Avenue, Suite 1200
Seattle, WA 98104-1023
206-287-1770

Related Sites

National Council of Education Opportunity Association   This program is designed to encourage undergraduate students from low-income families and from underrepresented minority groups to pursue doctoral degrees and careers in college teaching. It represents the largest and best pipeline in the nation of potential graduate students from these groups. Call them at 202-347-7430.

National Council of Higher Education Loan Programs Inc. (NCHELP)
1100 Connecticut Avenue NW, 12th Floor
Washington, D.C. 20036
1-202-822-2106

NCHELP represents a nationwide network of guaranty agencies, secondary markets, lenders, loan servicers, collection agencies, schools, and other organizations involved in the administration of the Federal Family Education Loan Program (FFELP).

National Representatives   This Web site will show you how to contact your congressperson. Visit the site for more information: **www.visi.comjuan/congress.**

NonProfit Gateway   NonProfit Gateway is literally a gateway into federal government Web sites and contains data on grants, federal laws, and federal agencies. Visit the site for more information: **www.nonprofit.org.**

Financial Aid Resources

There are literally hundreds of resources out there that you can use to find all types of financial aid. In this section, we list the primary ones to help you get started.

Chronicle of Higher Education   This is a good place to find information on changes in the financial aid process. Visit their Web site for more information: **www.chronicle.merit.edu.**

College Edge   This Web site includes advice from the experts on choosing a college! Visit the site if you need more information: **www.collegeedge.com.**

College Opportunities On-Line   This Web site links to over 9,000 colleges and universities in the United States. If you're thinking about a large university, a small liberal arts college, a specialized college, a community college, a career or technical college, or a trade school, you can find it here. College Opportunities On-Line is brought to you by the National Center for Education Statistics in the U.S. Department of Education. Visit the site for more information: **nces.ed.gov/ipeds/cool.**

Ecola Directories College Locator   This Web site contains more than 2,500 links to colleges and universities, including their libraries and alumni pages. Visit the site for more information: **www.ecola.comcollege.**

Highly Recommended

Fast Web   Fast Web is the largest and most comprehensive scholarship search engine on the Internet. It provides access to a searchable database of more than 400,000 private sector scholarships, fellowships, grants, and loans available to students. Visit their site for more information: **www.fastWeb.com.**

Educaid   Educaid provides you with all the information you need in order to understand the financial aid process and your aid options. Educaid, one of the nation's top 10 lenders and the student loan division of First Union National Bank, offers loans for undergraduates, graduates, parents, and continuing education and international students. Visit their Web site for more information: **www.educaid.com.**

Federal Student Aid Hotline   This hotline is a toll-free number that you can call if you have any questions regarding the financial aid process. Call 1-800-433-3243.

Financial Aid Information Page   This site is a major financial aid information page on the Internet. No other site even comes close to having the massive amount of guidance that this site provides. You can use their financial aid calculators, look up laws, locate lenders, find specialized scholarships, or browse top-drawer links to other great sites. Visit the site for more information: **www.finaid.com.**

Financial Aid Links   At about.com, you'll find a fairly comprehensive list of links about college financial aid. Visit their Web site for more information: **collegeapps. about.comeducation/collegeapps/msub1.html.**

Funding Services   College funding and financial aid sources, including scholarships, grants, loans, private sources, and work-study programs, are covered by the Funding Service Center. Coming up with all of the money you need to attend college can be a challenge. In reality, your college funds will probably be made up of a combination of funds from financial aid sources, private sources, and your own money. Visit their Web site for more information: **www.collegefundingonline.com.**

Objective Guidance   This comprehensive, content-rich site is dedicated to providing students and parents with objective guidance on financial aid. Visit their Web site for more information: **www.finaid.org.**

Pennsylvania Higher Education Assistance Agency (PHEAA)   This is a collaborative effort to use cutting-edge technology and business processes to dramatically transform the administration of student financial aid and improve both funding for education beyond high school and customer access to information. Visit their Web site for more information: **www.pheaa.org**.

Student Loans   This Web site includes excellent student loan counseling and interactive tools to plan your loan requirements. Visit the site for more information: **mapping-your-future.org**.

***U.S. News & World Report* Financial Aid Advice**   Get information and advice on financial aid, tools for comparing college costs, scholarship search services, and a list of "best value" schools, all from this Web site: **www.usnews.comusnews/edu/dollars/dshome.html**.

Yahoo's Financial Aid Search   This Web site allows you to locate online financial aid and provides Internet links to college financial aid offices, listed alphabetically by college. Visit the site for more information: **www.yahoo.com**.

Financial Planning

Without a financial plan for college, you can't know for sure whether you can afford the school of your choice. The following listings can help you get started on a financial plan.

Academic Management Services   Academic Management Services offers a Web site to help families plan and finance their kids' education. Visit the site for more information: **www.amsWeb.com**.

Financial Aid Calculators   Use these free, convenient worksheets with supporting calculators to help plan your strategy for financing college costs. Visit their Web site for more information: **www.collegeboard.org/html/calculator000.html**.

Financial Aid Guidance   This Web site offers financial aid guidance, homework, help for your kids, and more. Visit the site for more information: **www.geostudies.com**.

Mark's Financial Aid Calculators   These financial aid calculators were implemented by Mark Kantrowitz. They are free, accurate, and completely confidential. Playing "what-if" games with these calculators can provide you with a better understanding of college education financing and help you plan for the future. Visit this site for more information: **www.finaid.org/calculators**.

Frauds and Scams

Fortunately, financial aid frauds and scams seldom occur, but they are out there. Before hiring a consulting service or taking a too-good-to-be-true deal, make sure you check it out first.

Hotline   If you're suspicious about a financial aid "deal," call the U.S. Department of Education, Inspector General's Hotline at 1-800-647-8733.

Reporting Fraud   You can report any financial aid fraud situation to the Council of Better Business Bureaus by calling 703-276-0100.

Scholarship Scams   Learn how to recognize and protect yourself from financial aid scams. If you must pay money to get money, it might be a scam. Visit the following Web site for more information: **www.finaid.org/scholarships/scams.phtml**.

Graduate and Professional Student Loans

Less than half of all graduate students and students seeking professional degrees (lawyers, medical doctors, etc.) receive any financial aid. Here are several sources to check out if you are a postgraduate student seeking financial aid.

Achiever Loan   Knight College Resource Group offers loans to graduate students in any discipline. Write them at 855 Boylston Street, Boston, MA 02116; or call 1-800-225-6783.

Business Access Loan Program   This program is for business graduate students only. Write to the Access Group, P.O. Box 7430, Wilmington, DE 19803-0430; or call 1-800-282-1550.

CitiAssist   Graduate students in any discipline may apply for a loan. Write to Citibank Student Loan Corporation, 99 Garnsey Road, Pittsford, NY 14534; or call 716-248-7672 or 1-800-692-8200.

ENGLoans   Loans for engineering students only are available from United Student Aid Group. Write them at P.O. Box 6182, Indianapolis, IN 46206; or call 1-800-255-8374.

EXCEL   Write them at Nellie Mae, 50 Braintree Hill Park, Suite 300, Braintree, MA 02184; call 1-800-634-9308; or visit **info@nelliemae.org**.

Federal Stafford and Direct Student Loans   These loans are available to graduate students in any discipline. Write the U.S. Department of Education, Federal Student Aid Information Center, P.O. Box 84, Washington, D.C. 20044-0084; call 1-800-433-3243; or visit **www.ed.gov**.

GradSHARE   These loans are for graduate students in any discipline. Write the New England Loan Marketing Association, Nellie Mae, 50 Braintree Hill Park, Suite 300, Braintree, MA 02184; or call 1-800-634-9308.

Graduate Access Loans   Graduate students in any discipline may apply for these loans. Write the Access Group, P.O. Box 7430, Wilmington, DE 19803-0430; or call 1-800-282-1550.

Health Education Assistance Loan (HEAL)   These loans are limited to medical students only. Write the Division of Student Assistance HEAL Branch, Parklawn Building, Room 8–37, 5600 Fishers Lane, Rockville, MD 20857; or call 301-443-1540.

Law Access Loan   These loans are for law students. Write to the Access Group, P.O. Box 7430, Wilmington, DE 19803-0430; or call 1-800-282-1550.

LawLoans   Law students only may apply for these loans. Write to Sallie Mae, P.O. Box 59023, Panama City, FL 32402-9023; or call 1-800-282-1550.

LawSHARE   Only law students may apply for these loans. Write to the New England Loan Marketing Association, Nellie Mae, 50 Braintree Hill Park, Suite 300, Braintree, MA 02184; or call 1-800-634-9308.

MBASHARE   Business students may apply for these loans. Write to the New England Loan Marketing Association, Nellie Mae, 50 Braintree Hill Park, Suite 300, Braintree, MA 02184; or call 1-800-634-9308.

Medical Access Loans   These loans are for medical students. Write to the Access Group, P.O. Box 7430, Wilmington, DE 19803-0430; or call 1-800-282-1550.

MEDLOANS and Alternative Loan Program (ALP)   Medical students may apply for these loans. Write to the Association of American Medical Colleges, 2450 N Street NW, Washington, D.C. 20037; or call 202-828-0400.

MEDSHARE   These loans are limited to medical and dental students. Write to the New England Loan Marketing Association, Nellie Mae, 50 Braintree Hill Park, Suite 300, Braintree, MA 02184; or call 1-800-634-9308.

Option 4 Loan Program   This loan program focuses on graduate students in any discipline. Write to USAFunds, P.O. Box 6198, Indianapolis, IN 46206-6198; or call 1-800-635-3785.

PLATO   Graduate students in any discipline may apply for these loans. Write to the Classic Student Loan, 205 Van Buren Street, Suite 200, Herndon, VA 20170-5336; or call 1-800-467-5286, fax 703-709-8609.

Professional Education Plan   Applicants must be graduate and professional students, including but not limited to students in the chiropractic, osteopathic, optometric, veterinary, physical therapy, physician's assistant, nursing, or occupational therapy fields. Write to the Education Resources Institute, 330 Stuart Street, Suite 500, Boston, MA 02116-5237; or call 1-800-243-8886.

Signature Health Loan   These loans are designed for students in allopathic medicine, dentistry, optometry, osteopathic medicine, pharmacy, podiatry, and veterinary medicine only. Write to Sallie Mae, 1050 Thomas Jefferson Street NW, Washington, D.C. 20007-3871; or call 1-888-888-3461.

Graduate Study Financial Aid Programs

Graduate students can acquire financial aid from many of the same sources that undergraduate students do. In addition, many colleges award money to graduate students for fellowships and teaching assistant positions.

Distance Learning Programs   If you're thinking about graduate school, Peterson's excellent Web site offers information about distance learning programs, as well as a discussion area for graduate students. Visit their site for more information: **www.petersons.comgraduate/indexfa.html.**

Embark for Graduates   Embark's Web site provides information about financial aid for graduate schools, including student loans, scholarships, grants, and work-study programs. Visit the site for more information: **www.embark.comfa/sm/default.asp.**

Graduate Tests (GMAT, GRE, LSAT, MCAT)

If you decide that you want to go to graduate school, you'll probably have to take one of the following tests.

Graduate Management Assessment Test (GMAT)

It is used by graduate schools of business to assess the qualifications of applicants to graduate management programs. The GMAT is available only as a computer-adaptive test (CAT), where questions are displayed on a computer terminal and answers are entered directly into the computer.

GMAT Practice Test   The Web site includes "hot tips" on how to take the test and other information, which can be found at **www.petersons.com/testprep/gmat.html.**

GMAT Information and Registration
Educational Testing Service
PO Box 6103
Princeton, NJ 08541-6103
Telephone: 609-771-7330 Fax: 609-883-4349

Graduate Record Examination (GRE)

A multiple-choice test which most graduate schools use for admission into their graduate programs. The GRE is available only as a computer-adaptive test (CAT), where questions are displayed on a computer terminal and answers are entered directly into the computer.

GRE Practice Test   A practice test is available at **www.ets.org/cbtdemo.html.**

GRE Information and Registration   For information go to the Educational Testing Service Network Web site at **www.ets.org/** or write to:

Graduate Record Examination
Educational Testing Service
P.O. Box 6000
Princeton, NJ 08541
609-771-7670

Highly Recommended

The GRE Program provides practice tests, publications, and services. Visit their Web site at **www.gre.org** to learn more.

Law School Admission Test (LSAT)

Current fee for the test is $88.00. The LSAT is published by the Educational Testing Service. Call them at 215-968-1001 or visit their Web site at: **darkwing.uoregon.edu/~testing/lsat.html.**

Information and Registration Find it at **www.best.indiana.edu/LSAT.html.**

Medical College Admissions Test (MCAT)

Practice Test You can find a practice test at **www.geocities.com/~writing-tutor/mcat.html.**

Information and Registration For information, or to register, write to:

MCAT Registration
The American College Testing Program
P.O. Box 414
Iowa City, IA 52243

Highly Recommended

Petersons is a recognized name and publisher of a wide variety of student test materials. They offer GRE Practice Tests that include "hot tips" on how to take the test. Visit their Web site at **www.petersons.com/ testprep/gre/html** to learn more.

Highly Recommended

4Tests.com offers a number of practice tests for college entrance exams including one for the MSAT. Visit their Web site at **www.4tests.com/exams.asp.**

Handicapped Students Assistance Programs

The following section lists private organizations that offer assistance to handicapped persons. Also see Appendix C for the office which administers rehabilitation services in your state, where you can get information on special programs available in your area.

Alexander Graham Bell Association for the Deaf
3417 Volta Place NW
Washington, D.C. 20007

The association awards several outstanding scholarships annually to deaf students.

American Council of the Blind
1010 Vermont Avenue
Washington, D.C. 20005

This nonprofit organization works with colleges and universities throughout the country to provide the latest tools and technology to assist blind students in obtaining college degrees. The Council also awards several scholarships each year to qualified blind students.

Association on Handicapped Student Services
Programs in Post-Secondary Education
P.O. Box 21192
Columbus, OH 43221

This nonprofit, tax-exempt organization has been set up to assist handicapped students in finding financial aid. To learn more about their programs, visit their Web site at **www.narha.org/**.

Council of Citizens with Low Vision (CCLV)
1400 Drake Road, #218
Kalamazoo, MI 49006
616-381-9566

The CCLV is an advocacy membership organization for partially sighted people. The council aims to establish the right of these persons to receive financial aid. To learn more about their programs, visit their Web site at **www.healthfinder.gov/text/orgs/HR1 105.html**.

Deafness and Communicative Disorders Branch
Switzer Building, M/S 3228
330 C Street SW
Washington, D.C. 20202-2736

This national institute on deafness and other communication disorders offers several scholarship programs. To learn more about their programs, visit their Web site at **www. chid.nih.gov/ subfile/contribs/dc.html**.

Epilepsy Foundation
4251 Garden City Drive
Landover, MD 20785

The Epilepsy Foundation is a national charitable organization, founded in 1968 as the Epilepsy Foundation of America. It is the only such organization wholly dedicated to the welfare of people with epilepsy. To learn more about their scholarship programs, visit their Web site at **www.efa.org/**.

Foundation for Science and the Handicapped
1141 Iroquois Drive #14
Napierville, IL 60540

The following Web site lists several foundations for handicapped students who are interested in pursuing a degree in science. For more information, visit:

www.altavista.com/cgi-bin/ query?q=Foundation+for+Science+ and+the+Handicapped&kl=XX&pg=q &Translate=on.

Gallaudet University
800 Florida Avenue NE
Washington, D.C. 20002

The mission of Gallaudet University is to serve as a comprehensive, multipurpose institution of higher education for deaf and hard-of-hearing citizens of the United States and of the world. In addition to its undergraduate and graduate academic programs, the university also offers national demonstration elementary and secondary education programs. To learn more about their scholarship programs, visit their Web site at **www.gallaudet.edu/ university.html**.

Health Resources Center and Services Administration (HRSA)
One Dupont Circle NW
Washington, D.C. 20036-1193

The HRSA directs national health programs that improve the nation's health by ensuring equitable access to comprehensive, quality health care for all.

HRSA works to improve and extend life for people living with HIV/AIDS, provide primary health care for medically underserved people, serve women and children through state programs, and train a health workforce that is both diverse and motivated to work in underserved areas. To learn more about their scholarship programs, visit their Web site at **www.hrsa.dhhs.gov/**.

Helen Keller National Center
111 Middle Neck Road
Sands Point, NY 11050

Since the launch of the Interpreters' Network in September 1996, this Web site has been visited more than 60,000 times. It is rapidly becoming "information central" for interpreters whose working languages include a signed language. The site has been reviewed by Magellan and given a three-star rating and also by Look Smart; their banners are proudly displayed on the front page of the site. To learn more about their scholarship programs, visit: **www.terpsnet.com/cards/99c090. html**.

Immune Deficiency Foundation
25 W. Chesapeake Avenue, Suite 206
Towson, MD 21204
410-321-6647

This national nonprofit health organization is dedicated to improving the diagnosis and treatment of primary immune deficiency diseases through research. To learn more about their scholarship programs, visit their Web site at **www.primaryimmune.org/**.

Learning Disability Association of America
4156 Library Road
Pittsburgh, PA 15234
Fax: 412-344-0224

To learn more about the Learning Disability Association's scholarship programs, visit their Web site at **www.mdtap.org/tt/1998.08/ 3-art.html**.

National Technical Institute for the Deaf (NTID)
Office of the Dean
52 Lomb Memorial Drive
Rochester, NY 14623

The NTID is the world's largest technical college for deaf students. To learn more about their scholarship programs, visit their Web site at **www.rit.edu/ ~433www/**.

Office of Special Education Programs
U.S. Department of Education
600 Independence Avenue
Washington, D.C. 20202-2570

To learn more about the Department of Education's scholarship programs for the disabled, visit their Web site at **www.altavista.com/cgi-bin/query? q=Office+of+Special+Education+ Programs&kl=XX&pg=q&Translate= on&search.x=16&search.y=10**. Also see Appendix C for listings of state Departments of Education and other agencies offering rehabilitation programs.

Recording for the Blind and Dyslexic
20 Roszel Road
Princeton, NJ 08540

This nonprofit organization provides textbooks on cassette and computer disk to blind and visually impaired students. To learn more about their programs, visit their Web site at **www.princetonol.com/groups/rfb/ index.html**.

303

International Financial Aid Directory

Unfortunately, there are not a lot of financial aid sources for study abroad. However, we have listed several major points of contact in this section to help you get started.

American Institute for Foreign Study
102 Greenwich Ave.
Greenwich, CT 06830
1-800-727-2437

This organization arranges cultural exchange and study-abroad programs throughout the world for more than 40,000 students each year.

Canadian Opportunities   This completely Canadian Web site is chock-full of scholarships, grants, and bursaries available to Canadian students. For more information, visit: **www.studentawards.com**.

Council on International Educational Exchange
205 E. 42nd St.
New York, NY 10017
212-822-2600

The council offers a variety of programs, domestic and overseas, for U.S. faculty and administrators, focusing on global issues and regions of the world. Visit their Web site at **www.ciee.org/**.

Institute for International Education
809 United Nations Plaza
New York, NY 10017
212-883-8200

The institute provides detailed descriptions of their 250 grant programs, including the prestigious Fulbright Program. For more information, visit their Web site at **www.iie.org/**.

Major Fellowship Opportunities and Aid to Advanced Education for Foreign Nationals

In this section, we offer several Web sites and addresses for organizations that foreign students can contact for financial aid.

CISP International Studies Funding Book
Council for Intercultural Studies and Programs
60 E. 42nd St.
New York, NY 10017
1-800-316-2739

This book provides guidelines and identifies contacts for students who are interested in studying abroad. For more information, visit their Web site at **www.utoledo.edu/students.htmlx**.

Dan Cassidy's Worldwide College Scholarship Directory   This directory offers a complete listing of financial aid resources from Australia to Zanzibar. To order, contact the National Scholarship Research Service at 1-800-432-7827 or 707-546-6781.

Financial Resources for International Study This is a listing of funding sources for U.S. students seeking support for study abroad. For more information, contact the Institute for International Education, IIE Books, Box 371, Annapolis Junction, MA 20701; or call 1-800-445-0443.

International Student Guide This guide discusses many topics of interest to international students, including financial aid for specific colleges. To order the guide, contact College Board Publications, 2 College Way, Forrester Center, WV 25438; or call 1-800-323-7155.

The National Academy of Sciences of Belarus The Web site is maintained by Dr. Nikolai N. Kostyukovich, Deputy Chief Scientific Secretary of the Academy. The list is always in a developmental stage and updated regularly. Visit the site at **www.ac.by/world/index.html.**

National Academy of Sciences, Fellowship Office
2101 Constitution Ave. NW
Washington, D.C. 20418

Web site: **www.ac.by/world/index.html.**

Lenders of College Loans

Virtually all families regardless of their affluence can borrow the entire cost of their kid's college education. There are no restrictions on how much money you make; you can still get an unsubsidized loan. You can make a million dollars a year and still get a Federal Stafford or PLUS loan at preferred interest rates.

Almost all major banks and lending institutions in the country offer student loans. Some institutions specialize in them. Here's a partial list of lenders to contact:

Lenders of College Loans (Telephone Directory)

Access Group, 1-800-282-1550

American Express College Loan Program, 1-800-814-4595

Bank of America National Student Lending, 1-800-344-8382

Bank of America (Texas Student Loan Center), 1-800-442-0567

Bank of America (loans in Idaho and Washington), 1-800-535-4671

Bank of Boston, 1-800-226-7866

Bank One Educational Finance Group, 1-800-487-4404

Chase Manhattan Bank Educational Loans, 1-800-242-7339

College Board, 212-713-8000

College Savings Bank, 1-800-888-2723

Commerce Bank, 1-800-666-3910

Connecticut Student Loan Foundation (CSLF), 1-860-257-4001

Crestar Bank's Student Lending Department, 1-800-552-3006

EduServ Technologies, 1-800-445-4236

EduServ ConSern Loans for Education, 1-800-732-2178

Extra Credit Extra Time, 1-800-874-9390

First Union Education Loan Services, 1-800-955-8805

Fleet Education Finance, 1-800-235-3385

GATE Student Loan Program, 1-800-895-4283

Heal Loans (medical-graduate), 301-443-1540

Independent Federal Savings Bank, 1-800-733-0473

KeyBank USA, 1-800-539-5363

Law-Access Group, 1-800-282-1550

Massachusetts Educational Financing Authority, 1-800-842-1531

MBA Loans (graduate students), 1-888-440-4622

MED Loans, 1-800-858-5050

Mellon Bank EduCheck, 1-800-366-7011

Nellie Mae (Excel and Share Loan Programs), 1-800-634-9308

Wells Fargo Student Loan Center, 1-800-658-3567

PHEAA (Graduate Loan Center, division of Pennsylvania Higher Education Assistance Agency), 1-800-446-8210

Sallie Mae (College Answer Service), 1-800-239-4211

Sandy Spring National Bank, 301-774-8488

Signet Bank Educational Funding, 1-800-434-1988

TERI Supplemental (The Educational Resources Institute), 1-800-255-8374

United Student Aid Funds, 1-800-635-3785

Lenders of College Loans (Web Sites)

Many major lending institutions throughout the United States specialize in offering loans to college students. Although there isn't room here to list them all, we do list the Web sites of the major college lending institutions.

Bank of America   Bank of America offers an online student banking center that offers products and services. Their services cover a variety of financial needs. Visit their Web site at **www.bankofamerica.com/student banking.**

Chase Education Loans   Chase Bank is committed to helping high school students and their families in their search for education funding. For more information, visit their Web site at **www.chase.com/chase/gx.cgi/FTcs?pagename=Chase/Href&urlname=chasehome.**

Compare Loans   This Web site allows you to compare student loans online and includes comprehensive financial aid information with budgeting tools for loan analysis. Visit the site for more information: **www.knowledgefirst.com.**

Financial Aid Loan Links   This Web site links to various lender, school, and government sites about financial aid. Visit the site for more information: **www.4financialaid.com.**

Loan Database   This is the U.S. Department of Education's Web site that offers you access to student loan databases and a wealth of other information. For more information, visit: **www.nslds.ed.gov.**

PNC Bank   This bank consistently ranks in the top 10 of education loan providers in the United States. It offers a full range of products in the Federal Family Education Loan Program as well as private alternative loans. The bank also provides students with innovative discounted loan programs that will save them money, and it sponsors scholarships for students across the country. Visit their Web site at **www.finaid.org/loans/lenders/pncbank.phtml.**

> **Highly Recommended**
>
> **Citibank**   You can apply for a loan online through Citibank's Web site, or you can access a variety of financial tools and calculators that will help you determine exactly how much money you need to borrow for college. Visit them at **www.studentloan.com.**

Service Provider   AES is a guarantor and lender providing students with a single point of service from the application and delivery of loans, through the conclusion of a successful repayment period. Visit their Web site for more information: **www.aessuccess.org.**

Southwest Student Services Corporation   As one of the premier student lending companies serving students nationwide, Southwest Student Services Corporation offers a full array of loan choices. It is a nonprofit company that focuses solely on student lending. Southwest's interest rates and related fees are some of the most competitive in the marketplace. Visit their Web site at **www.sssc.com.**

Student Loan Funding   This Web site provides personalized solutions, including scholarships, financial aid calculators, and student loans. Visit them at **www.studentloanfunding.com.**

U.S. Bank   This Web site helps answer serious questions about attending college and applying for loans. It also offers a list of hotlinks on related topics. Visit **www.usbank.compersonal/index.html.**

Loan Consolidation and Forgiveness Programs

The following organizations can help you consolidate your loans into one manageable monthly payment. They can also provide you with information on loan forgiveness program options.

The National College Scholarship Foundation (NCSF)   You can find out about loan forgiveness programs by calling 301-548-9423.

Nellie Mae   Federal and private education loans for undergraduate and graduate students are processed through a program known as Nellie Mae. To learn more about the program, call 1-800-634-9308 or visit their Web site at **www.nelliemae.com/**.

PHEAA (Pennsylvania Higher Education Assistance Agency)   This agency is a full-service student financial aid organization and a national leader in educational assistance. To learn more about the program, call 1-800-692-7392 or visit their Web site at **www.pheaa.org/**.

Sallie Mae Educational Loan Center   Sallie Mae provides student loans and other financial aid services to make paying for a college education more affordable for students and their families. To learn more, call 1-800-524-9100 or visit their Web site at **www.salliemae.com/**.

Loan Programs

There is a wealth of information out there to help you determine whether a student loan is right for you. Here are several sources to contact:

Find-A-Loan   This Web site has a search function to help you find loans that are right for you. It explains what Stafford and Perkins Loans are all about, who is eligible, and how you apply for a loan. Visit the site for more information: **www.educaid.com**.

General Loan Information   This Web site offers you useful tools for submitting online loan applications and provides loan criteria, loan calculators to determine costs, and other useful financial aid tools. Visit the site for more information: **www.studentloan.com**.

Key Bank   For more information about Key Education Resources, call 1-1-800-KEY-LEND (539-5363) or visit their Web site: **www.key.comtemplates/t-le1.5. jhtml?nodeID=H-5**.

Parent or PLUS Loans   This Web site explains what PLUS loans are, who is eligible, and how you apply for a loan. Visit their Web site for more information: **www.finaid.org/loans/parentloan.phtml**.

Highly Recommended

Easy Access for Students and Institutions (EASI)   EASI neatly organizes all the major federal loans and grants into a concise list with links to their respective sites. The site exposes you to details that are commonly overlooked and covers what to do after college when you start giving back loan money. Visit their Web site for more information: **www.easi.ed.gov**.

Private or Alternative Loans   This Web site explains what private or alternative loans are all about and how you apply for a loan. Visit the site for more information: **www.finaid.org/loans/privateloan.phtml**.

Stafford and Perkins Loans   At this Web site you'll learn what Stafford and Perkins Loans are all about, who is eligible, and how you apply for a loan. Visit the site for more information: **www.finaid.org/loans/studentloan.phtml**.

Student Loan Specialists   Educaid specializes in student loans. They can provide you with answers to your financial aid questions and offer advice on how to get started in your search for a loan. Visit their Web site for more information: **www.educaid.com**.

USA Group   This Web site is especially helpful for student loan borrowers. It features calculators that determine how much it will cost to repay student loans. For more information, visit **www.usagroup.com**.

Military and Veteran Programs

The military and veteran organizations offer exciting scholarship opportunities that you may want to check out. Veterans Administration Centers are listed by state in Appendix C.

General Information   This Web site offers general information about military financial aid programs. Visit the site for more information: **www.nfx.net/~nqh1/pamphlets.html**.

GI Bill   This Web site explains the GI Bill and also covers military scholarships, education benefits, and school rankings, all from a military perspective. Visit the site for more information: **www.easi.ed.gov**.

Minority Programs

The following is just a partial list of whom to contact for more information about some of the excellent financial aid programs available for minorities.

American Institute of Certified Public Accountants   This organization offers financial assistance to qualified minority students. For more information, write to the Manager, Minority Recruitment, American Institute of Certified Public Accountants, 1211 Avenue of the Americas, New York, NY 10036-3775. Application deadlines are July 1 and December 1.

Bureau of Indian Affairs   This program provides financial aid to eligible Native American students. The awards are based on financial need. For further information, write to the Bureau of Indian Affairs Higher Education Grant Program, Bureau of Indian Affairs, 18th and C Street NW, Washington, D.C. 20245.

Congressional Hispanic Caucus   This organization provides fellowships to qualified Hispanic students to work with members of Congress. The fellowships are for one academic term. For further information on this program, contact the Congressional Hispanic Caucus, 504 C Street NE, Washington, D.C. 20002.

General Motors   The GM Corporation provides scholarship assistance to qualified minority undergraduate students through several colleges and universities in the United States. For more information, write to the General Motors Scholarship Program, General Motors Corporation, 8–163 General Motors Building, Detroit, MI 48202.

National Action Council for Minorities in Engineering (NACME)   This organization provides financial assistance to qualified undergraduate minority students pursuing degrees in engineering. The major funding is directed through corporate scholarships that are administered by NACME. For more information, write to the National Action Council for Minorities in Engineering, 3 W. 35th Street, New York, NY 10001; or call 212-279-2644, fax 212-629-5178.

Office of Indian Education Programs   The scholarship awards are based on financial need. For further information, write to Indian Fellowship Program, Office of Indian Education Programs, 1849 C Street NW, MS-Room 3525, Washington, D.C. 20242.

United Methodist Church   The Board of Higher Education and Ministry awards scholarships to qualified undergraduate and graduate minority students. Applicants must be U.S. citizens or permanent residents; must be Hispanic, Asian, or Native American; and must be active members of the Methodist church. The United Methodist church also sponsors several scholarship and loan programs for graduate students. A church-sponsored loan program is available to undergraduate as well as graduate students. For additional information, write to the United Methodist Church, Board of Higher Education and Ministry, Box 871, Nashville, TN 37202.

United Negro College Fund   This organization awards over a thousand scholarships a year to students attending United Negro College Fund schools. The awards are based on financial need and academic merit. For more information, write to the United Negro College Fund, 8260 Willow Oaks Corporate Drive, Fairfax, VA 22031. For a list of United Negro College Fund schools, see Chapter 13.

Prepaid Tuition Programs

Prepaid tuition plans are usually operated statewide and permit families to lock in a tuition rate years in advance of when their kids will be ready for college. The money you deposit is set aside in a state account. For more information, see the following list of phone numbers for states whose college institutions participate in prepaid tuition plans. If your state is not listed, call your state Department of Education (listed under your state in Appendix C) and ask whether they plan to offer a prepaid tuition plan in the near future. They may have added the program after this book was printed.

Alabama, 1-800-252-7228
Alaska, 907-474-7469
Colorado, 1-800-478-5651
Florida, 1-800-552-4723
Indiana, 317-232-6386
Kentucky, 1-800-928-8926
Louisiana, 1-800-259-5626, ext. 1012
Maryland, 1-800-903-7875
Massachusetts, 1-800-449-6332, option 1
Michigan, 1-800-243-2847
Mississippi, 1-800-987-4450
Ohio, 1-800-589-6882 or 1-800-233-6734
Pennsylvania, 1-800-440-4000
Tennessee, 1-888-486-2378
Texas, 1-800-445-4723
Virginia, 1-888-567-0540
Wisconsin, 888-338-3789

Private Tuition Payment Plans

Academic Management Services (AMS)   This company offers innovative educational payment programs for college students. It also offers loan origination, including federal loan programs. To learn more about AMS, call 1-800-635-0120 or visit their Web site at **www.amsweb.com/**.

EduServ Tuition Installment Plan   EduServ is supported by the Higher Education Funding Councils and provides tuition installment plans to qualified students. To learn more about EduServ, call 1-800-445-4236 or visit their Web site at **www.eduserv.ac.uk/**.

FACTS Tuition Management System   This company provides tuition management services to colleges and universities throughout the country. To learn more about FACTS, call 1-800-624-7092 or visit their Web site at **www.factsmgt.com/wccase.html**.

Key Education Resources and Knight College Resources Group   Key offers a range of education planning and financing products that can help you meet your education goals. For more information, call 1-800-225-6783.

Reference Books, Periodicals, and News Sources

This section has a selected list of excellent books, periodicals, and news sources that will help you learn more about the financial aid process.

Book Links   This Web site offers books, links, and resources to help you find the money you need for your education. For more information, visit **www.scholarstuff.com**.

Catalog of Federal Domestic Assistance (CFDA)   This is the federal government's guide to all funding programs. The catalog is a good place to start a grants search for federal funding. The CFDA number consists of two digits that identify the agency (for example, the Education Department is 84 and the Health and Human Services Department is 93). Visit their Web site for more information: **www.cfda.gov.**

College Financial Aid Handbook   This handbook is published by the American Legion and costs $3. To order, write National Emblem Sales, P.O. Box 1050, Indianapolis, IN 46206; or call 317-630-1200.

Community of Science   Federally funded research on science topics is the focus of this Web site. Visit it for more information: **www.cos.com.**

Complete College Financing Guide   This guide is published by Barron's and costs $14.95. Call 1-800-645-3476 to order.

Don't Miss Out: The Ambitious Student's Guide to Financial Aid   This guide is published by Octameron Association and costs $8. Call 703-836-5480 to order.

Financial Aid Newsletter   Those seeking financial assistance and other information regarding grants, scholarships, and loans for college attendance will be interested in subscribing to this free electronic newsletter (*FinAid Newsletter*). Visit their Web site for more information: **www.finaid.org.**

Foundation News & Commentary   This Web page answers frequently asked questions and offers information from the magazine of the same name. Visit the site for more information: **www.cof.org.**

Free Scholarship Resources   Free Scholarship Resources' Web site offers insider secrets about finding and winning scholarships, boosting financial aid, and minimizing tuition bills. Visit the site for more information: **www.usnews.comusnews/edu/ dollars/dshome.html.**

How to Buy a College Education   This guide is published by the Access Group and costs $14.95. Call 612-941-7103 to order.

Meeting College Costs: What You Need to Know Before Your Child and Your Money Leave Home   This guide is published by the College Board and costs $13.95. Call 1-800-323-7155 to order.

Paying for College: A Guide for Parents   This guide is published by the College Board and costs $14.95. Call 1-800-323-7155 to order.

Philanthropy Journal   Philanthropy topics and an extensive meta-index of links to other sites are presented in this Web site. Visit it for more information: **www.pj.org.**

Software Links   This Web site sells books and software for searching out sources of scholarships. Visit the site for more information: **www.educationpage.com.**

Student Guide   This is a free financial aid guide published by the U.S. Department of Education. You can order it by calling 1-800-433-3243, or view it on their Web site at: **www.ed.gov/prog_info/SFA/StudentGuide.**

The Student's Guide: Five Federal Financial Aid Programs   This free government publication is available from the Consumer Information Center, Dept. 511S, Pueblo, CO 81009.

Top 10 Financial Aid Questions   This is a free document published by the National Association for College Admission Counseling. Call 703-836-2222 or write NACAC, 1631 Prince Street, Alexandria, VA 22314-2818.

USA Today—Financial Aid for College: A Quick Guide to Everything You Need to Know   This guide is published by Peterson and costs $8.95. Call 1-800-EDU-DATA (338-3282) to order.

Scholarships, Grants, and Fellowships

There are literally thousands of scholarships, grants, and fellowships that you can apply for if you know where to find them. Fortunately, most funding opportunities are listed in one or more of several databases that you can access over the Internet. In this section, we have identified the best sites from which to start your search.

Arts and Writing Awards   Information on one of the most prestigious arts recognition programs in the country is offered by Scholastic Inc. Over 1,000 awards are given annually. Visit their Web site for more information: **www.scholastic. comartandwriting/index.html.**

Children's Scholarship Fund   This fund provides educational opportunities for low-income children. Visit their Web site for more information: **www.scholarshipfund. org/index.asp.**

College Admissions Scholarships   Scholarships and grants related to college admissions are offered through this Web site. For more information, visit **collegeapps. about.comeducation/collegeapps/msub13.html.**

College Board   Free online scholarship search service includes aid programs from 3,300 sponsors and also features college and career search capabilities. Visit their Web site for more information: **www.collegeboard.org/index_this/fundfinder/html/ ssrchtop.html.**

College Scholarships   Free scholarships are added to this Web site every month (since 1995) for undergraduate, graduate, and international students. Visit the site for more information: **www.collegescholarships.com.**

CollegeNet Mach25 Scholarship Database   This Web site features over 500,000 scholarships from 1,500 sponsoring organizations. The site allows students to save listings and create letters requesting more information. For more information, visit **www.collegenet.commach25.**

ExPAN Scholarship Search   ExPAN is an online version of the College Board's FUND FINDER scholarship database. After you enter information about yourself, the search returns a list of scholarships that you're eligible for. This service is free and includes thousands of colleges. Visit their Web site for more information: **www. collegeboard.org/fundfinder/bin/fundfindOl.pl.**

Financial Aid Information   This Web site provides links to sources of information about student financial aid. It is maintained by Mark Kantrowitz, author of the *Prentice Hall Guide to Scholarships and Fellowships for Math and Science Students*. It includes FastWEB (*Financial Aid Search Through the WEB*)—a searchable database of more than 180,000 private-sector scholarships, fellowships, grants, and loans. Visit the site for more information: **www.finaid.org.**

Florida Scholarships   Statewide scholarship programs for Florida students are covered in this Web site. Visit the site for more information: **www.floridaleader.comsoty.**

Foundation Center   The Foundation Center Web site contains information about foundations and corporate grant makers, philanthropic news, and frequently asked questions about grants and foundations. Visit the site for more information: **www. fdncenter.org.**

Foundation Directory   This directory is an annual reference source for information about private and community grant-making foundations in the United States. It provides basic descriptions and current fiscal data for the nation's largest foundations. For a free catalogue, write to the Foundation Center, 79 Fifth Avenue, New York, NY 10003-3076; or call 1-800-424-9836.

Free Scholarship Databases   In addition to searching FastWeb, you may want to search one of the other free scholarship databases. Visit this Web site for more information: **www.finaid.org/scholarships/other.html.**

FreeScholarships.Com   Win free scholarship money for school through this Web site at **www.freescholarships.com.**

Fresch Scholarships   This is an online database for thousands of sources of scholarships. It has tips on applying for and winning scholarships, and volunteers will answer your financial aid and scholarship questions. Visit their Web site for more information: **www.freschinfo.comindex.phtml.**

Grants   Search a collection of grants available at schools throughout the United States. Visit their Web site for more information: **planet.rtec.org/project/search.cgi.**

Grantsmanship Center   This Web site contains information about the center and its magazine, grant resources, and training classes. There are federal grant announcements and links to other grant sites. Visit the site for more information: **www.tgci.com.**

GrantsNet Scholarships   GrantsNet offers funding opportunities in the biological and medical sciences. Visit their Web site for more information: **www.grantsnet.org.**

Guide Star   This free service has information on the scholarship programs of thousands of American nonprofit organizations. Their Web site also features news stories on philanthropy. For more information, visit **www.guidestar.org.**

Help for Grant Writers   You'll find free online grant-writing classes, funding news, and Internet resources for grant writers, plus a glossary of grant-writing terms and acronyms. There's also a discussion section in which grant writers and nonprofit staff share ideas and experiences. Visit their Web site for more information: **tram.east. asu.edu/fund/index.html.**

McDonald's Scholarships   McDonald's Arching Into Education Scholarship program has more than $425,000 in scholarships available for students in the New York/New Jersey/Connecticut tri-state area. Visit their Web site for more information: **www.archingintoeducation.com.**

National Merit Scholarships   Sharpen those No. 2 pencils. The PSAT/NMSQT is good practice for the SAT and gives you a shot at several prestigious college scholarships. Visit their Web site for more information: **4scholarships.4anything. comnetwork-frame/0,1855,6206-34202,00.html.**

National Science Teachers Association Scholarships   Win scholarships for college by inventing something powered by Duracell brand batteries. The National Science Teachers Association sponsors the awards. Visit its Web site for more information: **www.nsta.org/programs/duracell.**

NEFE High School Finance Literary Awards   This annual award program is intended to help promote lifelong financial literacy and responsibility among today's high school students. Cash awards recognize teens for their creativity. Visit their Web site for more information: **www.nefe.org/hsfla/index.html.**

RAM-FIE   This organization is oriented toward federal programs and research, with an emphasis on scientific grants for researchers. Visit their Web site for more information: **www.fie.com.**

Sallie Mae's Online Scholarship Service   At this Web site, you'll have access to the College Aid Sources for Higher Education (CASHE) database, one of the oldest scholarship databases. Visit the site for more information: **www.salliemae.complanning/ scholarships.html.**

Scholaraid   Scholaraid's database contains over 2.5 million awards worth over $21.6 billion. Visit their Web site for more information: **scholaraid.studentadvantage.com.**

Scholarship Guide   This is a comprehensive guide to financial aid and scholarships for college. Visit their Web site for more information: **www.theoldschool.org.**

Scholarship Resource Network   This database features mostly private, portable, non–need-based scholarships. Visit their Web site for more information: **www.rams.comsrn/scholarships/index.cfm.**

Scholarships Express   This Web site offers personalized scholarship information. Visit **www.scholarship-page.com.**

Siebel Systems Scholarships   Siebel Systems, a California-based supplier of Web-based software, has donated $3 million toward the goal of allowing more students access to private and parochial school education. Visit their Web site for more information: **www.siebel.comabout-siebel.**

SRN Express   This is a free Web version of the Scholarship Resource Network (SRN) database. The SRN database focuses on private-sector, non-need-based aid and includes numerous scholarship opportunities. To find out about contests, grants, and other aid options, visit **www.studentservices.com.**

Tobias Foundation Scholarships   This foundation funds individual scholarships and is particularly interested in addressing the quality of K–12 education as well as related issues of education reform. Visit their Web site for more information: **www.rltfound.org.**

TRAM Research Funding   Research funding and specialized grant request forms are found on the TRAM Web pages. Visit the site for more information: **tram.east.asu. edu/fund/index.html.**

William E. Simon Foundation   This foundation provides support for scholarships and fellowships for academically qualified students in need of financial assistance. Visit their Web site for more information: **www.wesimonfoundation. org/wesf.nsf.**

Scholastic Aptitude Tests (SAT, PSAT, ACT)

Most of the country's major colleges and universities require students to take an aptitude test as part of their admissions requirement. Your score on these tests could be the determining factor as to whether or not you will be admitted. In this section, we list Web sites that will help you become familiar with the test and let you practice on demonstration tests.

American College Test (ACT)   This test is published by American College Testing to measure a student's ability in math, verbal comprehension, and problem solving. Usually students take this test during their junior or senior year of high school. All the studying in the world won't mean a thing on test day unless you know how to take the test. Much of what you need to know on the ACT is common sense. If you want to learn more about the test, visit this Web site: **testprep.embark.com/act/ freeinfo/act_article_tips.asp.**

Practice SAT Tests (PSAT)   The College Board provides a sample SAT test in their booklet "Taking the SAT by Flashpoints." Flashpoints is a comprehensive SAT study system that will familiarize you with the SAT exam format while sharpening your verbal and math reasoning skills. In addition, the College Board provides detailed explanations designed to improve your understanding of the exam material. By testing yourself with Flashpoints, you'll quickly be able to identify your strengths and weaknesses. This knowledge will enable you to focus on the types of questions and the subject areas you need to review most. Studying with Flashpoints will reinforce your test-taking skills and your retention of the information in an easy-to-use flashcard format. Visit their Web site for more information: **www.nalsa.comfpinfo.html.**

SAT Planner   Find out about the SAT Program test dates, deadlines, and fees. Use the SAT Planner to get all the critical dates you need to know for each test administration, including registration deadlines and score report mailings. Visit their Web site for more information: **www.collegeboard.comsat/html/students/clind001.html.**

SAT Program Information   The SAT Program Information Web site provides general information about the SAT test. Visit the site at **www.collegeboard.comsat/html/students/indx001.html.**

SAT Registration   Register online for any SAT Program test. New features make it faster and more convenient than ever. Visit their Web site for more information: **www.collegeboard.comsat/html/satform.html.**

Software for Financial Aid

ExPan   Take advantage of the free software offered by ExPAN. This comprehensive information-delivery system links schools, colleges, students, and parents. ExPAN software offers a searchable database with more than 3,200 two- and four-year colleges, plus graduate and professional schools. It has electronic application forms, financial planning, FUND FINDER—a financial aid tutorial with college cost data—and 3,300-plus scholarships verified annually. ExPAN isn't a product for home use but is available at high schools throughout the United States and many locations abroad. Visit their Web site for more information: **www.expan.com.**

Tax Deductions

You or your family members may be eligible for federal and/or state tax credits for attending a postsecondary school. It's worth looking into.

Scholarship and Lifetime Learning Tax Credits   Learn about the HOPE Scholarship and Lifetime Learning tax credits available as a result of the 1997 Tax Relief Act by visiting their respective Web sites: **www.ed.gov/offices/OPE/Students/hopegd.html** or **embark.wiredscholar.compaying/content/#lifetime.**

Tax Credits   For examples on how tax credits can work for you, visit the Internal Revenue Service Web site. Be sure to check with your state's Department of Education (see Appendix C) to find out whether similar higher-education tax credits are available. Visit the site for more information: **www.irs.ustreas.gov.**

Women's Financial Aid Publications

There are many excellent publications that recommend funding sources for women students. In addition to the range of financial aid available to all qualifying students, many aid programs are specifically for women.

317

Directory of Financial Aids for Women by Dr. Gail Ann Schlachter, Reference Service Press, 1100 Industrial Road, Suite 9, San Carlos, CA 94070.

Happier by Degrees: A College Re-Entry Guide for Women by Pam Mendelsohn, P.O. Box 4597, Arcata, CA 95518.

Higher Education Opportunities for Minorities and Women, available from the U.S. Department of Education, Superintendent of Documents, P.O. Box 37194, Pittsburgh, PA 15250-7954; or call 202-512-1800, fax 202-512-2250.

How to Get Money for Research by Mary Rubin, The Feminist Press, P.O. Box 1645, Hagerstown, MD 21741.

Professional Women's Groups, available from the American Association of University Women, 2401 Virginia Avenue NW, Washington, D.C. 20007.

Resources for Women in Science, free from the Association for Women in Science, 1346 Connecticut Avenue NW, Washington, D.C. 20036.

Women's Organizations: A National Directory, available from Garrett Park Press, P.O. Box 190, Garrett Park, MD 20896.

Women's Sports Foundation College Scholarship Guide, available from the Women's Sports Foundation, 342 Madison Avenue, Suite 728, New York, NY 10173.

Work-Study and Co-Op Programs

Work-study is a need-based program in which the federal government pays 50 percent of the student's wages for private sector work and 70 percent for on-campus employment. Work-study is administered by college financial aid offices. For state-funded programs, contact your state's Department of Education, listed by state in Appendix C.

Co-op (cooperative education) programs are not based on financial need. They combine classroom work with jobs in the private sector as well as for the federal government (the largest employer of co-op students).

Work-Study

Most of the work-study programs are determined by a needs analysis and will provide employment on campus for students who qualify. Priority will be given to students who have completed the necessary paperwork by June 1. You generally work 20 hours per week. Work-study grants of up to $5,000 per year are available to students who have a demonstrated financial need. Positions are available both on and off campus. The application process and hiring of work-study students takes place in August and September.

In addition to applying for work-study at your college's financial aid office or state Department of Education, the following Web site offers application instructions to students who are interested in applying for a work-study program. It also offers links to other financial aid programs. Visit it at: **www.grayson.edu/admin/stuserv/finaid/wstudy.html.**

Multimedia Learning Center (MMLC)   Its Web site will help you find an opportunity that's right for you. Visit it at **www.mmlc.nwu.edu/jobs/.**

To learn more about work-study grants, visit: **www.law.du.edu/finaid/continuing_students/workstudyc.html.**

Learn To Serve Directory   If you're interested in participating in a work-study program, this online directory will provide you with the names, addresses, and telephone numbers of sponsoring organizations to contact throughout the country. Visit their Web site if you need more information: **www.cns.gov/learn/about/k_12/k12_ca.html.**

University of Pennsylvania Work-Study Program   Most of the major colleges and universities offer work-study programs to their students. However, the programs vary significantly between the different institutions. Some are excellent, while others are, at best, fair. The University of Pennsylvania (UOP) offers one of the best work-study programs in the country. Visit their Web site at **www.psu.edu/dept/studentaid/** to learn more about their program. Then, contact the financial aid office at the college(s) you're interested in attending to see what they have to offer and how it compares with the UOP program.

Co-Op Programs

Co-op education students alternate between full-time work and full-time study, and are paid during their work term which helps offset the costs of tuition. Co-op education also provides career-related experience that extends the learning process beyond the limitations of the classroom and is valuable for entering the job market. Check with your state's financial aid office or Department of Education (listed by state in Appendix C) for information about programs in your state.

Approximately a thousand United States colleges and universities have co-op programs, so also check with your college's financial aid office, or contact the

National Commission for Cooperative Education
360 Huntington Avenue, 384 CP
Boston, MA 02115-5096
617-373-3770

See if a trade association related to your field is listed under "Associations Related to Financial Aid" in this Directory, and find out if any companies in your area participate in work-study programs.

Another good resource is *Gales Encyclopedia of Associations,* which lists trade associations for every field and area of business.

Eberly College of Science Co-Op Program   An example of a good resource is the Eberly College of Science Co-op Program. This program places students in government labs or industry, for pay and academic credit. Through the program, students can acquire hands-on experience in real-life situations. Co-op opportunities include, for example, astronomy research that emphasizes computer skills at government and industrial positions. Students planning to take advantage of this program should begin applying for Co-op positions during their sophomore year for Co-op rotations in the following summer or fall. For further information, contact:

Dr. David Burrows
Office of Cooperative Education
520 Thomas Building, University Park, PA 16802

NASA Johnson Space Center (JSC) Cooperative Education Program   The Cooperative Education Program at JSC is open to undergraduate and graduate students from around the country. As a co-op student, you alternate semesters at school with semesters at JSC working in a paid, full-time position directly related to your field of study. See JSC's Web site to learn more about the program: **www.jsc.nasa.gov/coop/jsccoop.html.**

Study Abroad Co-Op Programs   Science co-op and study abroad programs are available to students during their junior or senior year. You can learn more about the program at this site: **www.astro.psu.edu/deptinfo/undersciencecoop.html.**

Alphabetical State Financial Aid Listings

State government agencies, colleges, and universities all play an important role in the financial aid program. They are responsible for distributing the aid money that has been collected by the federal government and passed on to them. The state agencies and educational institutions must follow strict federal guidelines and regulations as they disperse the money.

In addition to the federal financial aid program, all states and most colleges offer their own independent financial aid programs to supplement the federal programs. That's why we decided to create this separate appendix dedicated to state financial aid.

Make sure you know about every financial aid program offered in your state so that you can take maximum advantage of any program that you qualify for. States are more generous than the federal government with their financial aid funds; thus you have a better chance of qualifying for a state program. Contact the state agencies listed in this appendix and all state colleges to learn more about any special aid programs that they may offer. Don't forget to contact the private institutions as well.

Under each state, we highlight special aid programs that may interest you, and we give you the addresses of each state's ...

➤ **Financial aid office.** State *aid offices* oversee most of your state's student aid. They have the most up-to-date and comprehensive information you can find on financial aid programs. A word of warning, however: Individual state programs such as scholarships and grants are in a continual state of change. Always check to find out whether the program you want to apply for is still available, or whether it's changed in any way that would affect your application.

➤ **Guaranty agency.** State *guaranty agencies* are nonprofit organizations that administer the FFEL (Federal Family Education Loan) and PLUS (Parent Loans for Undergraduate Students) loans that are covered in detail in Chapter 15, "The Inside Scoop on Student Loans."

➤ **Community service agency.** The office which administers *community service programs* in your state can lead you to work-study programs in your area.

➤ **Department of education.** State *Departments of Education* are sources of information for state grants, work-study programs, and minority programs. They also administer prepaid tuition plans in states which participate in them. See the "Prepaid Tuition Plans" section of Appendix B to see if your state is one of them.

➤ **Rehabilitation services.** The *rehabilitation service* in your state can lead you to special programs and assistance for handicapped students.

➤ **Veterans administration center.** Your state's *Veterans Administration* center can tell you about financial aid for students who are veterans.

Contents

Alabama

Alabama Student Assistance Program provides grants up to $2,500 per year. The awards are need based, and applicants must be Alabama residents. Interested applicants should file the FAFSA as early as possible to qualify for the program.

Alabama Student Grant Program gives grants of up to $1,200 per year to both full-time and part-time undergraduate students attending state colleges or universities. Applications are available from the school you plan to attend.

Junior and Community College Athletic Scholarship Program provides grant assistance for tuition and books at community colleges in Alabama. Awards are based on athletic ability, not financial need. Awards may be renewed based on continued participation in the designated sport. Further information may be obtained from the athletic director, coach, or financial aid counselor at any community college in Alabama.

Financial Aid Office and Guaranty Agency
Alabama Commission on Higher Education
P.O. Box 302000
Montgomery, AL 36130-2000
334-242-1998

Community Service Programs
Governor's Office on Volunteerism
Alabama State Capitol
600 Dexter Avenue
Montgomery, AL 36130
205-242-7174

Department of Education
Gordon Persons Building
50 N. Ripley St.
P.O. Box 302101
Montgomery, AL 36130
334-242-9700

Rehabilitation Services
Department of Education
50 N. Ripley St.
P.O. Box 302101
Montgomery, AL 36130
205-281-8780 or 205-281-8780 (294 TDD)

Department of Veterans Affairs
Regional Office
474 South Court Street
Montgomery, AL 36104

Alaska

Alaska's Student Loan Program is available to graduate, undergraduate, and vocational students who are state residents. Students must be in good academic standing to receive this loan. Loan forgiveness options are available under this program.

Teacher Scholarship Loan Program provides financial assistance to high school graduates who are planning to pursue teaching careers in rural elementary and secondary schools in Alaska and are nominated by a rural school district. To be eligible, students must be state residents.

Robert C. Thomas Memorial Scholarship Loan Fund offers loans to students enrolled in accredited colleges and universities and pursuing careers in education, public administration, or other related fields.

Financial Aid Office and Guaranty Agency
Alaska Commission on Postsecondary Education
3030 Vintage Boulevard
Juneau, AK 99801
907-465-2962

Community Service Programs
Department of Regional and Community Affairs
P.O. Box 112100
Juneau, AK 99811
907-465-4700

Department of Education
801 W. 10th St.
Juneau, AK 99801-1894
907-465-2800

Office of Vocational Rehabilitation
P.O. Box FMS 0581
Juneau, AK 99811
907-465-2814 or 907-465-2440 (TDD)

Department of Veterans Affairs
Regional Office
235 East Eighth Avenue
Anchorage, AK 99501

Arizona

Arizona State Student Incentive Grant Program provides funds to needy students who attend participating postsecondary educational institutions in Arizona. Awards are made to both undergraduate and graduate students. Recipients must be state residents and have financial need.

Bureau of Indian Affairs Grant Program provides annual grants to Native American students. The amount of the award varies and is need based. Contact your school's financial aid office for further information.

WICHE Student Exchange Program helps state residents obtain access to professional education not available in Arizona but made available at participating institutions in other western states at a reduced tuition rate. Contact your school's financial aid office for further information.

Financial Aid Office and Guaranty Agency
United Student Aid Group Arizona Education Loan Program
25 South Arizona Place, Suite 530
Chandler, AZ 85225
602-814-9988 or 1-800-551-1353

Community Service Programs
Governor's Office of Community Programs and Public Outreach
1700 West Washington, Third Floor
Phoenix, AZ 85007
602-542-3461

Department of Education
United Student Aid Group Arizona Education Loan Program
25 South Arizona Place, Suite 530
Chandler, AZ 85225
602-814-9988 1-800-551-1353

Rehabilitation Services Administration
1300 West Washington
Phoenix, AZ 85007
602-542-3323 (TDD) or 1-800-352-8161

Department of Veterans Affairs, Regional Office
3225 North Central Avenue
Phoenix, AZ 85012

Arkansas

MIA/KIA Dependents' Scholarship Program offers scholarship assistance to full-time undergraduate students who are dependents or spouses of persons killed in action, missing in action, or prisoners of war from 1960 to the present.

Law Enforcement Officers Dependents' Scholarship Program offers scholarship assistance to full-time students who are dependents of Arkansas state law enforcement officers.

Financial Aid Office
Arkansas Department of Higher Education
114 East Capitol
Little Rock, AR 72201-1884
501-371-2000

Guaranty Foundation of Arkansas
219 South Victory
Little Rock, AR 72201
501-372-1491

Community Service Programs
Arkansas Division of Volunteerism
103 East Seventh Street
Donaghey Building
Little Rock, AR 72201
501-682-6724

Department of Education
#4 Capitol Mall, State Education Bldg.
Little Rock, AR 72201
501-682-4260

Division of Rehabilitation Services
720 West Third Street
Little Rock, AR 72201
501-324-09106

Department of Veterans Affairs, Regional Office
Building 65, Ft. Roots
P.O. Box 1280
North Little Rock, AR 72115

California

Cal Grant A Program assists low- and middle-income students in meeting their educational expenses. Recipients are selected on the basis of grade-point average and financial need. Students must be enrolled at least half-time to be eligible for this program.

Cal Grant B Program provides financial assistance to very low income students. Most of the recipients of this grant are enrolled in public community colleges. The amount of the award varies but generally provides a living allowance and sometimes tuition and fee financial assistance.

Cal Grant C Program helps vocational school students with tuition and training costs. Recipients must be enrolled at a community college, independent college, or vocational school. Three-year, hospital-based nursing students are also eligible for this program.

State Work-Study Program offers eligible college and university students the opportunity to earn money to meet some of their expenses. Students may be placed with public institutions or nonprofit or profit-making enterprises.

Financial Aid Office and Guaranty Agency
California Student Aid Commission
P.O. Box 510845
Sacramento, CA 94245-0845
916-323-0435

Community Service Programs
California Commission on Improving Life Through Service
1121 L Street, Suite 600
Sacramento, CA 95814
916-323-7646

Department of Education
P.O. Box 944272
Sacramento, CA 94244-2720
916-327-0219

California Department of Rehabilitation
830 K Street Mall
Sacramento, CA 95814
916-445-1971

Department of Veterans Affairs, Regional Office
Federal Building
11000 Wilshire Boulevard
Los Angeles, CA 90024

Colorado

Virtually every college and university in Colorado offers a rich mixture of scholarships to students from all walks of life. For example:

The *University of Colorado (UC) Alumni Association* funds scholarships for undergraduate students at CU's Colorado Springs campus. The Association awards two scholarships of $1,000 each to be used for educational expenses.

Unfortunately, we don't have the space in this section to list all of the scholarships that are available from the institutions in Colorado. However, if you visit the following Web site, you will get a good idea of what's available: **www.co-ptk.org/page7.html.**

The Boettcher Foundation (303-534-1927) offers 40 renewable scholarships every year. Call them to get an application and to learn who is eligible to apply.

Financial Aid Office
Colorado Commission on Higher Education
1300 Broadway, Second Floor
Denver, CO 80203
303-866-2723

Guaranty Agency
Student Loan Program
999 Eighteenth Street, Suite 425
Denver, CO 80202
303-294-5050

Community Service Programs
Office of the Governor
136 State Capitol Building
Denver, CO 80203
303-866-2120

Department of Education
Office of the Colorado State Board of Education
201 East Colfax Avenue
Denver, CO 80203
303-866-6817

Rehabilitation Services
1575 Sherman, Fourth Floor
Denver, CO 80203-1714
303-866-5196 or 303-866-3258 (TDD)

Department of Veterans Affairs, Regional Office
44 Union Boulevard
P.O. Box 25126
Denver, CO 80225

Connecticut

The Connecticut College Library Scholarship Award was established to encourage the professional development of a Connecticut college senior or alumnus who wants to do graduate study in library science, book conservation, or archival management. Full- and part-time students are eligible. Candidates submit a current curriculum vitae and a short essay describing their plans for graduate study and explaining why they are interested in the field. If you are interested in learning more about the program, call 860-439-2672.

Connecticut Audubon Camp Scholarships are available to area educators from St. Joseph and Elkhart counties to attend the "Audubon Camp for Educators" in Greenwich. Three scholarships are provided by South Bend Audubon Society and include week-long camp sessions throughout the summer. The scholarships cover room and board at the camp.

Financial Aid Office
Connecticut Department of Higher Education
61 Woodland Street
Hartford, CT 06105-2391
860-566-2618

Guaranty Agency
Student Loan Foundation
P.O. Box 1009
Rocky Hill, CT 06067
860-257-4001

Department of Education
165 Capitol Avenue
Hartford, CT 06145
860-566-5677

Commission on Community Services
61 Woodland Street
Hartford, CT 06105
860-947-1800

Division of Rehabilitation Services
10 Griffin Road
North Windsor, CT 06095
203-298-2000 (V/TDD) or 1-800-537-2549 (CT)

Department of Veterans Affairs, Regional Office
Abraham Ribicoff Federal Building
450 Main Street
Hartford, CT 06103

Delaware

The University of Delaware awards over $25 million dollars annually in aid. Financial aid is based on a family's ability to pay, and academic scholarships are awarded on the basis of academic merit without regard to financial need. The University also offers The Delaware Plan, a group of innovative installment and financing options aimed at making it easier for families to budget for their children's education.

If you are an outstanding student academically, you may be eligible for academic scholarships, including those awarded without regard to financial need. At Delaware, all students who apply for fall freshman admission are reviewed for academic scholarships by the Scholarship Committee.

The most promising candidates are selected as University of Delaware semifinalists and are mailed the Application Supplement for Scholarship Semifinalists. As a general rule, semifinalists are in the top 20 percent of the pool of admitted freshmen. Approximately 57 percent of the students who are named scholarship semifinalists are offered scholarships. Awards range from $1,000 per year to full, four-year scholarships.

Academic merit is also recognized for students who are already enrolled at the University of Delaware. Students' transcripts are reviewed at the end of each academic year. Those excelling academically may be awarded additional monies.

Financial Aid Office
Delaware Higher Education Commission
Carvel State Office Building, Fourth Floor
820 North French Street
Wilmington, DE 19801
302-577-3240

Guaranty Agency
Education Loan Services
Carvel State Office Building, Fourth Floor
820 North French Street
Wilmington, DE 19801
302-577-6055

Community Service Programs
DHHS Campus, T Building
1901 North DuPont Highway
New Castle, DE 19720
302-577-4961

Department of Education
P.O. Box 1402
Dover, DE 19903
302-739-4696

Rehabilitation Services
Department of Health and Social Services
Biggs Building
1901 North Dupont Highway
New Castle, DE 19720
302-421-6748

Department of Veterans Affairs, Regional Office
1601 Kirkwood Highway
Wilmington, DE 19805

District of Columbia

The wealth of opportunities available in the Washington, D.C. area is unsurpassed.

The Latino Association of D.C. Interns (LADI) has compiled a list of fellowships, internships, and scholarships in order to directly present them to a larger minority audience. Their objective is to highlight programs that can fulfill the needs and interests of a diverse academic and professional candidacy.

Although the Latino Association primarily lists opportunities available in the Washington, D.C. area, students from other locations have also been included in the program. Visit their Web site at: www.eesc.sc.usp.br/sel/ladi/lading.html if you want to learn more about the program.

The University of Michigan Club of Washington, D.C. offers $5,000 merit and need-based scholarships to promising scholars from the Washington, D.C. metropolitan area who enroll as undergraduate students at the University of Michigan. A committee of Club members reviews the applications and selects a pool of finalists for interviews in March.

Financial Aid Office and Guaranty Agency
Office of Postsecondary Education Assistance
Department of Human Services
2100 Martin Luther King Jr. Avenue SE, Suite 401
Washington, D.C. 20020
202-727-3688

Community Service Programs for College Students
District of Columbia Youth Initiatives Office
717 Fourteenth Street NW, Suite 900
Washington, D.C. 20004
202-727-4970

U. S. Department of Education
400 Maryland Avenue, SW
Washington, D.C. 20202-0498
1-800-872-5327

Rehabilitation Services Administration
1120 G Street NW, Sixth Floor
Washington, D.C. 20005
202-727-8620

Department of Veterans Affairs, Regional Office
941 North Capitol Street, NE
Washington, D.C. 20421

Florida

Vocational Gold Seal Endorsement Scholarships is a scholarship program for outstanding high school graduates. The maximum award is $2,000 per year. Applicants must be state residents and enrolled full-time in an eligible public or private Florida college or university. Applications are available from your high school guidance office and must be received by April 1.

Jose Marti Scholarship Challenge Grant Fund is a need-based scholarship program for Hispanic Americans. Awards of $2,000 are available per academic year. Applicants must be of Hispanic heritage and have a minimum GPA of 3.0 to qualify. You must file a FAFSA to be considered for this program. Applications are available from your high school guidance office. The application deadline is April 1.

Nicaraguan and Haitian Scholarship Program is a one-time scholarship awarded to one Nicaraguan and one Haitian living in Florida, for attendance at a state university. To qualify for this program, you must have a GPA of at least 3.0 and demonstrate a willingness to serve the community.

Rosewood Family Scholarship Fund is a need-based scholarship program for up to 25 minority students per year to attend state universities or public and community colleges. Awards cannot exceed $4,000 per year. Applications are available from the Office of Student Financial Assistance and must be postmarked April 1 or earlier. The FAFSA is also required and must be processed by May 15.

Seminole-Miccosukee Indian Scholarship Program provides scholarship assistance for Seminole and Miccosukee Indians of Florida. The respective tribes determine the amount of the award.

Florida Resident Access Grant provides tuition assistance that is not based on need. The maximum amount is based on available funding and the eligible number of applicants. A minimum of one year of Florida residency is required.

Florida Work Experience Program is a need-based employment program that aims to complement a student's educational and career goals. Undergraduate students who are enrolled at least half-time at an eligible Florida institution may apply. It is necessary to file the FAFSA. Contact your school's financial aid office for further information.

Financial Aid Office, Guaranty Agency, and Department of Education
Office of Student Financial Assistance
Department of Education
P.O. Box 7019
Tallahassee, FL 32314-7019
1-800-366-3475

Governor's Commission on Community Service
1101 Gulf Breeze Parkway, Suite 331
Gulf Breeze, FL 32561
904-934-4000

Division of Vocational Rehabilitation
1709A Mahan Drive
Tallahassee, FL 32399-0696
904-488-6210 or 904-488-2867 (TDD)

Department of Veterans Affairs, Regional Office
144 First Avenue, South
P.O. Box 1437
St. Petersburg, FL 33731

Georgia

Georgia Tuition Equalization Grant Program provides grants, administered by the Georgia Student Finance Authority, for state residents who are attending approved schools. Interested students should complete the Georgia Student Grant Application and submit it to the financial aid office of the college or university they plan to attend.

State Direct Student Loan Program gives loans, with loan forgiveness options, to Georgia students enrolled in approved fields of study in which personnel shortages exist in the state.

Governor's Scholarship Program recognizes graduating Georgia high school seniors of exceptional academic accomplishments who plan to attend an eligible college or university located in Georgia. To be eligible for this program, a student must be selected by the Georgia Department of Education as a Georgia Scholar and must be enrolled or accepted for enrollment as a full-time student. The award covers tuition, up to a maximum of $1,575 per academic year.

Regents Scholarship Program provides scholarship assistance to state residents with superior ability and financial need. Recipients must be enrolled or accepted for enrollment as full-time students in a school of the Georgia university system. Contact your college financial aid office for further information.

Helping Outstanding Pupils Educationally (HOPE) is a program that provides scholarships and grants to students attending public and approved private institutions in Georgia. The awards are not based on need. For additional information, contact your high school guidance counselor.

PROMISE Teacher Scholarships and *HOPE Teacher Scholarship Programs* assist undergraduate students majoring in education. The awards are not based on financial need.

Georgia Public Safety Memorial Grant provides financial assistance to the children of Georgia public safety officers who were killed or permanently disabled in the line of duty. Applicants must attend a public college or university in Georgia. Contact your high school guidance counselor for further information.

Financial Aid Office and Guaranty Agency
Georgia Student Finance Commission
2082 East Exchange Place, Suite 200
Tucker, GA 30084
770-723-1029

Community Service Programs
Georgia Peach Corps
Georgia DCA
100 Peachtree Street
Atlanta, GA 30303
404-657-7827

Department of Education
1970 Twin Towers East
Atlanta, GA 30334-5040
404-657-9954

Division of Rehabilitation Services
878 Peachtree Street, Room 706
Atlanta, GA 30309
404-894-6670 (V/TDD)

Department of Veterans Affairs, Regional Office
730 Peachtree Street NE
Atlanta, GA 30365

Hawaii

Hawaii Student Incentive Grant Program provides tuition grants to full-time undergraduate students who are state residents. Recipients must have financial need and must be eligible to receive a Pell Grant. Contact your high school guidance counselor or college financial aid director for further information.

Regents Scholarships for Academic Excellence award scholarships to new students who are state residents. The awards are renewable. For application forms, contact the University of Hawaii financial aid office.

Financial Aid Office
State Postsecondary Education Commission
209 Bachman Hall
University of Hawaii
2444 Dole Street, Room 209
Honolulu, HI 96822
808-956-8213

Guaranty Agency
Hawaii Education Loan Program
P.O. Box 22187
Honolulu, HI 96823
808-593-2262

Hawaii Commission on National and Community Service
335 Merchant Street, Room 101
Honolulu, HI 96813
808-586-8675

Department of Education
P. O. Box 2360
Honolulu, HI 96804
808-586-3230

Rehabilitation Services
Department of Human Services
1901 Bachelot Street
Honolulu, HI 96817
1-800-548-6367

Department of Veterans Affairs, Regional Office
PJKK Federal Building
300 Ala Moana Boulevard
P.O. Box 50188
Honolulu, HI 96850

Idaho

The Idaho Scholarship Program provides financial assistance to graduating high school seniors who plan to attend an Idaho college or university. Recipients must be state residents and maintain satisfactory academic progress. Contact your high school guidance counselor for further information.

The Idaho Governor's Scholarship Program provides vocational scholarships to outstanding Idaho high school graduates who attend eligible technical schools in Idaho's colleges and universities. Contact your high school guidance counselor for more information.

Paul L. Fowler Memorial Scholarship Program awards scholarships on the basis of class rank and ACT scores. Recipients must be state residents and must enroll as full-time students in an institution of higher learning.

Education Incentive Fee Waiver Program provides financial assistance to state residents who graduated from a secondary school in Idaho and plan a career in teaching. Recipients must rank in the upper 15 percent of their graduating high school class to qualify. Contact your school's financial aid office for further information.

Financial Aid Office
Office of the State Board of Education
P.O. Box 83720
Boise, ID 83720-0037
208-334-2270

Guaranty Agency
Student Loan Fund of Idaho, Inc.
P.O. Box 730
Fruitland, ID 83619-0730
208-452-4058

Community Service Programs
Idaho Office of the State Board of Education
LBJ Building
650 West State Street, Room 307
Boise, ID 83720

Department of Education
650 W. State St.
Box 83720
Boise, ID 83720-0027
208-334-3300

Division of Vocational Rehabilitation
650 West State Street
Boise, ID 83702
208-334-3390 (V/TDD)

Department of Veterans Affairs, Regional Office
Federal Building & U.S. Courthouse
550 West Fort Street
Boise, ID 83724

Illinois

Monetary Award Program (MAP) provides grants to needy students. To be eligible, students must be state residents and must be enrolled at least half-time in an approved school. The amount of the award is based on financial need. Contact your high school guidance counselor or college financial aid director for further information and application materials.

The Illinois Merit Recognition Scholarship Program provides a one-time grant to state residents who rank in the top five percent of their high school class. Students must enroll in an approved Illinois school at least on a part-time basis to be considered for this program. Contact your high school guidance counselor for further information.

The Illinois Veterans Grant pays tuition and certain fee costs at all state colleges, universities, and community colleges. To be eligible, students must be state residents with at least one year of active duty in the Armed Forces.

Police, Fire Personnel, and Correctional Workers Grants provide grant assistance to the spouses and children of police, fire, and correctional personnel killed in the line of duty. For applications and further information, contact the Client Services Division of the Illinois State Scholarship Commission at 217-782-5053.

Financial Aid Office and Guaranty Agency
Illinois Student Assistance Commission
1755 Lake Cooke Road
Deerfield, IL 60015
847-948-8500

Community Service Programs
Lieutenant Governor's Office of Volunteerism
James R. Thompson Center
100 West Randolph
Chicago, IL 60601
312-814-5220

Department of Education
1755 Lake Cooke Road
Deerfield, IL 60015
847-948-8500

Illinois Department of Rehabilitation Services
623 East Adams Street
P.O. Box 19429
Springfield, IL 62794-9429
217-782-2093 or 217-782-5734 (TDD)

Department of Veterans Affairs, Regional Office
536 South Clark Street
P.O. Box 8136
Chicago, IL 60680

Indiana

Indiana's Minority Teacher Scholarship Program provides annual scholarships to African-American and Hispanic state residents. Recipients must be enrolled in a teacher certification program and agree to teach after graduation in an accredited Indiana elementary or secondary school. For applications and information, contact Indiana's State Department of Education (in following state office listings).

The State Summer Work-Study Program provides work opportunities, administered by the State Student Assistance Commission of Indiana, to eligible students. The employer determines wages and hours.

The Indiana Higher Education Grant awards scholarship assistance to residents who attend or plan to enroll in an eligible Indiana college or university as full-time students. Applicants must file the FAFSA since the awards are based on financial need.

The Hoosier Scholar Award is given to an Indiana high school student who ranks in the top 20 percent of his or her class. The award is a $500 scholarship.

The Special Education Services Scholarship awards financial aid to Indiana residents who are enrolled as full-time students in an eligible institution and who are planning to become special education teachers in Indiana. Contact your high school guidance counselor for further information.

The Nursing Scholarship Program provides financial assistance of up to $5,000 per academic year to Indiana residents who are enrolled either as part-time or full-time students in a nursing program. Recipients must agree to work in any type of health care setting in Indiana after graduation. Contact your high school guidance counselor for further information.

Financial Aid Office and Guaranty Agency
State Student Assistance Commission of Indiana
150 West Market Street, Suite 500
Indianapolis, IN 46204
317-232-2350

Community Service Programs
Student Assistance Commission of Indiana
ISTA Center
150 West Market Street, Fifth Floor
Indianapolis, IN 46204
317-232-2353

Department of Education
State House Room 229
Indianapolis, IN 46204
317-232-0570

Rehabilitation Services
Department of Human Resources
251 North Illinois Street
P.O. Box 7083
Indianapolis, IN 46207-7083
317-232-1147

Department of Veterans Affairs, Regional Office
575 North Pennsylvania Street
Indianapolis, IN 46204

Iowa

Iowa Scholarships provide scholarship assistance to high school seniors who rank in the upper 15 percent of their high school class. Interested high school students should complete the State of Iowa Scholarship application form in September or October of their senior year. Contact your high school guidance counselor for further information.

Iowa Tuition Grants provide need-based grants to eligible students. Recipients must be state residents and enrolled or planning to enroll in undergraduate programs at eligible schools. Contact your high school guidance counselor or college financial aid office for further information.

Iowa Vocational and Technical Tuition Grants provide grants to state residents who plan to attend an Iowa community college and pursue a vocational or technical career. Contact your local community college for additional information.

The Iowa Work-Study Program provides part-time employment to help students attending Iowa schools meet their college expenses. Contact your college financial aid director for further information.

The Partnership Loan Program provides loan assistance to middle-income families to help them meet the cost of postsecondary education. Borrowers must attend eligible Iowa schools and pass prescribed credit tests.

Iowa Corps is a program for state residents entering their senior year of high school. Applicants must design community service projects that will be completed with public or nonprofit agencies. Students whose applications are approved will receive $500 tuition credits upon the successful completion of their projects.

Financial Aid Office and Guaranty Agency
Iowa College Student Aid Commission
200 Tenth Street, Fourth Floor
Des Moines, IA 50309
515-281-4890

Community Service Programs
Governor's Office on Volunteerism
State Capitol
Des Moines, IA 50319
515-281-8304

Department of Education
State Office Bldg.
Des Moines, IA 50319
515-281-3575

Division of Vocational Rehabilitation Services
510 East Twelfth Street
Des Moines, IA 50309
515-281-4311 or 1-800-532-1486 (IA) or 515-281-6755 (TDD)

Community Service Programs
Department of Veterans Affairs, Regional Office
210 Walnut Street
Des Moines, IA 50309

Kansas

The Vocational Education Scholarship Program provides scholarships to students interested in pursuing careers in vocational education. Students interested in this grant must register to take a competitive examination.

The Kansas Ethnic Minority Scholarship Program is a need-based scholarship program for minority students. Applicants must meet the program's academic requirements and must be enrolled or plan to enroll full-time at a Kansas public or private college or university.

The Kansas Nursing Scholarship Program is a scholarship program for full-time students enrolled in nursing programs at Kansas postsecondary schools. Applicants are required to practice as nurses in Kansas for a specified period of time.

The Kansas Teacher Scholarship is a state-funded scholarship loan program designed to encourage teaching careers at both the elementary and the secondary school level. Applicants must be state residents and must be enrolled or plan to enroll in full-time teacher education programs.

The Regents Supplemental Grant provides grant assistance to needy state residents enrolled full-time at public universities. Award amounts range from $200 to $1,000. Applicants must file the FAFSA, and all applications must be received by April 1.

Financial Aid Office
Kansas Board of Regents
Student Financial Aid Section
700 Southwest Harrison Street, Suite 1410
Topeka, KS 66603
785-296-3517

Guaranty Agency
USA Services, Inc.
3 Townsite Plaza, Suite 220
120 S.E. Sixth Street
Topeka, KS 66603
785-234-0072

Community Service Programs
Kansas Commission on National and Community Service
120 S.E. Tenth Street
Topeka, KS 66612
913-575-8330

Department of Education
120 SE 10th Avenue
Topeka, KS 66612-1182
785-296-3201

Rehabilitation Services
Biddle Building, First Floor
300 Southwest Oakley Street
Topeka, KS 66606
913-296-3911 or 1-800-432-2326 (KS) or 913-296-7029 (TDD)

Department of Veterans Affairs, Regional Office
Boulevard Office Park
901 George Washington Boulevard
Wichita, KS 67211

Kentucky

The Kentucky Tuition Grant Program (KTG) provides grant assistance to students attending one of the state's independent nonprofit colleges. The awards are need based. Interested students must file a Kentucky Financial Aid Form to be considered.

The Teacher Scholarship Program provides financial assistance to attract academically talented students into the teaching profession. To be eligible, students must rank in the top 10 percent of their graduating class and must be accepted for enrollment at a Kentucky participating institution. Recipients are required to teach one semester in a Kentucky public school for each semester of scholarship assistance. Contact your high school guidance counselor for further information.

College Access Program (CAP) provides grants to the state's neediest residents to attend in-state public or private schools. The total family contribution cannot exceed $1,500, and the recipient may not receive other state or federal funds designated specifically for tuition.

The Kentucky Educational Savings Plan Trust assists parents, grandparents, or other benefactors to save in a planned way for the higher education of a child under the age of 15. The trust account can be opened with as little as $25. Earnings are exempt from Kentucky income tax.

The Kentucky Work-Study Program provides career-related work experience to state residents attending approved colleges and universities. Applicants must be enrolled at

341

least part-time and be making satisfactory academic progress. Interested students should contact their school's financial aid office for further information.

Financial Aid Office and Guaranty Agency
Kentucky Higher Education Assistance Authority
1050 U.S. 127 South, Suite 102
Frankfort, KY 40601
502-696-7200

Department of Education
1050 U.S. 127 South
Frankfort, KY 40601
502-564-7990

Office of Vocational Rehabilitation
Capital Plaza Tower
500 Mero Street, Ninth Floor
Frankfort, KY 40601
502-564-4440 or 1-800-372-7172 (KY) or 502-564-6817 (TDD)

Community Service Programs
Campus SERVE
1050 U.S. 127 South
Frankfort, KY 40601
502-564-3553

Department of Veterans Affairs, Regional Office
600 Federal Place
Louisville, KY 40202

Louisiana

The T. H. Harris Scholarship is a competitively awarded scholarship program based on academic ability. Awards are $400 per year of undergraduate study. Applicants must be U.S. citizens and state residents and must have graduated with a GPA of at least 3.0. Further information may be obtained from your high school guidance counselor's office.

The Louisiana Honors Scholarship Program awards tuition scholarships to top high school graduates. Applicants must be state residents and must graduate in the top five percent of their class and be enrolled as full-time students. Awards cover the basic cost of tuition at a public college or university or public postsecondary technical institute. Recipients who choose to enroll in approved private colleges or universities can be awarded the actual tuition of the independent institution or an amount equal to the highest tuition charged at a Louisiana public postsecondary school. Further information may be obtained from your high school guidance counselor's office.

Louisiana's "Start Smart" Program is a college savings plan designed to help families meet the high cost of college tuition. Participants save to meet future college costs at their own pace and in the amounts they can afford. Deposits made to individual accounts are pooled in the state treasury and managed by the treasurer.

Louisiana Tuition Assistance Plan (TAP) awards tuition to state residents who attend public colleges and universities and who meet specific academic standards and financial need criteria. The annual amount varies. Applicants must be U.S. citizens and state residents and must have graduated with at least a 2.5 GPA. Recipients must be enrolled at a Louisiana public postsecondary institution as full-time undergraduate students. Recipients must also have financial need. Further information may be obtained from your school's high school guidance counselor's office.

Financial Aid Office and Guaranty Agency
Louisiana Office of Student Financial Assistance
P.O. Box 91202
Baton Rouge, LA 70821-9202
504-922-1011

Community Service Programs
Office of the Lieutenant Governor
930 North Third Street
Baton Rouge, LA 70804
504-342-2038

Department of Education
P.O. Box 44064
Baton Rouge, LA 70804
504-922-1011

Department of Social Services Rehabilitation Services
1755 Florida Boulevard
P.O. Box 94371
Baton Rouge, LA 70804-9371
504-342-2285 or 504-342-2266 (TDD)

Department of Veterans Affairs, Regional Office
701 Loyola Avenue
New Orleans, LA 70113

Maine

The Maine Student Incentive Scholarship Program provides state residents who are full-time undergraduate or graduate students with need-based grant assistance. Interested students should submit a Maine Financial Aid Form by April 30. Contact your school's financial aid director for further details and application forms.

The Blain House Scholars Program provides loans to eligible students. The loans, which are competitive and based on academic merit, carry no interest charges. For applications, contact any high school guidance office or college financial aid office.

Indian Scholarships award tuition and fee waivers to eligible Native Americans attending postsecondary institutions in the University of Maine system. For application forms, contact the University of Maine's financial aid office.

The Tuition Waiver Program for Children of Firefighters and Law Enforcement Officers Killed in the Line of Duty provides tuition waivers for eligible dependents to attend any Maine public postsecondary educational institution.

Maine Education Loans are available to parents and students through the Maine Education Loan Authority. Loans at reduced rates are offered to creditworthy Maine residents and also to out-of-state residents attending Maine institutions.

Financial Aid Office and Guaranty Agency
Finance Authority of Maine
State House Station
1191 Weston Court
Augusta, ME 04333
207-287-2183

Community Service Programs
Maine State Planning Office
State House Station No. 38
Augusta, ME 04333
207-287-1489

Department of Education
23 Station House Station
Augusta, ME 04333-0023
207-287-5944

Bureau of Rehabilitation
35 Anthony Avenue
Augusta, ME 04333-0011
207-626-5300 or 207-626-5322

Department of Veterans Affairs, Regional Office
Togas, ME 04330

Maryland

The General State Scholarship Program provides scholarship assistance to qualified, full-time undergraduate students and part-time nursing students. The program is need-based and is available only to state residents. Contact your college's financial aid office for application forms and further details.

Senatorial Scholarships provide assistance to qualified undergraduate and graduate students. The awards are need-based and are available only to state residents. Contact your school's financial aid office for further information.

The House of Delegates Scholarship Program provides grant assistance to both full-time and part-time undergraduate and graduate students. The program is not based on need. Only state residents are eligible to apply.

Professional Scholarships provide scholarship aid to qualified graduate and undergraduate students. The awards are need-based and are available only to state residents. Contact your school's financial aid office for application forms and further details.

Tolbert Grants provide awards to full-time, non-degree-seeking students. The awards are based on need and are available only to state residents. Officials of private vocational or technical schools in Maryland must nominate recipients.

The Distinguished Scholar Program provides grant assistance to full-time, undergraduate students. The awards are made on the basis of SAT I scores and high school rank, not need. Contact your high school guidance counselor for further information.

The Teacher Education Distinguished Scholarship Program provides assistance to qualified full-time students. The awards, which are not based on need, are available only to state residents. Recipients must agree to teach one year in a Maryland public school for each year they receive the award.

Sharon Christa McAuliffe Memorial Critical Shortage Teacher Education Tuition Assistance Program provides financial assistance to qualified students who are state residents. Recipients must be full-time undergraduate students or public school teachers. The awards are not based on need. Students must agree to teach in a teacher shortage area for a specified period of time.

Nursing Grants provide grants of up to $2,000 to full-time and part-time graduate students enrolled in graduate nursing programs in Maryland. The awards are made only to state residents and are based on need. Recipients must agree to teach or serve in a shortage area. Contact your school's financial aid office for further information and application forms.

Edward Conroy Grants (War Orphans grants) provide grant assistance to undergraduate and graduate students who lost a parent in World War II or the Vietnam conflict. Up to $5,000 is available per year. The awards are not based on need.

The Firemen Reimbursement Program provides assistance to Maryland firefighters. The financial assistance covers up to full tuition costs at eligible Maryland institutions. The program is available to undergraduate and graduate students and is not need-based.

The Loan Assistance Repayment Program provides funds to graduates of Maryland institutions who are employed by the state or local government or by a nonprofit institution. Priority is given to employment fields in which there are critical shortages.

The Physical and Occupational Therapist Program gives grants to undergraduate students enrolled full-time in postsecondary institutions in approved programs of occupational or physical therapy leading to licenses in physical or occupational therapy.

The Child Care Provider Program makes awards to both full-time and part-time graduate and undergraduate students. Only students enrolled in eligible Maryland institutions with eligible childcare programs may apply for this program. There is a service obligation after graduation.

Financial Aid Office
Maryland State Scholarship Administration
16 Francis Street
Annapolis, MD 21401
410-974-5370

Guaranty Agency
United Student Aid Group
555 Fairmont Avenue
Towson, MD 21218
410-337-0274

Department of Education
200 W. Baltimore St.
Baltimore, MD 21201
410-767-0249

Community Service Programs
Governor's Commission on Service
301 West Preston Street, Room 1501
Baltimore, MD 21201
410-225-1216

Division of Vocational Rehabilitation
2301 Argonne Drive
Baltimore, MD 21218-1696
301-554-3276 or 301-544-3277 (TDD)

Department of Veterans Affairs, Regional Office
Federal Building
31 Hopkins Plaza
Baltimore, MD 21201

Massachusetts

The General Scholarship Program provides scholarship assistance to residents of at least one year. Recipients must be enrolled in approved postsecondary schools. The application deadline is May 1.

The Gilbert Matching Scholarship provides scholarship assistance determined by the school's financial aid director and is awarded to state residents. Contact your college's financial aid office for further details.

The Tuition Waiver Program provides tuition waivers for eligible state residents enrolled in state-supported colleges or universities. Each school's financial aid director determines the award amounts.

The Fire/Police/Corrections Scholarship and War Orphans Scholarship provide scholarship aid. Recipients must be state residents and the children of deceased fire, police, or corrections officers, or of war veterans whose death was service-related.

The Family Education Loan Program allows students or parents to borrow for college expenses. Home mortgage options are available. Borrowers have up to 15 years to repay loans. Repayment begins 30 days after loans are disbursed.

MassPlan is a loan program that allows borrowers to borrow from $2,000 up to the total cost of attendance minus other financial aid received. Both variable and fixed rates of interest are available. Applicants must be enrolled at participating colleges or universities and must be creditworthy.

The No Interest Loan (NIL) is a loan program for student borrowers with demonstrated financial need who are enrolled full-time at participating Massachusetts schools. Applicants must be state residents for at least one year. Loan amounts range from $1,000 to $4,000 per year. There are no application or origination fees and no interest charges. Applicants must file the FAFSA. Contact your school's financial aid office for further information on this program.

Financial Aid Office and Guaranty Agency
American Student Assistance
330 Stuart Street
Boston, MA 02116
617-426-9434

Community Service Programs
Office of the Governor
State House, Room 259
Boston, MA 02133
617-727-5787

Department of Education
350 Main Street
Malden, MA 02148-5023
781-338-3000

Massachusetts Rehabilitation Commission
Fort Point Place
27–43 Wormwood Street
Boston, MA 02110
617-727-2183 or 1-800-442-1171 (MA) or 617-727-9063 (TDD)

Department of Veterans Affairs, Regional Office
John F. Kennedy Federal Building Government Center
Boston, MA 02203

347

Michigan

The Michigan Competitive Scholarship Program provides scholarship assistance to Michigan students attending public and private in-state colleges and universities. Awards are based on ACT scores. Interested students must complete the FAFSA form. Contact your school's guidance counselor for further information.

The Michigan Tuition Grant Program provides financial need-based assistance to Michigan students attending nonpublic degree-granting in-state colleges and universities. The FAFSA is required for consideration for this program. Contact your high school's guidance counselor for further information.

The Michigan Education Trust (MET) guarantees payment of in-state tuition and fees. Purchasers sign agreements with MET for the guarantee of future Michigan college tuition costs. The families' money is invested by MET, and investment earnings are used to pay the college costs for students enrolled in the program.

The Tuition Incentive Program provides tuition and fee assistance to students from low-income families. To qualify, applicants must apply before graduating from high school and must be under the age of 20 and receiving (or have received) Medicaid from the Family Independence Agency.

Financial Aid Office and State Guaranty Agency
Michigan Guaranty Agency
P.O. Box 30047
Lansing, MI 48909-7547
517-373-0760

Michigan Community Service Commission
111 South Capitol Avenue
Olds Plaza Building
Lansing, MI 48909
517-335-4295

Department of Education
Cascade Road SE
Grand Rapids, MI 49546
616-493-8800

Rehabilitation Services
608 West Allegan
P.O. Box 30010
Lansing, MI 48909
517-373-3391 or 517-373-3980 or 1-800-292-5896 (MI)

Department of Veterans Affairs, Regional Office
Patrick V. McNamara Federal Building
477 Michigan Avenue
Detroit, MI 48226

Minnesota

The State Work-Study Program provides employment opportunities to eligible state residents enrolled at least half-time in undergraduate, graduate, or vocational programs. Contact your school's financial aid office for application forms.

The Student Educational Loan Fund (SELF) provides non-need-based loans to students who have limited access to other financial aid programs. Undergraduate students may borrow a maximum of $4,500 per year for the first two years of study and $6,000 per year thereafter, with a cumulative maximum of $25,000. Borrowers must be credit-worthy and are required to pay interest quarterly while in school.

Nursing Grants for Persons of Color assist students entering, or enrolled in, educational programs leading to licensure as registered nurses or to advanced nursing degrees. Grants range from $2,000 to $4,000 per year.

Non-AFDC Child Care Grants assist students who have children 12 years of age or younger and who have financial need. The maximum amount available to help pay childcare costs is $1,700 for each eligible child per academic year.

Financial Aid Office
Minnesota Higher Education Services Office
Capitol Square, Suite 400
550 Cedar Street
St. Paul, MN 55101-2292
612-296-3974 or 1-800-657-3866

Guaranty Agency
Northstar Guaranty Inc./Great Lakes Higher Education Guaranty Corp.
P.O. Box 64102
St. Paul, MN 55164-0102
612-290-8795 or 1-800-366-0032

Community Service Programs and Department of Education
Department of Education
923 Capitol Square Building
550 Cedar Street
St. Paul, MN 55101
612-296-1435

Division of Rehabilitation Services
390 North Robert
St. Paul, MN 55101
612-296-5616 or 1-800-328-9095 (MN) or 612-296-3900 (TDD)

Department of Veterans Affairs, Regional Office
Bishop Henry Whipple Federal Building
Fort Snelling
St. Paul, MN 55111

Mississippi

The State Student Incentive Program provides state-administered grant assistance to eligible state residents. Each school selects the recipients through its regular financial aid process. Contact your college financial aid office for further information.

The Nursing Education Scholarship Grant Program provides scholarships to registered state nurses who apply for accredited bachelor of science nursing degrees or graduate degrees in a nursing program. Upon completion of the college program, the recipient must work in nursing service or nursing education in Mississippi.

The Nursing Education Scholarship for Study in Baccalaureate Nursing Education Program awards need-based scholarships to state residents studying in Mississippi schools of nursing. To qualify, recipients must agree to work in the state for a specified period of time after graduation.

Law Enforcement Officers and Firemen Scholarships provide scholarship assistance to the children of full-time state law enforcement officers and firefighters who were fatally injured or totally disabled while performing their official duties. The scholarship may be used only in state-supported colleges and universities in Mississippi.

The Southeast Asia POW/MIA Scholarship Program provides four-year scholarships at any state-supported institution to children of Vietnam veterans who are missing in action, returned prisoners of war, or deceased prisoners of war.

The William Winter Teacher Scholar Loan Program offers financial assistance to students enrolled in teacher education programs leading to a Class A teaching certificate. To qualify, recipients must be enrolled in accredited public or private institutions in Mississippi and must agree to repay the scholarships by teaching full-time in Mississippi.

Financial Aid Office and Guaranty Agency
Mississippi Postsecondary Assistance Board
3825 Ridgewood Road
Jackson, MS 39211-6453
601-982-6663

Community Service Programs
Office of the Governor
P.O. Box 139
Jackson, MS 39205
601-359-2790

Department of Education
P.O. Box 771
Jackson, MS 39205
601-982-6611

Vocational Rehabilitation
P.O. Box 1698
Jackson, MS 39215
601-354-6677 or 1-800-443-1000 (MS) or 601-354-6830 (TDD)

Department of Veterans Affairs, Regional Office
100 West Capitol Street
Jackson, MS 39269

Missouri

The Missouri Student Grant Program provides need-based grant assistance to state residents enrolled as full-time undergraduate students at approved Missouri schools. Students may apply for this grant by completing the FAFSA.

The Higher Education Academic Scholarship Program provides scholarship assistance to high school seniors with superior academic achievement. A recipient must be a graduating high school senior planning on attending a Missouri postsecondary institution as a full-time undergraduate student.

The Teacher Education Scholarship Program provides scholarships to students who plan careers in teaching. To qualify, scholarship recipients must agree to teach in a Missouri public school for a specified period of time after graduation.

Financial Aid Office and Guaranty Agency
Coordinating Board for Higher Education CBHE/MSLP
P.O. Box 6730
Jefferson City, MO 65102
573-751-3940 or 1-800-473-6757

Department of Education
3024 West Truman Blvd.
Jefferson City, MO 65109
573-751-3251

Community Service Programs
Lieutenant Governor's Office
State Capitol, Room 121
Jefferson City, MO 65101
314-751-4727

Division of Vocational Rehabilitation
201 East McCarty Street
Jefferson City, MO 65101
314-751-3251 or 314-751-0881 (TDD)

Department of Veterans Affairs, Regional Office
Federal Building
1520 Market Street
St. Louis, MO 63103

Montana

The State Student Incentive Grant provides need-based grant assistance to eligible state residents. Contact your school's financial aid director for further details.

The Bureau of Indian Affairs Grant and Scholarship Programs offer several state-administered grants and scholarships to eligible state Native Americans. The programs are need-based.

The State Work-Study Program provides employment opportunities to state residents who are full-time undergraduate or graduate students. The program is based on need. Contact your school's financial aid office for more information.

The Fee Waiver Program grants waivers to a limited number of undergraduate and graduate students who meet specific requirements. The awards are based on financial need and academic achievement. For further information, contact personnel in the financial aid office of any unit of the Montana university system.

Financial Aid Office and Guaranty Agency
Montana Guaranteed Student Loan Program
2500 Broadway
Helena, MT 59620-3103
406-444-6594

Community-Service Coordinator Office of the Governor
State Capitol Building
Helena, MT 59620
406-444-5547

Department of Education
Office of Public Instruction
P.O. Box 202501
Helena, MT 59620-2501
406-444-3095

Department of Social and Rehabilitation Services
111 Sanders Street
P.O. Box 4210
Helena, MT 59604-4210
406-444-2590 (V/TDD)

Department of Veterans Affairs, Regional Office
Fort Harrison, MT 59636

Nebraska

The Edgar J. Boschult Memorial Scholarships Program provides annual scholarships to students enrolled in the Army, Air Force, and Naval Science courses at the University of Nebraska. The Executive Committee of the Nebraska American Legion selects recipients.

The Nebraska Mathematics and Science Teacher Tuition Assistance Act provides financial assistance to mathematics and science students who are enrolled in teacher training programs and who agree to teach in a public or private state school after graduation. Contact your school's financial aid office for more information.

Employment Programs provide state-administered employment opportunities through the Job Training Partnership Act. Under this program, economically disadvantaged, unemployed, and underemployed people can receive assistance to enroll in retraining programs.

The Bureau of Indian Affairs Grant (BIA) provides financial aid to eligible state Native Americans. The program is need-based. Contact your college's financial aid office for more information.

Financial Aid Office
Coordinating Commission for Postsecondary Education
P.O. Box 95005
Lincoln, NE 68509-5005
402-471-2847

Guaranty Agency
Nebraska Higher Education Loan Program
Educational Planning Center
13 "0" Street
Lincoln, NE 68508
402-471-2847

Nebraska Commission on National and Community Service
State Capitol, Sixth Floor
West Centennial Mall
Lincoln, NE 68509
402-471-6225

Department of Education
P.O. Box 82505
Lincoln, NE 68501
402-475-8686

Division of Rehabilitation Services
301 Centennial Mall South, Sixth Floor
P.O. Box 94987
Lincoln, NE 68509-4987

Nebraska Commission on National and Community Service
State Capitol, Sixth Floor
West Centennial Mall
Lincoln, NE 68509
402-471-6225

Department of Veterans Affairs, Regional Office
Federal Building
100 Centennial Mall North
Lincoln, NE 68508

Nevada

The Nevada Student Incentive Grant (NSIG) provides assistance to state residents with significant financial need who are enrolled at least half-time at the University of Nevada. The grant is available to both undergraduate and graduate students.

University of Nevada Freshman Scholarships provide scholarships based on academic merit to seniors in Nevada high schools. The University of Nevada also offers other scholarships. Some are based on academic accomplishment, while others are awarded to students pursuing work in particular colleges or departments.

In-State Grants-in-Aid gives University of Nevada grants to state residents each semester, based upon scholastic achievement, financial need, and the rendering of special services to the university. Contact the Office of Student Financial Services for further information.

Out-of-State Grants-in-Aid gives University of Nevada grants each semester to undergraduate students who are not Nevada residents. Recipients of these awards are not required to pay the nonresident tuition charge. A number of these grants are set aside for international students.

Financial Aid Office and Guaranty Agency
University of Nevada-Reno Student Financial Services
Mailstop 076
Reno, NV 89557
702-784-4666

Nevada Commission on National and Community Service
1830 East Sahara, Suite 230
Las Vegas, NV 89104
702-486-7997

Department of Education
700 East Fifth St.
Carson City, NV 89701
775-687-9200

Rehabilitation Services
505 East King, Room 502
Carson City, NV 89701
775-684-4067 or 775-687-4440 (V/TDD)

Department of Veterans Affairs, Regional Office
1201 Terminal Way
Reno, NV 89550

New Hampshire

The New Hampshire Incentive Grant Program provides grant assistance to eligible state residents. Students must be enrolled full-time in private, public, vocational, or technical schools. Scholarships may be applied to schools within the six New England states. Satisfactory academic progress is required. Contact your school's financial aid director for more information.

Financial Aid Office and Guaranty Agency
New Hampshire Higher Education Assistance Foundation
P.O. Box 877
Concord, NH 03302
603-225-6612

Community Service Programs
New Hampshire Job Training Council
64 Old Suncook Road
Concord, NH 03301
603-228-9500

Department of Education
101 Pleasant St.
Concord, NH 03301
603-271-3739

Division of Vocational Rehabilitation
78 Regional Drive, Building 2
Concord, NH 03301
603-271-3471 or 1-800-992-3312 (TDD) (NH)

Department of Veterans Affairs, Regional Office
Norris Cotton Federal Building
275 Chestnut Street
Manchester, NH 03101

New Jersey

The Tuition Aid Grants (TAG) Program provides grant assistance based on the student's financial need. Eligible students must be state residents and must be enrolled or planning to enroll in approved schools. Recipients should file the FAFSA to be considered for the program. For applications, contact your high school guidance office or college financial aid office.

Educational Opportunity Fund Grants (EOF) provide financial assistance to students from disadvantaged backgrounds who have exceptional financial need. The grants are renewable. Recipients must file the FAFSA to be considered.

The Garden State Scholars Program provides scholarships to high school students with outstanding academic achievement. The awards are based on SAT I scores and high school grades. Applicants must also have financial need and must plan to enroll as full-time undergraduate students. Recipients should file the FAFSA to be considered. For applications, contact your high school guidance office or college financial aid office.

The Distinguished Scholars Program awards scholarships to high school seniors with the highest records of academic achievement. The awards are based on SAT I scores and high school grades. Candidates are selected by their high school principals or guidance counselors. Recipients must be state residents. Financial need is not taken into consideration.

The Public Tuition Benefit Program pays for the actual cost of tuition up to a maximum of the tuition charged at New Jersey public institutions. Eligible students must be state residents enrolled in New Jersey institutions of higher learning at least half-time and must be the dependents of service personnel or law enforcement officers killed in the line of duty.

The New Jersey Class Loan allows students and parents to borrow up to the cost of education minus other financial assistance. Borrowers must be creditworthy. There is no interest subsidy, and a need analysis is required. The interest rate may be fixed or variable, and three payment options are available.

Financial Aid Office and Guaranty Agency
New Jersey Office of Student Assistance
P.O. Box 543
Trenton, NJ 08625
609-588-3200 or 1-800-792-8670

Community Service Programs
New Jersey State Department of Education
CN500
Trenton, NJ 08625
609-292-1083

Department of Education
4 Quakerbridge Plaza
Trenton, NJ 08625
609-292-1083

Division of Vocational Rehabilitation
Labor Building
Sixth Floor CN 398
Trenton, NJ 08625
609-292-5987 or 609-292-2919 (TDD)

Department of Veterans Affairs, Regional Office
20 Washington Place
Newark, NJ 07102

New Mexico

New Mexico Student Choice Grants provide funds to needy state residents attending eligible independent institutions of higher education in New Mexico.

The New Mexico Work-Study Program provides employment opportunities to needy students. Eligible students must be state residents and be enrolled at least half-time at institutions of higher learning.

The Three Percent Scholarship Program provides grant assistance to state residents enrolled as undergraduate or graduate students at public colleges or universities. At least one-third of the scholarship is based on financial need. For further information, contact financial aid personnel of any New Mexico public postsecondary institution.

The New Mexico Competitive Scholarship Program gives scholarships to state residents who graduated in the upper 5 percent of their high school class or who scored at least 25 on the ACT examination or 1020 on the SAT I. Awards cover the cost of tuition, fees, and books. They are renewable for four years of college if the recipient maintains academic progress. Eligibility also includes financial need.

The New Mexico Nursing Student Loan Program is designed to increase the number of nurses in medically underserved areas. The loan is based on financial need, and recipients must agree to practice in an underserved area for a specified period of time. Students enrolled in an approved nursing education program or working for a Master of Science degree in nursing are eligible to apply for this loan program.

The New Mexico Legislative Endowment Program provides financial assistance to full-time and part-time transfer and returning students. Amounts vary. Contact financial aid office personnel.

Financial Aid Office
Commission on Higher Education
1068 Cerrillos Road
Santa Fe, NM 87501-4295
505-826-7383

Guaranty Agency
New Mexico Educational Assistance Foundation
P.O. Box 27020
Albuquerque, NM 87125
505-345-3371

New Mexico Commission for National and Community Service
Governor's Office
State Capitol, Suite 400
Santa Fe, NM 87503
505-827-3042

Department of Education
Special Education Office
State Education Bldg.
Santa Fe, NM 87501
505-827-6541

Division of Vocational Rehabilitation
604 West San Mateo Drive
Santa Fe, NM 87503
505-827-3511 or 1-800-235-5387 (NM) or 505-827-3510 (TDD)

Department of Veterans Affairs, Regional Office
Dennis Chavez Federal Building
U.S. Courthouse
500 Gold Avenue SW
Albuquerque, NM 87102

New York

The Tuition Assistance Program (TAP) provides grant assistance to needy students. The awards are based on family income and tuition costs. Contact your high school guidance counselor or college financial aid office for further information.

Aid for Part-time Study (APTS) provides financial assistance to eligible students enrolled for part-time study in New York state schools. The awards are based on income and tuition costs. Contact your high school guidance counselor or college financial aid office for more information.

Educational Opportunity Programs (HEOP, CD, SEEK, EOP) provide financial assistance to eligible students studying in New York state schools. The programs provide counseling, tutorial assistance, and help in meeting living expenses. The amount of the award depends upon the program.

Children of Veterans, Police Officers, Firefighters, and Correction Officers Program provides financial assistance to the children of deceased or disabled veterans, prisoners of war, or service persons missing in action. The children of New York state firefighters, police officers, and corrections officers who died as a result of service-related injuries are also eligible for assistance under this program.

Regents Scholarships are based on special tests taken by high school seniors. High school performance, class rank, and high school grades are also taken into consideration. Contact your high school guidance counselor for more information.

Empire State Scholarships of Excellence are awarded to outstanding high school seniors. High school rank, class grades, and high school performance are some of the criteria considered. Contact your high school guidance counselor for further information.

Financial Aid Office and Guaranty Agency
New York State Higher Education Services Corporation Loans Division
99 Washington Avenue
Albany, NY 12255
518-473-1574 or 1-800-642-6234

Governor's Office for Voluntary Service
Empire State Plaza
Agency Building Four, Seventh Floor
Albany, NY 12224
518-473-8882

Department of Education
Boards of Cooperative Educational Services
Education Bldg., Room 503
Albany, NY 12234
518-474-3936

Office of Vocational and Educational Services for Individuals with Disabilities
One Commerce Plaza, Room 1606
Albany, NY 12234
518-474-2714 or 1-800-222-5627 (NY) or 518-473-9333 (TDD)

Department of Veterans Affairs, Regional Office
Federal Building
111 West Huron Street
Buffalo, NY 14202

North Carolina

The North Carolina Student Incentive Grant (NCSIG) makes grant awards to eligible state residents. The awards are based on financial need. Interested students must file a FAFSA to be considered.

The North Carolina Teaching Fellows Scholarship Program makes awards to qualified students. Applicants are chosen on the basis of high school grades, class rank, SAT I scores, and extracurricular activities. The scholarships are available at select North Carolina postsecondary institutions. For applications, contact your high school guidance counselor.

The North Carolina Legislative Tuition Grant Program provides financial assistance to state residents who attend North Carolina private colleges or universities. Students must be enrolled full-time in undergraduate programs. The amount of the award varies and is not based upon need.

The North Carolina Student Loan Program for Health, Science, and Mathematics provides assistance to legal residents of the state who are accepted as full-time students in accredited schools and are working toward a degree in mathematics, health sciences, allied health fields, or clinical psychology. Loan amounts vary. Contact your school's financial aid director for further details.

Prospective Vocational Teacher Scholarships are awarded to qualified state residents enrolled in accredited North Carolina colleges who plan to become vocational education teachers. The program is not based on financial need. Contact your high school guidance counselor for further information and application forms.

The North Carolina Community Scholarship Program provides scholarships to state residents enrolled at least part-time in community colleges. Priority is given to students with the greatest financial need and to minority students.

Financial Aid Office
North Carolina State Education Assistance Authority
P.O. Box 2658
Chapel Hill, NC 27515
919-549-8614

Guaranty Agency
College Foundation
P.O. Box 12100
Raleigh, NC 27605-2100
919-821-4721

Community Service Programs
Governor's Office of Citizen Affairs
116 West Jones Street
Raleigh, NC 27603
919-715-3470

Department of Education
Department of Public Instruction
301 N. Wilmington Street
Raleigh, NC 27601
919-715-1000

Division of Vocational Rehabilitation Services
805 Ruggles Drive
P.O. Box 26053
Raleigh, NC 27611
919-733-3364 or 919-733-5924 (TDD)

Department of Veterans Affairs, Regional Office
Federal Building
251 North Main Street
Winston-Salem, NC 27155

North Dakota

The North Dakota Merit Scholar Program provides tuition scholarships to high school seniors who rank in the top 20 percent of their high school graduating class and in the top 5 percent of all students who take the ACT. Contact your high school guidance counselor for more information.

The Nurse Education Scholarship Loan Program awards financial assistance through the financial aid offices of those North Carolina colleges and universities that offer nurse education programs leading to a nursing certificate or a degree as a licensed practical nurse or registered nurse. The awards are based upon financial need and academic merit.

Financial Aid Office and Guaranty Agency
Bank of North Dakota Student Loan Program
P.O. Box 5509
Bismarck, ND 58506-5509
701-328-5660 or 1-800-472-2166

Community Service Programs
Department of Human Services
State Capitol
Bismarck, ND 58505
701-224-2310

Department of Education
State Capitol
Bismarck, ND 58505
701-224-2310

Office of Vocational Rehabilitation
State Capitol
600 East Boulevard Avenue
Bismarck, ND 58505-0250
701-224-2907 or 1-800-472-2622 or 701-224-2699 (TDD)

Department of Veterans Affairs, Regional Office
655 First Avenue, North
Fargo, ND 58102

Ohio

The Ohio Instructional Grant Program provides need-based tuition assistance to full-time undergraduate students from low- and moderate-income families. Recipients must be state residents. Award amounts vary and are based on family income and the number of dependents in the family. You may apply for this program by completing the FAFSA.

The Ohio Student Choice Grant Program provides financial assistance to full-time students enrolled in baccalaureate programs in Ohio private nonprofit colleges and universities. Recipients must be state residents. Eligibility is not based on need or academic merit. No application is necessary. The program is designed to close the tuition gap between the state's public and private nonprofit colleges and universities. Contact your school's financial aid office for further information.

The Ohio Academic Scholarship Program provides competitive, merit-based financial assistance to the state's most academically outstanding high school students who enroll as full-time students in Ohio institutions of higher learning. The program is intended to provide an incentive for students to remain in Ohio to attend college. Eligibility is determined by a selection formula that considers a student's high school GPA and ACT test scores. Scholarships provide $1,000 each year for up to four years of undergraduate study. Approximately 4,000 students receive assistance from this program each year. Applications may be obtained from high school guidance offices.

The Ohio War Orphans Scholarship Program awards tuition assistance to the children of deceased or severely disabled war veterans. To be eligible, applicants must be enrolled for full-time undergraduate study at an eligible college or university. State residency is also required. The application deadline is July 1.

The Ohio Safety Officers Memorial Fund provides tuition assistance to the children of Ohio peace officers, firefighters, and certain other safety officers who were killed in the line of duty. Recipients may enroll for full-time or part-time study at any participating Ohio postsecondary institution. This program provides benefits that cover the full instructional and general fee charges at public and private colleges and universities.

The Nurse Education Assistance Loan Program provides financial aid to students enrolled in approved nursing education programs in Ohio colleges, universities, hospitals, and vocational schools. Recipients must be enrolled at least part-time. Debt cancellation provisions are available if borrowers are employed in Ohio.

Financial Aid Office and Guaranty Agency
Great Lakes Higher Education Corp.
P.O. Box 182174
Columbus, OH 43218-2174
614-755-7400

Governor's Community Service Commission
51 North High Street, Suite 481
Columbus, OH 43215
614-728-2916

Department of Education
65 S. Front St., Room 810
Columbus, OH 43215-4183
614-644-3175

Rehabilitation Services Commission
400 East Campus View Boulevard
Columbus, OH 43235-4604
614-438-1200 or 1-800-282-4536 (OH) or 614-438-1391 (TDD)

Department of Veterans Affairs, Regional Office
Anthony J. Celebrezze Federal Building
1240 East Ninth Street
Cleveland, OH 44199

Oklahoma

The Oklahoma Tuition and Grant Program gives grants to state residents enrolled at least part-time as graduate or undergraduate students at approved schools in Oklahoma. The grants are based on financial need. Students should file the FAFSA to be considered for the program. Contact your college's financial aid office for application forms and further information.

The Future Teachers Scholarship Program awards scholarships to outstanding state residents who graduated in the top 15 percent of their high school class. Recipients must be interested in pursuing a career in teaching.

The Academic Scholars Program provides scholarship assistance for students who attend the University of Oklahoma, Oklahoma State University, the University of Tulsa, or Oral Roberts University. A recipient must be a National Merit Scholar, National Achievement Scholar, National Hispanic Scholar, or Presidential Scholar.

The Oklahoma Higher Learning Access Program (OHLAP) awards financial aid to academically talented and financially needy students. The award must be used at an Oklahoma public or private school, and parental income may not exceed $24,000.

The Oklahoma State Regents' Regional University Baccalaureate Degree Scholarship Program provides scholarship assistance to academically talented students. An award of $3,000 is available. Qualified applicants must have an ACT composite score of at least 30 and an exceptional GPA.

The Oklahoma State Regents' Heartland Scholarship Program was created after the bombing of the Alfred P. Murrah Federal Building. Recipients must be dependent children who lost a parent or guardian in the bombing or who were themselves injured in the bombing. All educational expenses are covered by the award.

Financial Aid Office and Guaranty Agency
Oklahoma Guaranteed Student Loan Program
P.O. Box 3000
Oklahoma City, OK 73101-3000
405-858-4300

Governor's Commission for Community Service
1515 North Lincoln Street
Oklahoma City, OK 73104
405-271-4218

Department of Education
2500 North Lincoln Boulevard
Oklahoma City, OK 73105-4599
405-521-3308

Rehabilitation Services
2409 North Kelley, Fourth Floor Annex
P.O. Box 25352
Oklahoma City, OK 73125
405-424-4311 or 405-424-2794 (TDD)

Department of Veterans Affairs, Regional Office
Federal Building
125 South Main Street
Muskogee, OK 74401

Oregon

The Need Grant Program makes grants available to eligible state residents attending any institution of higher education in Oregon. Recipients must be full-time undergraduate students. The awards are based upon need. Students must complete the FAFSA.

The Nursing Loan Program provides loans to qualified state residents enrolled as full-time nursing students at the Oregon Health Sciences University.

The Oregon Teacher Corps Loan Program provides forgivable loans to prospective teachers. Recipients must rank in the top 20 percent of their class, must have completed at least two years of undergraduate study, and must be enrolled in an approved teacher education program at an Oregon college or university.

Financial Aid Office and Guaranty Agency
Oregon State Scholarship Commission
1500 Valley River Drive, Suite 100
Eugene, OR 97401
503-687-7400 or 1-800-452-8807

Oregon Commission on Community Service
Portland State University
Neuberger Hall, Room 491A
724 Southwest Harrison Avenue
Portland, OR 97207
503-725-5903

Department of Education
255 Capitol St. NE
Salem, OR 97310-0203
503-378-3569

Rehabilitation Services
2045 Silverton Road NE
Salem, OR 97310
503-378-3830 (V/TDD)

Department of Veterans Affairs, Regional Office
Federal Building
1220 Southwest Third Avenue
Portland, OR 97204

Pennsylvania

The State Grant Program provides grant assistance to state residents enrolled full-time in approved academic programs of at least two years. The amount of the award varies and is based on financial need. Contact your high school guidance counselor or financial aid office for further information and application forms.

Scholars in Education Awards (SEA) provide financial assistance to eligible state residents who are pursuing careers in teaching mathematics or science. Recipients must agree to teach mathematics or science after graduation for a specified period of time.

The Pennsylvania Work-Study Program provides employment opportunities for eligible state residents enrolled in Pennsylvania postsecondary institutions. Contact your school's financial aid office for further information.

Financial Aid Office and Guaranty Agency
Pennsylvania Higher Education Assistance Agency
PHEAA Loan Division
1200 North Seventh Street
Harrisburg, PA 17102
717-720-2654 or 1-800-692-7392

Community Service Programs
PennSERVE
Labor and Industry Building
Harrisburg, PA 17120
717-787-1971

Department of Education
333 Market Street
Harrisburg, PA 17126-0333
717-783-6788

Office of Vocational Rehabilitation
Seventh and Forster Street
Harrisburg, PA 17120
717-787-4256 or 1-800-442-6351 (PA) or 717-783-8917 (TDD)

Department of Veterans Affairs, Regional Office
5000 Wissahickon Avenue
P.O. Box 8079
Philadelphia, PA 19101

Rhode Island

The Rhode Island State Scholarship Program rewards outstanding high school students. Awards are based on SAT I scores and financial need. Contact your high school guidance counselor for more information. It is necessary to file the FAFSA to qualify for this program.

The Rhode Island State Grant Program provides grants to students whose family resources are not sufficient to meet the costs of higher education. Recipients must be state residents and must attend a postsecondary institution on at least a half-time basis. Applicants must complete the FAFSA form to be considered.

The Rhode Island Higher Education Scholarship Program recognizes outstanding high school students based on their SAT I scores. Awards are also based on financial need. The FAFSA is required. Further information may be obtained from your high school guidance counselor's office.

Financial Aid Office and Guaranty Agency
Rhode Island Higher Education Assistance Authority
560 Jefferson Boulevard
Warwick, RI 02886
401-736-1100 or 1-800-922-9855

Community Service Programs
Governor's Office
State House
Providence, RI 02903
401-277-2080

Department of Education
560 Jefferson Blvd.
Warwick, RI 02886
401-783-6788

Department of Vocational Rehabilitation
40 Fountain Street
Providence, RI 02903
401-421-7005 or 1-800-752-8088 (RI) or 401-421-7016 (TDD)

Department of Veterans Affairs, Regional Office
380 Westminster Mall
Providence, RI 09203

South Carolina

The South Carolina Tuition Grants Program provides grants to state residents who are accepted for enrollment in eligible private institutions in South Carolina. The awards are based on financial need. Contact your school's financial aid office for further information. The FAFSA serves as your application.

The South Carolina Teacher Loan Program provides financial assistance to eligible state residents who plan to teach in certain geographic areas or to teach mathematics or science. Awards are available to both undergraduate and graduate students. The amounts of the loans vary, and loans are forgiven under certain conditions. For applications, contact your college's financial aid office.

Children of deceased or disabled South Carolina firefighters, law officers, and members of the Civil Air Patrol or Organized Rescue Squad can apply for financial assistance at the state's financial aid office. The awards are not based on financial need, and the amount of the award varies. Contact your school's financial aid office for further information and application materials.

Financial Aid Office
Higher Education Tuition Grants Commission
Keenan Building, Room 811
Box 12159
Columbia, SC 29211
803-734-1200

Guaranty Agency
South Carolina Student Loan Corporation
Interstate Center, Suite 210
P.O. Box 21487
Columbia, SC 29221
803-798-0916

Community Service Programs
Governor's Office on Volunteerism
1205 Pendleton Street
Columbia, SC 29201
803-734-0398

Department of Education
Keenan Building
P.O. Box 12159
Columbia, SC 29211
803-734-1200

Vocational Rehabilitation Department
1330 Boston Avenue
West Columbia, SC 29201
803-822-5319 (V/TDD)

Department of Veterans Affairs, Regional Office
1801 Assembly Street
Columbia, SC 29201

South Dakota

The South Dakota Student Incentive Grant Program provides grant assistance to eligible state residents with financial need. Recipients must be enrolled in an accredited institution on at least a half-time basis. The amount of the award varies according to individual financial need. For applications, contact your school's financial aid office.

The South Dakota Tuition Equalization Grant Program provides grant assistance to eligible state residents who are enrolled at accredited South Dakota private schools as full-time undergraduate students. The awards are based upon financial need.

Financial Aid Office
Department of Education and Cultural Affairs
Office of the Secretary
700 Governor's Drive
Pierre, SD 57501
605-773-3134

Guaranty Agency
Education Assistance Corporation
115 First Avenue SW
Aberdeen, SD 57401
605-225-6423 or 1-800-592-1802

Community Service Programs
Governor's Office of Operations
500 East Capitol Avenue
Pierre, SD 57501
605-773-3661

Department of Education
700 Governor's Drive
Pierre, SD 57501
605-773-3134

Division of Rehabilitation Services
700 Governor's Drive
Pierre, SD 57501-2291
605-773-3195 or 605-773-4544 (TDD)

Department of Veterans Affairs, Medical and Regional Office Center
2510 West 22nd Street
P.O. Box 5046
Sioux Falls, SD 57117

Tennessee

The Tennessee Academic Scholars Program encourages academically superior state high school graduates to attend colleges or universities in Tennessee. Recipients must be state residents. For more information, contact your school's financial aid office.

The Tennessee Student Assistance Award provides grant assistance to needy state residents who are enrolled or accepted for enrollment at eligible educational institutions in Tennessee. Contact your school's financial aid office for more information.

The Tennessee Teacher Loan and Scholarship Program provides financial assistance for up to the full cost of tuition to students who plan careers in teaching. Priority is given to students planning to teach mathematics or science in Tennessee public schools. Students planning to teach music or art and certified state teachers are also eligible to apply. The awards are based on academic performance. Recipients must agree to teach for a specified period of time in a critical shortage area after graduation.

Financial Aid Office and Guaranty Agency
Tennessee Student Assistance Corp.
404 James Robertson Parkway Towers, Suite 1950
Nashville, TN 37243-0820
615-741-1346 or out of state: 1-800-257-6526

Tennessee Commission on National and Community Service
State Capitol, Governor's Office G-12
Nashville, TN 37243
615-741-4131

Department of Education
9th Floor Andrew Johnson Tower
710 James Robertson Parkway
Nashville, TN 37243
615-741-2966

Division of Rehabilitation Services
400 Deaderick Street, Fifteenth Floor
Nashville, TN 37249-0060
615-741-2019

Department of Veterans Affairs, Regional Office
110 Ninth Avenue South
Nashville, TN 37203

Texas

The State Student Incentive Grant provides grant assistance to eligible state residents attending private and public nonprofit institutions of higher education. For applications, contact your school's financial aid office.

The Tuition Equalization Grant helps students attending independent colleges meet costs. Applicants must be state residents or National Merit Scholarship finalists, and must be enrolled at least half-time in approved colleges or universities. The awards are need-based, and grants vary according to financial need. Contact your school's financial aid office for further information.

The Texas Public Educational Grant provides financial aid to needy students enrolled in public institutions that participate in the program. Contact your school's financial aid office for more information.

The State Scholarship Program for Ethnic Recruitment provides financial aid to eligible minority students who have financial need. Contact your school's financial aid office for more information.

The Hinson-Hazelwood College Student Loan Program makes loan funds available to eligible undergraduate and graduate students, and students studying the professions. Students must demonstrate financial need to be considered. Loan forgiveness provisions are available. Contact the college's financial aid office for further information and application forms.

The College Access Loan Program provides loans to students who do not qualify for Federal Stafford Loans. Contact your school's financial aid office for more information.

The Texas College Work-Study Program provides part-time employment for students attending public or private institutions in Texas on at least a half-time basis. The amount of the award is based upon financial need. Jobs may be on- or off-campus and are arranged through the student's college or university financial aid office.

Financial Aid Office
Texas Higher Education Coordinating Board
Student Services Division
P.O. Box 12788
Austin, TX 78711
512-483-6340

Guaranty Agency
Texas Guaranteed Student Loan Corp.
P.O. Box 201725
Austin, TX 78720-1725
512-219-5700

Community Service Programs
Governor's Office
201 East Fourteenth Street, Sixth Floor
Sam Houston Building
Austin, TX 78701
512-463-2198

Department of Education
1001 Trinity St.
Austin, TX 78701-2603
1-888-863-5880

Rehabilitation Commission
4900 North Lamar Boulevard
Austin, TX 78751-2316
512-483-4000 or 512-483-4884 (TDD)

Department of Veterans Affairs, Regional Office
2515 Murworth Drive
Houston, TX 77054

Utah

The State Student Incentive Grant Program provides financial assistance to needy state residents. Contact your school's financial aid office for more information.

Financial Aid Office and Guaranty Agency
Utah System of Higher Education
P.O. Box 45202
Salt Lake City, UT 84145-0202
801-321-7100

Utah Commission on National and Community Service
324 South State Street, Room 240
Salt Lake City, UT 84114
801-538-8610

Department of Education
3 Triad Center
355 W. North Temple
Salt Lake City, UT 84145
801-321-7200

Office of Rehabilitation
250 East 500 South
Salt Lake City, UT 84111
801-538-7522 or 1-800-662-9080 (TDD) (UT)

Department of Veterans Affairs, Regional Office
Federal Building
125 South State Street
P.O. Box 11500
Salt Lake City, UT 84147

Vermont

Vermont Incentive Grants provide financial aid to undergraduate state residents enrolled in eligible degree programs. Recipients may receive up to $5,200. Awards are based on financial need and are made on a first-come, first-served basis. Applicants must complete the FAFSA to apply.

The Vermont Part-Time Grant Program is designed to assist students enrolled in eligible degree programs and taking fewer than 12 credit hours. Awards are based on financial need. Applicants should complete the FAFSA.

The Vermont Value Program allows borrowers of Federal Stafford or PLUS Loans to receive interest rebates equivalent to one percent of the principal balance every year that the loan is in repayment.

Financial Aid Office and Guaranty Agency
Vermont Student Assistance Corporation
Champlain Mill
P.O. Box 2000
Winooski, VT 05404
802-655-9602 or 1-800-642-3177

Community Service Programs
Office of the Governor
109 State Street
Montpelier, VT 05609
802-828-3333

Department of Education
Office of the Governor
109 State Street
Montpelier, VT 05609
802-828-3333

Vocational Rehabilitation Division
Osgood Building
103 South Main Street
Waterbury, VT 05671-2301
802-241-2186 (V/TDD)

Department of Veterans Affairs, Medical and Regional Office Center
White River Junction, VT 05001

Virginia

The Undergraduate Student Financial Aid Program (Last Dollar) gives grants to needy minority undergraduate students who are state residents and who are enrolled for the first time in a public college or university in Virginia. The amount of the award ranges from $400 to the full cost of tuition and fees.

The Virginia College Scholarship Assistance Program aids needy undergraduate students who are enrolled at least half-time at Virginia's public and private schools and who are state residents. Grants range from $400 to $5,000.

The Virginia Graduate and Undergraduate Scholarship Assistance Program provides financial aid to state residents who are full-time students at Virginia's public colleges and universities. Awards are based on academic performance.

Virginia Student Financial Assistance Programs provide financial assistance to needy Virginia residents who are undergraduate students enrolled at least half-time in Virginia's public colleges and universities. Award amounts vary but can be as much as tuition and fees.

The Virginia Transfer Grant Program provides grants of up to full tuition and fees to minority students who enroll in historically white public institutions, or minority transfer students who enroll in historically black public institutions. Applicants must meet minimum merit criteria and qualify for entry as first-time transfer students.

The Virginia Tuition Assistance Grant Program is a non–need-based grant program for Virginia residents who attend accredited colleges or universities in Virginia. The amount of the award varies.

The Lee-Jackson Foundation Scholarship Program awards scholarships to high school students who plan to enroll in Virginia public or private institutions. Further information on this program may be obtained from your high school guidance counselor.

The Academic Common Market is an arrangement among 13 southern states. It allows students to pay in-state tuition at non-Virginia colleges and universities while studying in certain programs that are not available at public institutions in Virginia. Students must be state residents and accepted into a participating program.

Financial Aid Office
State Council of Higher Education for Virginia
James Monroe Building
101 North Fourteenth Street
Richmond, VA 23219
804-225-2624

Guaranty Agency
Educational Credit Management Corp.
411 East Franklin, Suite 300
Richmond, VA 23219
804-644-6400

Community Service Programs
Governor's Office of Volunteerism
730 East Broad Street, Ninth Floor
Richmond, VA 23219
804-692-1952

Department of Education
James Monroe Building, Ninth Floor
101 North Fourteenth Street
Richmond, VA 23219
804-225-2600

Department of Rehabilitative Services
4901 Fitzhugh Avenue
Richmond, VA 23230
804-367-0316 or 1-800-552-5019 (VA) or 804-367-0315 (TDD)

Department of Veterans Affairs, Regional Office
210 Franklin Road SW
Roanoke, VA 24011

Washington

The Washington Need Grant Program provides grant assistance to needy state residents enrolled in accredited colleges or universities or accredited vocational/technical institutions. The awards are based on financial need. The amounts of the awards vary. Contact your institution's financial aid office for further information and application forms.

The State Work-Study Program provides employment opportunities to qualified state residents who are financially needy. Students must be enrolled at least half-time to be considered for the program. Contact your college's financial aid office for further information and application forms.

The Tuition Waiver Program allows public colleges and universities to waive all or part of the tuition and fee costs of needy or disadvantaged students. Recipients of this program must be state residents and must be enrolled in Washington public institutions. Contact your college's financial aid office for further information and application forms.

The Future Teachers' Conditional Scholarship Program encourages outstanding students to enter the teaching profession. Eligible students must be state residents and enrolled in a graduate or undergraduate program.

The Nurses Conditional Scholarship provides financial assistance to nursing students who agree to serve in a designated state shortage area. The program is not based on financial need. For further information, contact either your high school guidance counselor or college financial aid office.

Financial Aid Office
Higher Education Coordinating Board
Financial Aid Office
P.O. Box 43430
Olympia, WA 98504-3430
360-753-7800

Guaranty Agency
Northwest Education Loan
500 Colman Building
811 First Avenue
Seattle, WA 98104
206-461-5470

Washington Commission on National and Community Service
P.O. Box 43113
Olympia, WA 98504
206-752-1814

Department of Education
Superintendent of Public Instruction
Old Capital Building
P.O. Box 47200
Olympia, WA 98504
360-753-6738

Vocational Rehabilitation Services
Office Building 2, OB-21C
Olympia, WA 98504
206-753-0293 or 1-800-637-5627 (V/TDD) (WA)

Department of Veterans Affairs, Regional Office
Federal Building
915 Second Avenue
Seattle, WA 98174

West Virginia

The West Virginia Higher Education Grant Program provides grant assistance to state residents enrolled full-time in accredited postsecondary schools. The awards are based upon financial need and vary in amount. Applicants must submit the FAFSA to apply for the grant.

The Underwood-Smith Teacher Scholarship provides financial assistance to graduate and undergraduate students. The awards are based on academic merit and are awarded to students in the top 10 percent of their class. Recipients must agree to teach in West Virginia.

Financial Aid Office
West Virginia Higher Education Grant Program
1018 Kanawha Boulevard East, Suite 700
Charleston, WV 24301
304-588-4614

Guaranty Agency
West Virginia Education Loan Services
P.O. Box 591
Charleston, WV 25301
304-345-7211

West Virginia Commission for National and Community Service
305 Stewart Hall
West Virginia University
Morgantown, WV 26505
304-293-8187

Department of Education
West Virginia Department of Education
1900 Kanawha Boulevard East
Charleston, WV 25305
804-225-2600

Division of Rehabilitation Services
P.O. Box 1004
Institute, WV 25305
304-766-4600 or 304-766-4969 (TDD)

Department of Veterans Affairs, Regional Office
640 Fourth Avenue
Huntington, WV 25701

Wisconsin

The Wisconsin Higher Education Grant (WHEG) Program provides financial assistance for undergraduate students who are state residents and are enrolled at least half-time in the University of Wisconsin system or at a vocational or technical institution. The awards are based on financial need.

The Wisconsin Tuition Grant (WTG) Program provides grant assistance to undergraduate students enrolled in independent nonprofit institutions in Wisconsin. The awards are based on financial need. Recipients must be state residents. Contact your institution's financial aid office for more information.

The Wisconsin Handicapped Program provides grant assistance to undergraduate students who are state residents and are legally blind or deaf. The awards are based upon financial need.

The Minority Retention Grant Program provides financial assistance to black, Hispanic, Native American, and certain Southeast Asian students who are upperclassmen enrolled in Wisconsin independent colleges or universities or in the Wisconsin technical college system.

The Minnesota-Wisconsin Reciprocity Agreement makes public colleges and universities more accessible to residents of Minnesota and Wisconsin by allowing students from these states to pay special reciprocity tuition.

The Academic Excellence Scholarship Program provides tuition and fee scholarships to Wisconsin's top high school students who must have at least a 3.0 GPA.

Financial Aid Office
Wisconsin Higher Educational Aids Board
P.O. Box 7885
Madison, WI 53707-7885
608-267-2206

Guaranty Agency
Great Lakes Higher Education Corp.
2401 International Lane
Madison, WI 53704
608-246-1800

Community Service Programs
Department of Health and Social Services
One West Wilson Street, Room 631
Madison, WI 53707
608-267-7796

Department of Education
Great Lakes Higher Education Corporation
2401 International Lane
Madison, WI 53704
608-246-1800

Division of Vocational Rehabilitation
One West Wilson Street
P.O. Box 7852
Madison, WI 53707
608-266-1281 or 608-266-9599 (TDD)

Department of Veterans Affairs, Regional Office
5000 West National Avenue, Building 6
P.O. Box 6
Milwaukee, WI 53295

Wyoming

The State Student Incentive Grant Program (SSIG) provides grant assistance to financially needy state residents. Awards are available each academic year.

The Scholarship Loan Fund for Superior Students provides financial assistance to Wyoming high school graduates with high scholastic achievement who plan to teach in Wyoming schools after graduation. Eligibility is based on ACT scores, high school grades, high school activities, and letters of recommendation. Contact your high school's guidance counselor for further information.

The County Commissioners Scholarship Program provides scholarship assistance to students who are state residents and graduates of Wyoming high schools. Application should be made directly to the Board of County Commissioners in the applicant's county of residence. The scholarship may be used at any public institution in Wyoming.

The Wyoming High School Honor Scholarship Program provides scholarships to state high school seniors with high scholastic achievement. The scholarship is usually equal to the full tuition and fees at any state community college, as well as at the University of Wyoming. Contact your high school's guidance counselor for further information.

The Scholarship/Loan Fund for Superior Students provides assistance to state high school graduates with high scholastic merit and leadership qualities who plan to teach in state public schools. Recipients must attend the University of Wyoming or any community college in the state, and must major in education. The awards are renewable, depending on academic achievement.

The President's Honor Scholarship Program awards scholarships to state residents who are high school seniors and who have demonstrated academic achievement and leadership. Each high school's principal makes nominations, and the number of awards depends on the size of the graduating class. The awards are renewable if the scholar maintains an acceptable GPA. For further information, contact your high school guidance counselor.

Financial Aid Office
Student Financial Aid Office
University of Wyoming
P.O. Box 3335
Laramie, WY 82071-3335
307-766-3886

Guaranty Agency
United Student Aid Group
1912 Capitol Avenue, Suite 320
Cheyenne, WY 82001
307-635-3259

Community Service Programs
Office of the Governor
Capital Building
Cheyenne, WY 82002
307-777-7437

Department of Education
2300 Capitol Avenue
Hathaway Building, 2nd Floor
Cheyenne, WY 82002-0050
307-635-3259

Division of Rehabilitation Services
1100 Herschler Building
Cheyenne, WY 82002
307-777-7389 (V/TDD)

Department of Veterans Affairs, Regional Office
2360 East Pershing Boulevard
Cheyenne, WY 82001

Index

F

Q-R

U

V

W

401

X–Z

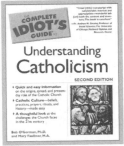

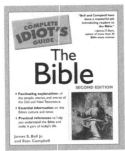

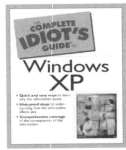